CZECH
PHRASEBOOK

Eugenia Janáčková

Czech phrasebook
1st edition – September 2001

Published by
Lonely Planet Publications Pty Ltd ABN 36 005 607 983
90 Maribyrnong St, Footscray, Victoria 3011, Australia

Lonely Planet Offices
Australia Locked Bag 1, Footscray, Victoria 3011
USA 150 Linden St, Oakland CA 94607
UK 72-82 Rosebery Ave, London, EC1R 4RW
France 1 rue du Dahomey, 75011 Paris

Cover illustration by Anne Marie Graham

ISBN 1 86450 184 7

text © Lonely Planet Publications Pty Ltd 2001
cover illustration © Lonely Planet Publications Pty Ltd 2001

10 9 8 7 6   4 3 2 1

Printed through The Bookmaker International Ltd
Printed in China

About the Author

Eugénia Mocnay was born and educated in Czechoslovakia, and has been living in Australia since 1983. She holds a Magister in Translating and Interpreting and gained a Masters Degree in Applied Linguistics at Monash University in 1993. Together with Prof Michael Clyne she conducted and published research on German/Hungarian/English trilingualism. At present Eugénia works as a freelance translator and interpreter, as well as part-time at Monash University Library, where she enjoys the acquisition and cataloguing of monographs in many European languages.

From the Author

Thanks to my Czech language consultant Mgr Milena Koreňová and my dear friend Brian Gerrard for their invaluable assistance.

Thanks also to my husband Paul and my children Lukáš, Lucia, Tamara and Christina. It was their support, help and patience that made my work on this phrasebook possible.

From the Publisher

Our Phrasebooks Team did it again, and did it together! Go team! This book is the result of a joint effort by the following people: Emma Koch immersed herself in the Czech language and edited. Patrick Marris designed and laid out, while Anne Marie Graham created both cover and illustrations. Belinda Campbell helped out with layout and Fabrice Rocher oversaw the design before skipping off to *La Douce France*. Sarah Curry proofread and assisted with editing. Annelies Mertens and Sophie Putman checked the layout. Cartographer Natasha Velleley provided the map and Karina Coates coordinated and oversaw production. Karin Vidstrup Monk, as usual, gladly provided assistance. Richard Nebesky wrote the introduction and Sally Steward and Peter D'Onghia initiated the project.

CONTENTS

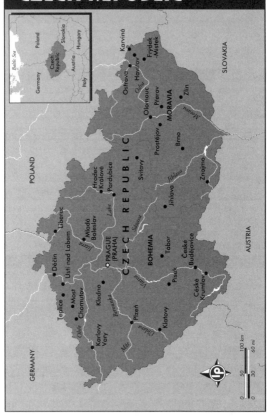

INTRODUCTION

Czech, or *čeština*, is a Slavonic language in the same language group as Russian. However, Czech belongs to the Western Slavonic subgroup, along with Slovak, Polish and Lusatian, to which it is more closely related. It's the mother tongue of around 10 million people in the Czech Republic and there are another one to one and a half million people of Czech descent spread around the world, most of whom live in the USA (1.3 million), with much smaller groups in Slovakia, Germany, Canada, Austria and Australia, among other countries.

You'll need to abandon a few linguistic habits in order to learn Czech. It is, however, mostly spelled the way it's spoken and once you get to know the sounds it's easy to read. The sound of the letter *ř* is a bit tricky and doesn't exist in any other language. Another peculiarity of the language is a frequent absence of vowels – many words lack them totally and are composed only of consonants. A well-known tongue twister is *strč prst skrz krk*, which means 'stick your finger through your neck'.

The primary influence of Czech, as of many other European languages, is Latin. The Czechs arrived in their present homeland around the 6th century, and the first major foreign influence came with the arrival of the Christian missionaries Cyril and Methodius in 864. They introduced the Bible written in Old Church Slavonic (which was based on a dialect of Slavic tribes that was understood by the Czechs) and using the Cyrillic script, thus giving the Czechs an alphabet. However, by the 11th century, the use of the Czech language and Latin script dominated literary works. Then came the rise of German influences on the Czech language, influences that were successfully minimized by the preacher Jan Hus, who helped to create a standard of the literary Czech language in the 15th century. The scholar Jan Ámos Komenský (known also as Comenius) took part in the next revision of Czech during the 17th century. His work was almost undone as the Czech language nearly disappeared during the next 300 years of Austrian domination, when Czech was mainly spoken by the peasants, while German dominated among the nobility and in the cities.

INTRODUCTION

The 18th century saw the revival of the Czech language, initiated by Josef Dobrovský and Josef Jungamann, who separately developed a Czech literary language close to the vernacular. This effort was part of a movement known as the Czech National Revival which resulted in the formation of Czechoslovakia in 1918, where Czech and Slovak became the two official languages. The relatively short union lasted only until 1993. Today, the Czech language, like many other languages around the world, is battling to keep out the overwhelming influences of the English language.

Not many people realise that Czech has also influenced other languages. The word 'robot' comes from the word *robota* meaning 'work' and was used by Karel Čapek in his novel 'Rossum's Universal Robots'. Some of the most well-known Czech literature translated into English is Jaroslav Hašek's *The Good Soldier Švejk*. There are also novels available by other contemporary authors such as Milan Kundera, Václav Havel, Ivan Klíma and, perhaps the best-known Czech author of the 20th century, Bohumil Hrabal.

ABBREVIATIONS USED IN THIS BOOK

adj	adjective	neut	neuter
f	feminine	pl	plural
inf	informal	pol	polite
lit	literal	sg	singular
m	masculine	v	verb
n	noun		

PRONUNCIATION

Once you become familiar with the sounds, Czech is quite easy to pronounce. Each letter always has the same sound, and all letters in each word are pronounced, even at the end of the word. When you've become accustomed to its diacritical marks, ´ (*čárka*), ˇ (*háček*) and ° (*kroužek*), you should have little trouble reading Czech.

VOWELS

Czech has a simple vowel system: five vowels, *a, e, i, o, u*, and a set of matching long vowels written as *á, é, í, ó, ú*, and in the case of *u*, a second long vowel, *ů*. The length of vowels is very important because it can completely change the meaning of a word, eg, *rada* (advice), *ráda* (I like).

a	a	as the 'u' in 'cut'
e	e	as the 'e' in 'bet'
i/y	i	as the 'i' in 'hit'
o	o	as the 'o' in 'dot'
u	u	as the 'u' in 'put'

The long vowels are marked with the acute sign ´ (*čárka*) and are pronounced twice as long as the short vowels.

á	aa	as the 'a' in 'father'
é	eh	as the 'ai' in 'fair'
í/ý	ee	as the 'ee' in 'breeze'
ó	aw	as the 'aw' in 'thaw'
ú/ů	oo	as the 'oo' in 'noodle'

> ## THE CZECH ALPHABET
>
> a, á, b, c, č, d, ď, e, é, ě, f, g, h, ch, i, í, j, k, l, m, n, ň, o, ó, p, r, ř, s, š, t, ť, u, ú, ů, v, w, y, ý, z, ž.

Diphthongs (Vowel Combinations)

There are three diphthongs in Czech: *au*, *eu* and *ou*. Each vowel is pronounced as a separate sound. The only native Czech diphthong is *ou*. The other two, *au* and *eu*, only appear in loan words, eg, *auto* (ow-to) 'car'.

ou	oh	as the 'o' in 'dot' followed by the 'u' in 'put'
au	ow	as the 'ow' in British English 'how'
eu	e-oo	as the 'e' in 'bet' followed by the 'oo' in 'noodle'

The letter *ě* and some combinations of letters are also pronounced like diphthongs.

ě	ye	as the 'ye' in 'yet'

The combinations *aj*, *ej*, *ij*, *oj*, *uj*, and *yj* which appear at the end of words are pronounced as the initial vowel followed by a 'y', eg, *čaj* (chai), *stroj* (stroy), *můj* (mooy).

aj	ai	as the ' i' in 'ice'
ej	ey	as the 'ey' in 'hey'
ij/yj	iy	as the 'ee' in 'breeze' followed by the 'y' in 'year'
oj	oy	as the 'o' in 'dot' followed by the 'y' in 'year'
uj	uy	as the 'u' in 'put' followed by the 'y' in 'year'
ůj	ooy	as the 'oo' in 'noodle' followed by the 'y' in 'year'

CZECH OR NOT?

It is a common error in English to say Czech instead of the Czech Republic. However, Czech in English can only be used as an adjective or the name of the language. If you want to save time, the relatively new and fashionable word *Czechia*, can be used for the Czech Republic.

CONSONANTS

Czech consonants are similar to English consonants. Most of them are pronounced in the same way as their English counterparts. The following consonants have the same sound as in English: *b, f, g, h, l, m, s, v, z*. The consonants *p* and *k* are also similar to English, although they are never accompanied by aspiration, ie, they are pronounced with no puff of breath after them. Consonants that differ from English are:

d	d	as in English, except when followed by *i* or *í*, when it's pronounced as the 'dy' sound in British English 'duty'
n	n	as in English, except when followed by *i* or *í*, when it's pronounced as the 'ny' in 'canyon'
t	t	as in English, except when followed by *i* or *í*, when it's pronounced as the 'ty' sound in British English 'tune'
r	r	rolled, like the Scottish r
ř	rzh	a sound unique to Czech; produced by pronouncing 'r' and the 's' in 'measure' simultaneously
c	ts	as the 'ts' in 'its'
č	ch	as the 'ch' in 'cheese'
š	sh	as the 'sh' in 'she'
ž	zh	as the 's' in 'measure'
j	y	as the 'y' in 'year'
ch	kh	as the 'kh' sound in Scottish *loch*
ď	dy	as the 'dy' sound in British English 'duty'
ň	ny	as the 'ny' in 'canyon'
ť	ty	as the 'ty' sound in British English 'tune'

For the English speaker, there are many 'tongue-twisting' Czech words, consisting of consonant clusters, eg, *zmrzlina*, 'ice'; *sprcha*, 'shower'; *čtvrtek*, 'Thursday'; *vlk*, 'wolf'; *krk*, 'neck'.

PRONUNCIATION

STRESS

The stress or accent always falls on the first syllable, eg, *pivo*: *pi*-vo; *víno*: *vee*-no. In words of more than three syllables, there is a secondary accent on the third syllable, eg, *milovati*: *mi*-lo-*va*-ti; *politika*: *po*-li-*ti*-ka.

Prepositions in Czech are usually pronounced together with the word that follows, eg, *ve škole*: *ve*-shko-*le*.

CHECK YOUR CZECH

While there is only one word in English for the word Czech, there are seven different forms to cover the word in the Czech language:

čeština	the Czech language (noun)
Češka	a Czech woman (feminine noun)
Čech	a Czech man (masculine noun)
Český les	a Czech forest (masculine adjective)
Česká republika	the Czech Republic (feminine adjective)
české občanství	Czech citizenship (neuter adjective)
česky	Czech (adverb)

In this book, the formal (polite) and informal (familiar) forms of pronouns and verbs (when both appear) are separated by a slash. In most cases, only the form considered most appropriate for the particular situation is used.

For nouns, the feminine ending is usually *-ka* and for verbs the most common ending is *-a*. Where considered important, the feminine ending of a word is separated from the masculine form by a slash, followed by (m/f).

GRAMMAR

Czech is a highly inflected language which, simply stated, means 'everything changes'. Nouns, adjectives, pronouns, numerals and verbs take various endings depending on their grammatical function in the sentence. Even foreign words undergo this treatment.

WORD ORDER
Generally, the order of words in Czech sentences is rather flexible. The words which are most important in the sentence, or which receive the strongest emphasis, are at the beginning or at the end of the sentence. This relatively free word order is possible due to the highly-developed inflectional system which gives little scope for ambiguity. This system means words have different forms, depending on their case, or their role in the sentence. The position of adjectives, however, is relatively rigid – they come before the nouns that they describe. Often the word order of Czech sentences is the same as in English.

ARTICLES
In Czech there are no articles, ie, 'a/an/the'. *Pivo* can mean 'a beer' or 'the beer' or just 'beer', depending on the context.

NOUNS
Gender
All Czech nouns belong to one of three grammatical genders: masculine, feminine or neuter.

The grammatical terms masculine, feminine and neuter have nothing to do with sex: *děvče*, 'girl', for example, is neuter, and so is *prase*, 'pig' regardless of whether the animal is male or female. The two capitals *Londýn* and *Praha* are masculine and feminine respectively. Masculine nouns also have subcategories of animate (living) and inanimate (non-living). All living and formerly living beings – animals, reptiles and insects – are animate nouns. Everything else, including trees, bushes, flowers and bacteria, falls into the inanimate category. Eg, your brain is 'dead', *neživotný*, but you as a whole person are 'alive', *životný*.

Masculine nouns generally end in a consonant, feminine nouns end in *-a*, *-e* or a soft consonant and neuter nouns end in *-o*, *-e* or *-í*:

MASCULINE		FEMININE		NEUTER	
umbrella	*deštník*	school	*škola*	bike	*kolo*
letter	*dopis*	garage	*garáž*	animal	*zvíře*
bread	*chléb*	tram	*tramvaj*	cabbage	*zelí*

The most common way of creating the feminine form of a noun is to add the suffix *-ka* to the masculine form:

male teacher	*učitel*	female teacher	*učitelka*
male traveller	*cestovatel*	female traveller	*cestovatelka*

However, there are some exceptions to this rule:

male Czech	*Čech*	female Czech	*Češka*
male office worker	*úředník*	female office worker	*úřednice*

Similarly, surnames in Czech have different forms for males and females. The majority of female surnames are formed from the male form by adding the ending *-ová*, eg, *pan Navrátil*, *pani Navrátilová*. The literal translation of this ending is 'belongs to', and is similar to the English 'Mr Smith's wife/daughter'.

If the male surname ends with *-ý*, the female form ends with *-á*, eg, *pan Černý*, *pani Černá*.

Plurals

Unlike English, Czech nouns belong to different groups and have different plural endings. The most common plural endings are:

-y	woman	žena	women	ženy
	hotel	hotel	hotels	hotely
-a	luggage (sg)	zavazadlo	luggage (pl)	zavazadla
-e	room	pokoj	rooms	pokoje
-i	thing	věc	things	věci

CASE

In English, we recognise the 'role' of a noun in a sentence – who is performing an action, to whom, with what and so on – by its position in a sentence and/or by the use of prepositions.

However, like Latin, German and many other languages, Czech uses what is known as 'case' to make these distinctions. Different suffixes known as 'case endings' act like labels on nouns to indicate their relationship to other words in a sentence. Other parts of the sentence such as pronouns, proper nouns and adjectives, also change their endings depending on the case.

Don't worry, though – if you stick to the nominative case, you'll be understood. We've included an explanation of how case affects noun endings so you'll be aware of it when you hear people speaking.

Czech has seven cases:

1	nominative	Paul	Pavel
2	genitive	from Paul	Pavla
3	dative	to Paul	Pavlovi
4	accusative	Paul	Pavla
5	vocative	Paul!	Pavle!
6	locative	about Paul	o Pavlovi
7	instrumental	with Paul	s Pavlem

GRAMMAR

In Czech grammar books and dictionaries, cases are usually referred to by the numbers given in the box above. Here's a brief explanation of each case:

The **nominative** case refers to the subject of a verb in a sentence and is also the form you'll find in a dictionary. It indicates what or who is performing an action:

The audience threw flowers to the dancer on the stage, stomped the ground with their feet and yelled 'Encore!'.

The **genitive** case refers to possession, a bit like English 'of' or the possessive 's' ('s). It indicates 'whose' or 'of what/of whom':

The audience threw flowers to the dancer on the stage, stomped the ground with *their feet* and yelled 'Encore!'.

In Czech, the genitive case is also used after certain prepositions, *do*, 'to, into', *z*, 'out of, from', *od*, 'from, away from', *u* 'at, by, near':

Prague	*Praha*	(lit: Prague+nominative)
from Prague	*z Prahy*	(lit: from Prague+genitive)
brother	*bratr*	(lit: brother+nominative)
from my brother	*od bratra*	(lit: from brother+genitive)

The genitive is also used in expressions of quantity, eg, *mnoho papíru*, 'a lot of paper'.

The **dative** case refers to the indirect object. It tells us for whose benefit the action is performed and answers the question 'to/for whom?':

The audience threw flowers to *the dancer on the stage*, stomped the ground with their feet and yelled 'Encore!'.

It is also used with certain prepositions, *k*, *ke*, *proti* and *kvůli*, and also with certain adjectives:

Mother is cold.   *Matce je zima.* (lit: mother+dative is cold)

Most nouns have dative case endings similar to the locative case endings.

The **accusative** is the direct object of a sentence. It indicates what or whom the verb refers to:

The audience threw *flowers* to the dancer on the stage, stomped the ground with their feet and yelled 'Encore!'.

| I see a house. | *Vidím dům.* | (lit: see-I house+accusative) |
| I see Mary. | *Vidím Marii.* | (lit: see-I Mary+accusative) |

The **vocative** is used for directly addressing living things or objects:

The audience threw flowers to the dancer on the stage, stomped the ground with their feet and yelled '*Encore!*'.

In Czech, even proper names are inflected for case:

Peter	*Petr*	(lit: Peter+nominative)
Peter!	*Petře!*	(lit: Peter+vocative)
boy	*hoch*	(lit: boy+nominative)
Boy!	*Hochu!*	(lit: boy+vocative)

The **locative** case is used to express location (where something is):

The audience threw flowers to the dancer *on the stage*, stomped the ground with their feet and yelled 'Encore!'.

GRAMMAR

In Czech, the locative is always a prepositional case. It is used to express location or place, ie, 'in', 'on', 'about', 'at', as opposed to destination or goal, ie, 'on', 'to' (expressed in Czech by the accusative).

| Prague | *Praha* | (lit: Prague+nominative) |
| in Prague | *v Praze* | (lit: Prague+locative) |

The **instrumental** case is used to answer 'with whom', 'with what', 'by what means', 'how' and 'where':

The audience threw flowers to the dancer on the stage, stomped the ground *with their feet* and yelled 'Encore!'.

I write with a pen.	*Píšu perem.*
	(lit: write-I pen+instrumental)
We are going by car to Prague.	*Jedeme autem do Prahy.*
	(lit: going-we car+instrumental to Prague+genitive)

The prepositions *s* and *se,* which mean 'with', 'by', 'along with', always take the instrumental case:

| I live with my brother. | *Bydlím s bratrem.* |
| | (lit: live-I with brother+instrumental). |

The prepositions *mezi, nad, pod, před* and *za* take the instrumental case to indicate the place where something is:

| before the bridge | *před mostem* |
| | (lit: before bridge+instrumental) |

ADJECTIVES

Adjectives in Czech have different endings depending upon whether the noun they relate to is masculine, feminine or neuter, singular or plural. They also agree with the case of the noun. As in English, adjectives come before the nouns that they describe.

In dictionaries, you'll find adjectives listed in the nominative case and the masculine gender.

MASCULINE	good day	*dobrý den*
FEMININE	good night	*dobrá noc*
NEUTER	good morning	*dobré ráno*

Comparatives

Comparatives use the basic endings: *-ejší*, *-ější*, *-ší* or *-čí*.

fast	*rychlý*	faster	*rychlejší*
beautiful	*hezký*	more beautiful	*hezčí*

Superlatives

The superlative is formed by adding *nej-* before the comparative:

the fastest	*nejrychlejší*
the most beautiful	*nejhezčí*

There are a few irregular forms:

good	*dobrý*	small	*malý*
better	*lepší*	smaller	*menší*
the best	*nejlepší*	the smallest	*nejmenší*
bad	*špatný*	large	*velký*
worse	*horší*	larger	*větší*
the worst	*nejhorší*	the largest	*největší*

GRAMMAR

PRONOUNS
Subject

The subject pronouns are:

PRONOUNS			
SINGULAR		**PLURAL**	
I	já	we	my
you (sg)	ty	you (pl)	vy
he/she/it	on/ona/ono	they (m/f/n)	oni/ony/ona

The verb ending indicates whether the subject is first, second or third person, singular or plural. Therefore, personal pronouns are not necessary if they are functioning as the verb's subject. They can be used, however, to emphasise the subject or for clarity.

(Já) Hledám taxík.   I am looking for a taxi.
(lit: (I) look-I taxi+accusative)

Like many other European languages, Czech distinguishes between the familiar 'you' *(ty)* and the formal 'you' *(vy)*. The second person singular pronoun *ty* is used when speaking to someone whom you know very well (they may specifically ask you to after a while) and also with people younger than you. You may be specifically asked to use *ty*, and it is generally the woman or the older person who says *Mohli bychom si tykat*, 'We should start using *ty*'. In all other cases the second person plural *vy* is appropriate. Formal situations and relationships always demand that you use *vy*, and no first names. Some people prefer to keep a distance – regardless of how well they know each other – and insist on the *vy* form of address. This phrasebook uses the most appropriate form for each situation.

Reflexive Pronouns

English has a separate reflexive pronoun for each personal pronoun, eg, I wash myself, They wash themselves. Czech has only one, *se*, which can refer to any subject. It can also mean 'each other'.

Hledáme se.   We are looking for each other.
(lit: search-we ourselves)
představit se   to introduce oneself
(lit: to-introduce oneself)

GRAMMAR

VERBS

The tense system of Czech verbs is quite simple. It's refined by the Slavic aspects, ie, the imperfective/perfective opposition. Aspect indicates the way a verb relates to time. The perfective aspect typically specifies completion of an act. The imperfective expresses the verbal action as a process.

Present

The infinitive form of verbs generally ends in *-t*: *dělat*, 'to do', *mluvit*, 'to speak', *pracovat*, 'to work'. The person is expressed primarily by inflections and secondarily by personal pronouns:

I drink	*(já) piju*	we drink	*(my) pijeme*
you drink (sg)	*(ty) piješ*	you drink (pl)	*(vy) pijete*
he/she/it drinks	*(on/ona/ono) pije*	they drink	*(oni) pijou*

TO BE

Like other languages, Czech has a few irregularities. One of them is *být* (to be) which is an irregular verb:

I am	*jsem*	I am not	*nejsem*
you are	*jsi*	you are not (sg, inf)	*nejsi*
he/she/it is	*je*	he/she/it is not	*není*
we are	*jsme*	we are not	*nejsme*
you are	*jste*	you are not (pol sg or pl)	*nejste*
they are	*jsou*	they are not	*nejsou*

Other examples of irregular verbs are: *jíst*, 'to eat', *vědět*, 'to know', *chtít*, 'to want'.

TO HAVE

The verb *mít*, 'to have' is entirely regular:

I have	*mám*	I have not	*nemám*
you have	*máš*	you have not (sg, inf)	*nemáš*
he/she/it has	*má*	he/she/it has not	*nemá*
we have	*máme*	we have not	*nemáme*
you have	*máte*	you have not (pol sg or pl)	*nemáte*
they have	*mají*	they have not	*nemají*

GRAMMAR

Verbs belong to five main verb classes. Which class they fall into is indicated by the third person present tense ending:

-e	to carry	*nést*
	he/she carries	*nese*
-ne	to print	*tisknout*
	he/she prints	*tiskne*
-je	to buy	*kupovat*
	he/she buys	*kupuje*
-í	to ask	*prosit*
	he/she asks	*prosí*
-á	to do	*dělat*
	he/she does	*dělá*

Past

The past tense in Czech represents the English present perfect 'I have done', simple past 'I did', imperfect 'I was doing', and pluperfect 'I had done'. It is formed from the infinitive by removal of the final *-t* which is usually replaced with the particle *-l*: *dělat*, 'to do' – *dělal jsem*, 'I did'.

Future

The future tense is formed with the auxiliary verb *budu* (the future tense of *být*, 'to be'), plus the actual verb: *budu dělat*, 'I will work'. It has the following conjugation:

I will be	*budu*		we will be	*budeme*
you will be	*budeš*		you will be	*budete*
he/she/it will be	*bude*		they will be	*budou*

POSSESSION

Possession may be expressed in the same two basic ways as in English, with *mít*, 'to have':

We have a new flat.   *Máme nový byt.*
(lit: have-we new flat)

or by using a possessive pronoun, such as *můj*, 'my', *svůj*, 'one's own', *náš*, 'our', and *váš*, 'your':

He/She loves his/her car.   *Miluje svoje auto.*
(lit: loves-he/she own car).

Possessive Adjectives

Possessive adjectives can be formed from masculine animate nouns by adding the suffixes *-ův* (m), *-ova* (f), *-ovo* (neut):

| Charles | *Karel* | Charles' | *Karlův* |
| brother | *bratr* | brother's | *bratrův* |

and from feminine nouns by adding *-in* (m), *-ina* (f), *-ino* (neut):

| sister | *sestra* | sister's | *sestřin* |
| mother | *matka* | mother's | *matčin* |

Proper nouns ending in *-ý*, eg, pan Hrbatý, have no special possessive form, but are declined like adjectives:

the house of   *dům pana Hrbatého*
Mr Hrbatý   (lit: house Mr Hrbatý+genitive)

The suffix added relates to the gender of the noun.

QUESTIONS

Questions are formed by using a question word and they usually have the same word order as in English:

Where is ...?	*Kde je ...?*
	(lit: where is ...?)
What are you doing?	*Co děláte?*
	(lit: what doing-you?)
How are you?	*Jak se máte?*
	(lit: how self have-you?)
When are you getting up?	*Kdy vstáváš?*
	(lit: when getting-up-you?)

As in English, a question may have the same word order as the corresponding statement. The difference lies in the intonation used.

QUESTION WORDS		
where?	gde?	kde?
what?	tso?	co?
why?	proch?	proč?
who?	gdo?	kdo?
how?	yak?	jak?
when?	gdi?	kdy?

NEGATIVES

Negatives in Czech are formed by prefixing the particle *ne-* to the verb:

I don't speak	*nemluvím*
	(lit: not-speak-I)
I am not	*nejsem*
	(lit: not-am-I)

The negative of *je*, 'he/she is', is *není*.

Is he at home?	*Je doma? Ne, není doma*
No, he is not at home.	(lit: is home? no, not home)

GRAMMAR

MODALS

Modal verbs are used with the infinitive form of another verb to modify that verb's meaning. They express need, desire, ability, etc.

can, to be able
Can you pay?

moci
Můžeš zaplatit?
(lit: can-you to-pay?)

will, want to
I want to buy a beer.

chtít
Chci koupit pivo.
(lit: want-I to-buy beer)

must, have to, to be obliged
I have to study Czech.

muset
Musím se učit česky.
(lit: must-I self to-teach Czech)

to be allowed, may
May I ask?

smět
Smím prosit?
(lit: may-I to-beg?)

have to, must
You are supposed to
eat vegetables.

mít
Máš jíst zeleninu.
(lit: have-you to-eat vegetables)

GRAMMAR

LIKING VS LOVING

In English, you can love everything from your socks to your boss. This is not so in Czech – if you are in love, you may say *Miluju tě,* ' I love you' (lit: love-I you+accusative). But you should avoid the 'loving' verb, *milovat,* with food, drinks, material possessions and particularly when asked if you enjoy doing something. Here you can use the liking verb *mít rád* (lit: to-have like). To say 'I like beer', you'd say *Mám rád pivo* (lit: I-have like beer) or even *Pivo mi chutná* (lit: beer to-me tastes-good), but you wouldn't say that you are in love with beer.

SPOLEČENSKÝ STYK

MEETING PEOPLE

The Czechs are friendly people. They like to demonstrate this by exchanging a cordial handshake and between friends you'll also notice a warm and hearty pat on the shoulder. Between family and relatives, a kiss on both cheeks is the usual greeting.

YOU SHOULD KNOW

BĚŽNÉ FRÁZE

Hello/Hi.	na-zdar/a-hoy	*Nazdar/Ahoj.*
Goodbye.	na-shle-da-noh	*Na shledanou.*
Yes.	a-no/yo/no	*Ano/Jo/No.*
No.	ne	*Ne.*
Excuse me.	pro-mi-nye/-te	*Promiňte.*
		(inf/pol)
Please.	pro-seem	*Prosím.*
Thank you	dye-ku-yi	*Děkuji*
(very much).	(mots-kraat)	*(mockrát).*

VERSATILE PLEASE

Prosím (**pro-seem**) could mean 'Please', 'Here you are', 'What did you say?', 'You're welcome' or 'I'll have ...'. It's a very useful word!

GREETINGS & GOODBYES

POZDRAVY & LOUČENÍ

The most common greeting you can use at any time during the day is *dobrý den* or *ahoj* between friends. *Dobré ráno,* 'good morning' is used only early in the morning, and *dobré odpoledne,* 'good afternoon' is not often used. *Dobrý večer,* 'good evening' is used for late evenings only, and *dobrou noc,* 'good night' only when parting for the night.

Good morning.	dob-reh raa-no	*Dobré ráno.*
Good day. (noon)	dob-ree den	*Dobrý den.*
Good afternoon.	dob-reh ot-po-le-dne	*Dobré odpoledne.*
Good evening.	dob-ree ve-cher	*Dobrý večer.*
Good night	dob-roh nots	*Dobrou noc*
Hello/Hi.	na-zdar/a-hoy	*Nazdar/Ahoj.*
Goodbye.	na-shle-da-noh	*Na shledanou.*
Bye.	a-hoy	*Ahoj.*

YOU MAY HEAR ...

budy/-te (pro-seem) tak las-kav/-a ...	Would you be so kind ... (inf/pol) (m/f)
dye-ku-yi, naa-po-dob-nye	Thanks, same to you.
ne-nyee zach	You're welcome.
be-ze vshe-ho!	No problem/Of course!
to ye ma-lich-kost!	That's nothing!

Civilities   Zdvořilostní fráze

Thank you (very much).	dye-ku-yi (mots-kraat)	*Děkuji (mockrát).*
You're welcome.	pro-seem	*Prosím.*
Excuse me/Sorry.	pro-mi-nye/-te	*Promiň/te.* (inf/pol)
May I?/Do you mind?	do-vo-lee-te?	*Dovolíte?*

FORMS OF ADDRESS   OSLOVENÍ

In Czech there are two different ways of addressing people – informal or familiar (inf) and polite (pol). When addressing close friends or relatives, first names are used with the familiar form of you, *ty*, and the verb in the singular (see Verbs, page 23). All other people are addressed as 'Mr/Mrs', *pan/paní*, with the polite form of you, *vy*, and the verb in the plural.

The use of academic titles has not died out and is still quite widespread. You'll hear titles like *pane doktore* or *paní učitelko*. There is a different ending and/or word for addressing males and females.

MEETING PEOPLE

Mr	pan	*pan*
Mrs	pa-nyee	*paní*
Miss	slech-na	*slečna*
friend (male)	przhee-tel	*přítel*
friend (female)	przhee-tel-kinye	*přítelkyně*
partner(male)	part-ner	*partner*
partner (female)	part-ner-ka	*partnerka*

BODY LANGUAGE   GESTIKULACE

A hearty handshake or pat on the shoulder is a sign to show that you are sincerely glad to meet someone.

Answering *ano*, 'yes' is usually supported by repeatedly nodding, while when answering *ne*,'no' you shake your head from side to side. *Ano* is often shortened to *no*, sometimes resulting in cross-language confusion.

When you visit someone at home, it's better to leave your shoes at the door – you might even be offered a pair of 'guest slippers'.

When giving flowers (a common custom in the Czech Republic), always give an odd number and take the wrapping paper off before presenting them.

FIRST ENCOUNTERS   SETKÁNÍ

How are you?
    yak se maash/maa-te?   *Jak se máš/máte?* (inf/pol)
Fine. And you?
    dob-rzhe. a ti/vi?   *Dobře. A ty/vy?* (inf/pol)
What's your name?
    yak se yme-nu-yesh/   *Jak se jmenuješ/*
    yme-nu-ye-te?   *jmenujete?* (inf/pol)
My name is (Karel).
    yme-nu-yi se (ka-rel)   *Jmenuji se (Karel).*
I'd like to introduce you to ...
    mo-hu tye/vaas   *Mohu tě/vás*
    przhed-sta-vit ...   *představit ...* (inf/pol)
I'm pleased to meet you.
    tye-shee mye   *Těší mě.*

MEETING PEOPLE

MAKING CONVERSATION   DOROZUMĚNÍ

Do you live here?
bid-leesh ta-di?   *Bydlíš tady?*

Where are you going?
kam ye-desh?   *Kam jedeš?*

What are you doing?
tso dye-laash?   *Co děláš?*

What's this called?
yak se to yme-nu-ye?   *Jak se to jmenuje?*

Beautiful, isn't it?
to ye przhe-kraa-sneh tso?   *To je překrásné, co?*

It's great here!
ye ta-di hez-ki!   *Je tady hezky!*

What a cute baby!
to ye hez-keh dye-tyaat-ko!   *To je hezké děťátko!*

Are you waiting too?
che-kaa-te ta-ki?   *Čekáte taky?*

That's strange!
to ye dyiv-neh!   *To je divné!*

That's funny. (amusing)
to ye sran-da   *To je sranda.*

Just joking!
ye-nom zher-tu-yi!   *Jenom žertuji!*

Are you here on holiday?
ysi/yste ta-di na do-vo-le-neh?   *Jsi/Jste tady na dovolené?*
                                        (inf/pol)

I'm here ...	ysem ta-di ...	Jsem tady ...
for a holiday	na do-vo-le-neh	na dovolené
on business	pra-tsov-nye	pracovně
to study	na stu-di-yeekh	na studiích

How long are you here for?
na yak dloh-ho ysi/yste ta-di?   *Na jak dlouho jsi/jste tady?*
                                        (inf/pol)

I'm/We're here for ... weeks /days.
   przhi-yel ysem na ...
   dnoo/tee-dnoo
        Přijel jsem na ...
        dnů/týdnů.
Do you like it here?
   lee-bee se tyi/
   vaam ta-di?
        Líbí se ti/
        vám tady? (inf/pol)
I/We like it here very much.
   mne/naam se ta-di
   ve-li-tse lee-bee
        Mně/Nám se tady
        velice líbí.
We're here with our family.
   ysme ta-dis na-shee ro-di-noh
        Jsme tady s naší rodinou.
I'm here with my partner.
   ysem ta-dis part-ner-em/
   part-ner-koh
        Jsem tady s partnerem/
        partnerkou. (m/f)

Useful Phrases   Užitečné fráze

Sure.	yi-stye	*Jistě.*
Just a minute.	mo-ment	*Moment.*
It's OK.	to yev po-rzhaad-ku	*To je v pořádku.*
It's important.	ye to doo-le-zhi-teh	*Je to důležité.*
It's not important.	ne-nyee to doo-le-zhi-teh	*Není to důležité.*
It's possible.	ye to mozh-neh	*Je to možné.*
It's not possible.	ne-nyee to mozh-neh	*Není to možné.*
I'm ready.	ysem przhi-pra-ve-nee/-aa	*Jsem připravený/á.* (m/f)
Good luck!	mno-ho shtye-stee!	*Mnoho štěstí!*

MEETING PEOPLE

NATIONALITIES   NÁRODNOSTI

In addition to Czechs, Moravians and Silesians, some Slovaks, Poles, Germans and Roma live in the Czech Republic. In recent years, Prague has also been a temporary home to many thousands of Americans who moved there to live and work and to enjoy the relatively low-cost/high-value life that contemporary Prague offers them.

You might find that some people like to distinguish themselves from the Czechs proper and call themselves Moravians. There are about two million people living in the region called Moravia, located in the eastern part of the Czech Republic, with Brno being the capital.

Where are you from?
  ot-kud ysi/yste?   *Odkud jsi/jste? (inf/pol)*

I'm from ...	ysem ...	*Jsem ...*
We're from ...	(mi) ysme ...	*(My) jsme ...*
Australia	sow-straa-li-ye	*z Austrálie*
Canada	ska-na-di	*z Kanady*
England	san-gli-ye	*z Anglie*
Europe	sev-ro-pi	*z Evropy*
Ireland	sir-ska	*z Irska*
Japan	zya-pon-ska	*z Japonska*
New Zealand	sno-veh-ho zeh-lan-du	*z Nového Zélandu*
Scotland	ze skot-ska	*ze Skotska*
the USA	ze spo-ye-neekh staa-too	*ze Spojených států*
Wales	zva-le-su	*z Walesu*

| CULTURAL DIFFERENCES | KULTURNÍ ROZDÍLY |

In general, Czechs are warm and emotional people. It's quite natural for them to touch each other on the arm and shoulder and to stand close to each other. In queues especially, you'll see people almost standing on the back of the person in front of them!

The Czechs enjoy their beer in the local pub – *hospoda* – and mostly discuss politics (while sport comes in second place), probably because it was illegal to discuss political topics publicly during the communist era. They can get quite animated during their political discussions as they're only slowly getting used to accepting opposing opinions and beliefs. This might be a consequence of the communist regime enforcing the slogan 'Who is not with us is against us' for over 40 years.

The Czechs are basically peaceful people. This was demonstrated in 1989 during the revolution against the communist regime, known to the world as the 'Velvet Revolution', and once again during the 'Velvet Divorce' in 1993 when the Czechs and the Slovaks peacefully split to form their independent and separate republics.

How do you do this in your country?
    yak to dye-laa-te u vaas?   *Jak to děláte u vás?*
Is this a local or national custom?
    ye to meest-nyee ne-bo   *Je to místní nebo*
    naa-rod-nyee zvik?   *národní zvyk?*
I don't want to offend you.
    nekh-tsi vaas u-ra-zit.   *Nechci vás urazit.*
I'm sorry, it's not the custom
in my country.
    ye mi lee-to u naas to   *Je mi líto, u nás to*
    ne-nyee zvi-kem   *není zvykem.*
I don't mind watching, but I'd
prefer not to participate.
    bu-du se koh-kat a-le ra-dye-yi   *Budu se koukat, ale raději*
    se ne-zoo-chast-nyeem   *se nezúčastním.*

MEETING PEOPLE

I'm sorry, it's	pro-mi-nye-te ye	*Promiňte, je*
against my ...	to pro-tyi meh ...	*to proti mé ...*
beliefs	vee-rzhe	*víře*
culture	kul-tu-rzhe	*kultuře*
religion	naa-bo-zhen-stvee	*náboženství*
(But) I'll give it a go.	(a-le) sku-seem to	*(Ale) zkusím to.*

OUT OF THE MUD ...

As cool as a cucumber.
S klidem Angličana.
As calm as an Englishman.

In the middle of nowhere.
Místo, kde lišky dávají dobrou noc.
A place where foxes say good night.

Out of the frying pan into the fire.
Dostat se z bláta do louže.
Out of the mud into the puddle.

It's as old as the hills.
To je starý jak Praha.
It's as old as Prague.

AGE

How old ...?	ko-lik ...?	*Kolik ...?*
are you	ye tyi let	*je ti let*
		(to a child)
are you	ye vaam let	*je vám let*
		(to an adult)
is your son	let ye vaa-she-mu si-novi	*let je vášmu synovi*
is your daughter	let ye vaa-she-mu de-tse-rzhi	*let je vaší dceři*
I'm ... years old.	ye mi ... let	*Je mi ... let.*

(See Numbers & Amounts, page 201, for your age.)

VĚK

OCCUPATIONS   ZAMĚSTNÁNÍ

The list below includes some occupations that people you meet
may have, as well as a few common Western occupations.

What (work) do you do?
ya-keh maa-te		*Jaké máte*
za-myest-naa-nyee?		*zaměstnání?*

I'm (a/an) ...	ysem ...	*Jsem ...*
artist	u-mye-lets/	*umělec/*
	u-mye-lki-nye	*umělkyně* (m/f)
businessperson	pod-nyi-ka-tel/-ka	*podnikatel/ka* (m/f)
chef	ku-kharzh/-ka	*kuchař/ka* (m/f)
doctor	leh-karzh/-ka	*lékař/ka* (m/f)
engineer	in-zhe-neer/-ka	*inženýr/ka* (m/f)
farmer	ze-mye-dye-lets/	*zemědělec/*
	ze-mye-dye-lki-nye	*zemědělkyně* (m/f)
homemaker	v do-maa-tsno-styi	*v domácnosti*
journalist	no-vi-naarzh/-ka	*novinář/ka* (m/f)
labourer	dyel-nyeek/	*dělník/*
	dyel-nyee-tse	*dělnice* (m/f)
lawyer	ad-vo-kaat/-ka	*advokát/ka* (m/f)
mechanic	ow-to-me-kha-nik	*automechanik*
nurse	o-shet-rzho-va-tel/	*ošetřovatel/*
	zdra-vo-tnyee	*zdravotní*
	se-stra	*sestra* (m/f)
office worker	u-rzhed-nyeek/	*úředník/*
	oo-rzhed-nyi-tse	*úřednice* (m/f)
scientist	vye-dets/vyed-kin-ye	*vědec/vědkyně* (m/f)
student	stu-dent/-ka	*student/ka* (m/f)
teacher	u-chi-tel/-ka	*učitel/ka* (m/f)
university lecturer	a-sis-tent/-ka	*asistent/ka* (m/f)
unemployed	ne-za-mye-stna-nee/-aa	*nezaměstnaný/á* (m/f)
waiter	cheesh-nyeek/	*číšník/*
	cheesh-nyi-tse	*číšnice* (m/f)
writer	spi-so-va-tel/-ka	*spisovatel/ka* (m/f)

MEETING PEOPLE

What are you studying?
	tso stu-du-yesh?	*Co studuješ?*

I'm studying ...	stu-du-yi ...	*Studuji ...*
art	u-mye-nee	*umění*
arts/humanities	hu-ma-nit-nyee	*humanitní*
	smye-ri	*směry*
business	biz-nis	*biznis*
engineering	stro-yarzh-stvyee	*strojařství*
English	an-glich-tyi-nu	*angličtinu*
languages	ya-zi-ki	*jazyky*
law	praa-vo	*právo*
medicine	me-di-tsee-nu	*medicínu*
science	przhee-rod-nyee	*přírodní*
	vye-di	*vědy*
teaching	u-chi-tel-stvee	*učitelství*

FEELINGS

POCITY

I'm afraid.	bo-yeem se	*Bojím se.*
Are you afraid?	bo-yeesh se?	*Bojíš se?*
I'm angry.	zlo-beem se	*Zlobím se.*
Are you angry?	zlo-beesh se?	*Zlobíš se?*
I'm in a hurry.	po-spee-khaam	*Pospíchám.*
Are you in a hurry?	po-spee-khaash?	*Pospícháš?*
I'm keen to ...	raad bikh ...	*Rád bych ...*
Are you keen to ...?	raad bis ...?	*Rád bys ...?*
I'm sorry. (regret)	mrzee mye	*Mrzí mě.*
Are you sorry? (regret)	mrzee tye?	*Mrzí tě?*

I'm ...	maam ...	*Mám ...*
Are you ...?	maash ...?	*Máš ...?*
depressed	de-pre-si	*depresi*
hungry	hlad	*hlad*
right	pra-vdu	*pravdu*
thirsty	zhee-ze-nye	*žízeň*
well	se do-brzhe	*se dobře*
worried	sta-ros-tyi	*starosti*

I'm ...	ysem ...	*Jsem ...*
Are you ...?	ysi ...?	*Jsi ...?*
grateful	vdyech-nee/-aa	*vděčný/á* (m/f)
happy	stya-stnee/-aa	*šťastný/á* (m/f)
sleepy	o-spa-lee/-aa	*ospalý/á* (m/f)
tired	u-nh-ve-nee/-aa	*unavený/á* (m/f)

I'm ...	ye mi ...	*Je mi ...*
Are you ...?	ye tyi ...?	*Je ti ...?*
cold	zi-ma	*zima*
hot	hor-ko	*horko*
sad	smut-no	*smutno*
sorry (condolence)	lee-to	*líto*

BREAKING THE LANGUAGE BARRIER
JAZYKOVÉ PROBLÉMY

Do you speak English?
mlu-veesh/
-te an-glits-ki?
Mluvíš/te anglicky?
(inf/pol)
Yes, I do.
yo mlu-veem
Jo, mluvím.
No, I don't.
ne ne-mlu-veem
Ne, nemluvím.
Does anyone speak English?
mlu-vee ta-di nye-gdo
an-glits-ki?
*Mluví tady někdo
anglicky?*
I speak a little.
yaa tro-khu mlu-veem
Já trochu mluvím.

Do you understand?
  ro-zu-meesh?   *Rozumíš?*
I don't understand.
  ne-roz-u-meem   *Nerozumím.*
Could you speak more slowly?
  moo-zhe-te mlu-vit po-ma-lu?   *Můžete mluvit pomalu?*
Could you repeat that?
  moo-zhe-te to zo-pa-ko-vat?   *Můžete to zopakovat?*
Please write it down.
  pro-seem na-pish-te to   *Prosím, napište to.*
How do you say ...?
  yakh se rzhee-ka ...?   *Jak se říka ...?*
What does ... mean?
  tso zna-me-naa ...?   *Co znamená ...?*

CESTOVÁNÍ

GETTING AROUND

FINDING YOUR WAY

DOTAZY NA CESTU

Where's the ...?	gde ye ...?	*Kde je ...?*
bus station	ow-to-bu-so-veh	*autobusové*
	naa-dra-zhee	*nádraží*
train station	vla-ko-veh	*vlakové*
	naa-dra-zhee	*nádraží*
road to Brno	vee-pa-dov-ka	*výpadovka*
	na brno	*na Brno*

What time does the ... leave/arrive?	fko-lik ho-dyin ... od-yeezh-dyee/ przhi-yee-zdyee?	*V kolik hodin ... odjíždí/ přijíždí?*
boat	lo-dye	*loď*
bus	ow-to-bus	*autobus*
train	vlak	*vlak*

What time does the aeroplane leave/arrive?

    fko-lik ho-dyin le-ta-dlo
od-leh-ta/przhi-leh-ta?

V kolik hodin letadlo odléta/přiléta?

How do we get to ...?

    yak se do-sta-ne-me do ...?

Jak se dostaneme do ...?

Is it far from/near here?

    ye to da-le-ko/blees-ko?

Je to daleko/blízko?

Can we walk there?

    do-sta-ne-me se tam pye-shki?

Dostaneme se tam pěšky?

Can you show me (on the map)?

    moo-zhe-te mi to u-kaa-zat
(na ma-pye)?

Můžete mi to ukázat (na mapě)?

Are there other means of getting there?

    mo-hu se tam do-stat
yesh-tye nye-yak yi-nak?

Mohu se tam dostat ještě nějak jinak?

Directions

Turn at ...	za-to-chte na ...	*Zatočte na ...*
the next corner	dal-sheem ro-hu	*dalším rohu*
the traffic lights	se-ma-fo-ru	*semaforu*

Straight ahead.	przhi-mo/ro-vnye	*Přímo/Rovně.*
To the right.	fpra-vo	*Vpravo.*
To the left.	vle-vo	*Vlevo.*

behind	za	*za*
in front of	przhed	*před*
far	da-le-ko	*daleko*
near	blees-ko	*blízko*
opposite	na-pro-tyi	*naproti*
here	ta-di	*tady*
there	tam	*tam*
north	se-ver	*sever*
south	yih	*jih*
east	vee-khod	*východ*
west	zaa-pad	*západ*

Pokyny Na Cestu

CH IS ONE LETTER IN CZECH!

When using a Czech index, remember that *ch* is considered to be a single letter and comes after *h* in the alphabet. Similarly, *č, ď, ř, š, ť* and *ž* are listed separately and they each immediately follow their non-accented mates.

ADDRESSES   ADRESY

The vast majority of the population lives in *činžáky* or *bytovky*, apartment block buildings. A written Czech address starts with the street name, then comes the building number, followed by the entry number, floor number and the apartment number.

BUYING TICKETS

JÍZDENKY – U POKLADNY

Where can I buy a ticket?
  gde-se pro-daa-va-yee
  yeez-den-ki?

Kde se prodávají jízdenky?

We want to go to ...
  khtse-me yeet do ...

Chceme jít do ...

Do I need to book?
  po-trzhe-bu-yi mees-ten-ku?

Potřebuji místenku?

I'd like to book a seat to ...
  pro-sil/-a bikh
  mees-ten-ku do ...

Prosil/a bych místenku do ... (m/f)

It's full.
  ye op-sa-ze-no

Je obsazeno.

I'd like ...   khtyel/-a bikh ...   *Chtěl/a bych ...*
                                                (m/f)

  a one-way ticket   ye-dno-smyer-noh   *jednosměrnou*
                      yeez-den-ku   *jízdenku*
  a return ticket   spaa-tech-nyee   *zpáteční*
                      yeez-den-ku   *jízdenku*
  two tickets   dvye yeez-den-ki   *dvě jízdenky*
  a student's fare   stu-dent-skoh   *studentskou*
                      sle-vu   *slevu*
  a child's/   dyet-skoh/   *dětskou/*
    pensioner's fare pen-zis-ti-tskoh   *penzistickou*
                      sle-vu   *slevu*

1st class   prv-nyee trzhee-du   *první třídu*
2nd class   dru-hoh trzhee-du   *druhou třídu*

AIR

CESTOVÁNÍ LETADLEM

When's the next flight to ...?
   gdi le-tyee przhee-shtee
   le-ta-dlo do ...?

*Kdy letí příští
letadlo do ...?*

What time do I have to check in
at the airport?
   fko-lik ho-dyin se mu-seem
   do-sta-vit kod-ba-ve-nyee na
   le-tyi-shti?

*V kolik hodin se musím
dostavit k odbavení na
letišti?*

Where's the baggage claim?
   gde ye vee-dey za-va-za-del?

Kde je výdej zavazadel?

My luggage hasn't arrived.
   mo-ye za-va-za-dla
   ne-przhi-shli

*Moje zavazadla
nepřišly.*

SIGNS

CELNICE	CUSTOMS
INFORMACE	INFORMATION
KONTROLA	CHECK POINT
LETIŠTĚ	AIRPORT
MÍSTENKY	BOOKING OFFICE
NÁDRAŽÍ	STATION
NÁSTUPIŠTĚ	PLATFORM
NOUZOVÝ VÝCHOD/	EMERGENCY EXIT
ÚNIKOVÁ CESTA	
ODJEZDY	DEPARTURES
POKLADNA	TICKET OFFICE
PŘÍJEZDY	ARRIVALS
REZERVACE	RESERVATIONS
VCHOD	ENTRANCE
VSTUP ZAKÁZÁN	NO ACCESS
VÝCHOD	EXIT
ZÁKAZ KOUŘENÍ	NO SMOKING

At Customs

Na Celnici

I have nothing to declare.
    ne-maam nits kpro-tsle-nyee

Nemám nic k proclení.

I have something to declare.
    maam nye-tso kpro-tsle-nyee

Mám něco k proclení.

Do I have to declare this?
    mu-seem to przhih-laa-sit
    kpro-tsle-nyee?

*Musím to přihlásit
k proclení?*

This is all my luggage.
    to ysoh maa fshekh-na
    za-va-za-dla

*To jsou má všechna
zavazadla.*

That's not mine.
    to ne-nyee mo-ye

To není moje.

I didn't know I had to declare it.
    ne-vye-dyel/-a ysem zhe to
    mu-seem przhih-laa-sit
    kpro-tsle-nyee

*Nevěděl/a jsem, že to
musím přihlásit
k proclení.* (m/f)

BUS

CESTOVÁNÍ AUTOBUSEM

Where's the bus stop?
    gde ye ow-to-bu-so-vaa
    za-staaf-ka?

*Kde je autobusová
zastávka?*

Which bus goes to ...?
    kte-ri ow-to-bus ye-de do ...?

Který autobus jede do ...?

How often do buses come?
    yak cha-sto yez-dee ow-to-bus?

Jak často jezdí autobus?

What time is	gdi ye-de ...	*Kdy jede ...*
the ... bus?	ow-to-bus?	*autobus?*
first	prv-nyee	*první*
last	po-sled-nyee	*poslední*
next	przhee-shtyee	*příští*

Could you let me know
when we get to ...?
    mol bi-ste mi pro-seem rzhee-tsi
    azh przhi-ye-de-me do ...?

*Mol by ste mi prosím říci
až přijedeme do ...?*

TRAIN   VE VLAKU

What station is this?
  yak se yme-nu-ye   *Jak se jmenuje*
  tah-le sta-nyi-tse?   *tahle stanice?*
Does this train stop at (Plzen)?
  sto-yee ten-to vlak f(plz-nyi)? *Stojí tento vlak v (Plzni)?*
The train is delayed/cancelled.
  vlak maa spozh-dye-nyee/   *Vlak má zpoždění/*
  ye zru-shen   *je zrušen.*
How long will it be delayed?
  ko-lik bu-de spozh-dye-nyee?   *Kolik bude zpoždění?*
Is it a direct route?
  ye to przhee-maa tse-sta bez   *Je to přímá cesta bez*
  przhe-stu-po-vaa-nyee?   *přestupování?*
Is that seat taken?
  ye to-to mees-to op-sa-ze-no?   *Je toto místo obsazeno?*
I want to get off at ...
  khtsi vi-stoh-pit v ...   *Chci vystoupit v ...*
I'd like a luggage locker.
  khtyel/-a bikh skrzhee-nku na   *Chtěl/a bych skřínku na*
  za-va-za-dla   *zavazadla.* (m/f)
Where's the last stop?
  gde ye ko-ne-chnaa?   *Kde je konečná?*
Where's platform three?
  gde ye trzhe-tyee   *Kde je třetí*
  naa-stu-pi-shtye?   *nástupiště?*

BOAT   CESTOVÁNÍ LODÍ

Where does the boat leave from?
  ot-kud ta lo-dye od-yeezh-dye? *Odkud ta loď odjíždí?*
What time does the boat arrive?
  gdi ta lo-dye przhi-yeezh-dye? *Kdy ta loď přijíždí?*

dock   przhee-sta-vi-stye/   *přístaviště/*
                przhe-stav/dok   *přístav/dok*

TAXI

Where can I get a taxi?
  gde nai-du ta-ksi?

Kde najdu taxi?

Please take me to ...
  pro-seem od-ves-te mye do ...

Prosím odvezte mě do ...

How much is it to go to ...?
  ko-lik sto-yee tses-ta do ...?

Kolik stojí cesta do ...?

Do we pay extra for luggage?
  pla-tee-me zvlaa-shtye za
  za-va-za-dla?

*Platíme zvlášť za
zavazadla?*

TAXI

Instructions

Continue!
  po-kra-chuy-te!

Pokračujte!

The next street to
the left/right.
  przhee-shtyee u-li-tsi
  vle-vo/fpra-vo

*Příští ulici
vlevo/vpravo.*

Please slow down.
  spo-mal-te pro-seem

Zpomalte, prosím.

Please wait here.
  po-chkey-te zde pro-seem

Počkejte zde, prosím.

Stop here!
  za-sta-fte!

Zastavte!

Stop at the corner.
  za-sta-fte na ro-hu

Zastavte na rohu.

Pokyny

GETTING AROUND

CAR

CESTOVÁNÍ AUTEM

Where can I rent a car?
gde si mo-hu pro-nai-moht ow-to?
Kde si mohu pronajmout auto?

How much is it daily/weekly?
ko-lik to sto-yee na den/tee-den?
Kolik to stojí na den/týden?

Does that include insurance/mileage?
ye ftse-nye zahr-nu-ta po-yist-ka/po-pla-tekh za na-ye-teh ki-lo-me-tri?
Je v ceně zahrnuta pojistka/poplatek za najeté kilometry?

Where's the next petrol station?
gde-ye przheesh-tyee ben-zee-no-vaa pum-pa?
Kde je příští benzínová pumpa?

Please fill the tank.
pl-noh naa-drzh pro-seem
Plnou nádrž, prosím.

I'd like ... litres.
khtyel bikh ... li-troo
Chtěl bych ... litrů.

Please check the ...	**pro-seem skon-tro-luy-te ...**	*Prosím zkontrolujte ...*
oil	**o-leye**	*olej*
tyre pressure	**tlak**	*tlak*
water	**vo-du**	*vodu*

Can I park here?
    mo-hu zde par-ko-vat?

Mohu zde parkovat?

How long can we park here?
    yak dloh-ho zde moo-zhe-me
    par-ko-vat?

Jak dlouho zde můžeme parkovat?

Does this road lead to ...?
    ve-de ta-to tses-ta do ...?

Vede tato cesta do ...?

air	vzdukh	*vzduch*
battery	ba-te-ri-ye	*baterie*
brakes	brz-di	*brzdy*
clutch	spoy-ka	*spojka*
driver's licence	rzhi-dyich-skee proo-kaz	*řidičský průkaz*
engine	mo-tor	*motor*
garage	ow-to-ser-vis	*autoservis*
indicator	smye-ro-vaa svye-tla	*směrová světla*
leaded/regular	spe-tsi-al	*special*
leaded	soo-per	*super*
lights	svye-tla	*světla*
oil	o-le-ye	*olej*
puncture	de-fekt	*defekt*
radiator	khla-dyich	*chladič*
seatbelt	bez-pech-no-stnyee paas	*bezpečnostní pás*
self-service	sa-mo-op-slu-ha	*samoobsluha*
tyres	pne-u-ma-ti-ki	*pneumatiky*
unleaded	na-tu-ral	*natural*
windscreen	przhe-dnyee sklo	*přední sklo*

Car Problems

We need a mechanic.
   po-trzhe-bu-ye-me
   ow-to-me-kha-ni-ka

What make is it?
   yak-aa ye to zna-chka?

The car broke down at ...
   ow-to se po-ka-zi-lo na ...

The battery is flat.
   ba-te-ri-e ye vi-bi-ta

The radiator is leaking.
   khla-dyich te-che

I have a flat tyre.
   maam de-fekt

It's overheating.
   mo-tor-se przhe-hrzhee-vaa

It's not working.
   ne-fun-gu-ye-to

I've run out of petrol.
   do-shel mi ben-zeen

Poruchy a Opravy

*Potřebujeme
automechanika.*

Jaká je to značka?

Auto se pokazilo na ...

Baterie je vybita.

Chladič teče.

Mám defekt.

Motor se přehřívá.

Nefunguje to.

Došel mi benzín.

BICYCLE

Is it within cycling distance?
do-sta-nu se tam na ko-le?
Is there a bike path?
ye ta-di stes-ka pro tsi-klis-ti?
Is there a guide to bicycle paths?
maa-te ma-pu
tsi-klis-tits-keekh tra-tyee?
Where can I find second-hand
bikes for sale?
gde pro-daa-va-yee
pow-zhi-taa ko-la?
Where can I hire a bicycle?
gde si mo-hu pooy-chit
yeezd-nyee ko-lo?

NA KOLE

Dostanu se tam na kole?

Je tady stezka pro cyklisty?

*Máte mapu
cyklistických tratí?*

*Kde prodávají
použitá kola?*

*Kde si mohu půjčit
jízdní kolo?*

BUTTER ON THE HEAD

Don't let people walk all over you.
Nenechat si srát na hlavu.
Don't let people shit on your head.

His mouth is going a hundred miles an hour.
Huba mu jede jak kolovrátek.
His mouth is going like a spinning wheel.

It's double Dutch to him.
Je to pro něj španělská vesnice.
It's a Spanish village to him.

to be up the creek without a paddle
ani svěcená voda mu nepomůže
not even holy water can help him

to drink like a fish
pít jak houba
to soak like a sponge

to have a chip on the shoulder
mít máslo na hlavě.
to have butter on the head

GETTING AROUND

How much is it for ...?	ko-lik to sto-yee na ...?	*Kolik to stojí na...?*
an hour	ho-dyi-nu	*hodinu*
the morning	do-po-led-ne	*dopoledne*
the afternoon	ot-po-led-ne	*odpoledne*
the day	den	*den*

I have a flat tyre.
maam peekh-loh
pne-u-ma-ti-ku
Mám píchlou
pneumatiku.

The brakes don't work.
brzdi ne-fun-gu-yee
Brzdy nefungují.

bike	ko-lo	*kolo*
bicycle path	ste-ska pro tsi-kli-sti	*stezka pro cyklisty*
to cycle	yez-dyit na ko-le	*jezdit na kole*
gear stick	rikh-lo-stnyee paa-ka	*rychlostní páka*
handlebars	rzhee-dyeet-ka	*řídítka*
helmet	hel-ma	*helma*
inner tube	du-she	*duše*
lights	svyet-la	*světla*
mountain bike	hor-skeh ko-lo	*horské kolo*
padlock	zaa-mek	*zámek*
pump	pum-pi-chka	*pumpička*
puncture	de-fekt	*defekt*
racing bike	zaa-vo-dnyee ko-lo	*závodní kolo*
saddle	sed-lo	*sedlo*
tandem	tan-dem	*tandem*
wheel	ko-lo	*kolo*

UBYTOVÁNÍ
ACCOMMODATION

Accommodation of all types, offering a range of facilities, is available. Information about accommodation is obtainable from information outlets in individual cities or towns. Many private homes offer *privát* or *Zimmer frei*. They usually have a sign in the window. Accommodation there is generally equivalent to that at a bed and breakfast.

FINDING ACCOMMODATION

SEHNÁNÍ UBYTOVÁNÍ

See In the Country, page 143, for words and phrases on camping.

I'm looking for a ...	hle-daam ...	*Hledám ...*
guesthouse	pen-zi-awn	*penzión*
hotel	ho-tel	*hotel*
motel	mo-tel	*motel*
youth hostel	u-bi-tov-nu/ho-stel/	*ubytovnu/ hostel/*
	stu-de-nts-koh	*studentskou*
	nots-le-haa-rnu	*noclehárnu*
Where can I find a ... hotel?	gde ye ... ho-tel?	*Kde je ... hotel?*
clean	chi-stee	*čistý*
good	do-bree	*dobrý*
nearby	ney-blizh-shee	*nejbližší*
Where's the ... hotel?	gde ye ... ho-tel?	*Kde je ... hotel?*
best	ney-lep-shee	*nejlepší*
cheapest	ney-lev-nyey-shee	*nejlevnější*

ACCOMMODATION

What's the address?
ya-koh maa a-dre-su? *Jakou má adresu?*

Could you write the address, please?
moo-zhe-te mi na-psat *Můžete mi napsat*
a-dre-su pro-seem? *adresu prosím?*

BOOKING AHEAD   REZERVACE

I'd like to book a room, please.
khtyel/-a bikh *Chtěl/a bych*
ob-yed-nat po-koy *objednat pokoj.* (m/f)

Do you have any rooms/
beds available?
maa-te vol-neh *Máte volné*
po-ko-ye/po-ste-le? *pokoje/postele?*

For (three) nights.
na (trzhi) no-tsi *na (tři) noci.*

How much for ...?	**ko-lik sto-yee ..?**	*Kolik stojí ..?*
one night	**yed-na nots**	*jedna noc*
a week	**tee-den**	*týden*
two people	**pro dva li-dyi**	*pro dva lidi*

I'll/We'll be arriving at ...
przhi-ye-du/przhi-ye-de-me v ... *Přijedu/Přijedeme v ...*

My name's ...
yme-nu-yi se ... *Jmenuji se ...*

Can I pay by credit card?
mo-hu pla-tyit kre-dit-nee *Mohu platit kreditní*
kar-toh? *kartou?*

CHECKING IN

NA RECEPCI

Do you have any rooms available?
  maa-te vol-neh po-ko-ye?

Máte volné pokoje?

Do you have a room with two beds?
  maa-te dvoh-loo-zhko-vee
  po-koy?

*Máte dvoulůžkový
pokoj?*

Do you have a room
with a double bed?
  maa-te po-koy sman-zhel-
  skoh po-ste-lee?

*Máte pokoj s manželskou
postelí?*

Where's the bathroom?
  gde ye koh-pel-na?

Kde je koupelna?

Is there hot water all day?
  ye ta-di te-plaa vo-da tse-lee den?

Je tady teplá voda celý den?

I'd like ...   khtyel/-a bikh ...   *Chtěl/a bych ...* (m/f)
  a single room   yed-no-loozh-ko-vee   *jednolůžkový*
                   po-koy   *pokoj*
  to share a dorm spo-le-chnoh   *společnou*
                   lo-zhnyi-tsi   *ložnici*

Sorry, we're full.
  bo-hu-zhel maa-me
  ob-sa-ze-no

*Bohužel máme
obsazeno.*

ACCOMMODATION

SIGNS

HOTEL	HOTEL
KEMPINK	CAMPING
MOTEL	MOTEL
PENZIÓN	GUESTHOUSE
PRIVÁT	BED & BREAKFAST
PRONÁJEM	RENT
STUDENTSKÁ KOLEJ	DORMITORY
TURISTICKÁ UBYTOVNA/	BACKPACKERS HOSTEL
NOCLEHÁRNA	
ZIMMER FREI	ROOM FOR RENT

I want a room with a ...	khtyel/-a bikh po-koy s ...	*Chtěl/a bych pokoj s ... (m/f)*
bathroom	koh-pel-noh	*koupelnou*
shower	se spr-khoh	*se sprchou*
TV	te-le-vi-zee	*televizí*
window	ok-nem	*oknem*

Can I see it?
  mo-hu se na nye po-dyee-vat? — *Mohu se na něj podívat?*
Are there any others?
  maa-te ye-shtye yi-neh
  po-koy-ye? — *Máte ještě jiné pokoje?*

Is there a discount for children/ students?
  maa-te sle-vu pro dye-tyi/
  stu-den-ti? — *Máte slevu pro děti/ studenty?*
It's fine. I'll take it.
  to ye fpo-rzhaat-ku.
  be-ru to — *To je v pořádku. Beru to.*

REQUESTS & QUERIES

ŽÁDOSTI A REKLAMACE

Where's the bathroom?
  gde ye koh-pel-na? — *Kde je koupelna?*
Is there somewhere to wash clothes?
  ye ta-di praa-del-na? — *Je tady prádelna?*
Can we use the kitchen?
  moo-zhe-me poh-zhit
  kukh-i-nyi? — *Můžeme použít kuchyni?*
Can we use the telephone?
  moo-zhe-me poh-zhit te-le-fon? — *Můžeme použít telefon?*
Do you have a safe where I can leave my valuables?
  maa-te ta-di sayf kde si moo-zhu
  ne-khat tsen-neh vye-tsi? — *Máte tady sejf kde si můžu nechat cenné věci?*
Could I have a receipt for them?
  moo-zhe-te mi daat na nye
  po-tvrze-nyee? — *Můžete mi dát na ně potvrzení?*

Do you change money here?
mye-nyee-te ta-di pe-nyee-ze? *Měníte tady peníze?*

Do you arrange tours?
or-ga-ni-zu-ye-te zaa-yez-di? *Organizujete zájezdy?*

Is there a message board?
ye tam ta-bu-le na vzka-zi? *Je tam tabule na vzkazy?*

Can I leave a message?
mo-hu ta-di ne-khat vzkaz? *Mohu tady nechat vzkaz?*

Is there a message for me?
ye tam pro mne nye-ya-kee
vzkaz? *Je tam pro mne nějaký vzkaz?*

Please wake us at (seven).
vzbu-dye-te naas v (sedm)
pro-seem *Vzbuďte nás v (sedm), prosím.*

Please change the sheets.
vi-me-nye-te pro-seem praa-dlo *Vyměňte prosím prádlo.*

The room needs to be cleaned.
po-koy pot-rzhe-bu-ye uk-li-dyit *Pokoj potřebuje uklidit.*

I've locked myself out of my room.
vim-kl/-a ysem se *Vymkl/a jsem se. (m/f)*

No, we left the key at reception.
ne ne-kha-li sme kleech
na re-tsep-tsi *Ne, nechali jsme klíč na recepci.*

ACCOMMODATION

YOU MAY HEAR ...

u-kazh-te mi pas pro-seem?
May I see your passport, please?

vi-plny-te pro-seem ten-to for-mu-laarzh
Please fill out this form.

ta-di se pod-pish-te
Sign here.

ya-koh maa-te poz-naa-va-tsee znach-ku?
What is your car registration number?

ACCOMMODATION

COMPLAINTS   STÍŽNOSTI

I can't open/close the window.
ne-mo-hu o-te-vrzheet/
za-vrzheet ok-no

*Nemohu otevřít/
zavřít okno.*

I don't like this room.
ten-hle po-koy se mi ne-lee-bee

Tenhle pokoj se mi nelíbí.

The toilet won't flush.
zaa-khod ne-splakh-u-ye

Záchod nesplachuje.

Can I change to another?
mo-hu se przhe-stye-ho-vat
do yi-neh-ho?

*Mohu se přestěhovat
do jiného?*

It's too ...	ye mots ...	*Je moc ...*
cold	stu-de-nee	*studený*
dark	tma-vee	*tmavý*
expensive	dra-hee	*drahý*
light/bright	svyet-lee	*světlý*
noisy	hluch-nee	*hlučný*
small	ma-lee	*malý*

This ... is not clean.	to-hle ne-nyee chi-steh ...	*Tohle není čisté ...*
blanket	de-ka	*deka*
pillow	pol-shtaarzh	*polštář*
pillowcase	po-vlak na pol-staarzh	*povlak na polštář*
sheet	pro-stye-ra-dlo	*prostěradlo*

CHECKING OUT

ODCHOD Z HOTELU

What time do we have to check out?
do gdi maa-me
vi-kli-dyit po-koy?

*Do kdy máme
vyklidit pokoj?*

I'm/We're leaving now.
od-yeezh-dim/-e

Odjíždím/e.

I'd like to pay the bill.
za-pla-tyeem

Zaplatím.

Can I pay with a travellers cheque?
mo-hu za-pla-tyit
tse-sto-vnyeem shek-em?

*Mohu zaplatit
cestovním šekem?*

Can I pay by credit card?
mo-hu pla-tyit u-vye-ro-voh
kar-toh?

*Mohu platit úvěrovou
kartou?*

There's a mistake in the bill.
voo-chtye ye o-mil

V účtě je omyl.

Can I leave my backpack
here until tonight?
mo-hu ta-di do ve-che-ra
ne-khat mooy ruk-sak?

*Mohu tady do večera
nechat můj ruksak?*

We'll be back in (three) days.
vraa-tyi-me se za (trzhi) dni

Vrátime se za (tři) dny.

RENTING

PRONÁJEM

I'm here about your ad for a
room to rent.
przhi-shel sem se po-dee-vat na
ten po-koy tso ste in-ze-ro-va-li
zhe ye na pro-naa-yem

*Přišel jsem se podívat na
ten pokoj co jste inzerovali,
že je na pronájem.*

Do you have any flats to rent?
maa-te nye-yak-eh bi-ti na
pro-naa-yem?

*Máte nějaké byty na
pronájem?*

I'm looking for a flat to rent for
(two) months.
hle-daam bit na pro-naa-yem
na (dva) mye-see-tse

*Hledám byt na pronájem
na (dva) měsíce.*

ACCOMMODATION

ACCOMMODATION

I'm looking for something close
to the city centre/railway station.

hle-daam nye-tso po-blee-zh k
tsen-tru mye-sta/naa-dra-zhee

Hledám něco poblíž k
centru města/nádraží.

Is there anything cheaper?

maa-te nye-tso lev-nyey-shee-ho?   *Máte něco levnějšího?*

Could I see it?

mo-hu se na to po-dee-vat?   *Mohu se na to podívat?*

How much is it per ...?	ko-lik ye to na ...?	*Kolik je to na ...?*
week	tee-den	*týden*
month	mye-seets	*měsíc*

Do you require a deposit?

pot-rzhe-bu-ye-te zaa-lo-hu?   *Potřebujete zálohu?*

I'd like to rent it for (one) month.

khtyel/-a bikh to pro-nai-moht
na (ye-den) mye-seets

Chtěl/a bych to pronajmout
na (jeden) měsíc. (m/f)

apartment	a-part-maan/bit	*apartmán/byt*
house	doom	*dům*
room	po-koy	*pokoj*
furnished	zarzh-ee-ze-nee	*zařízený*
partly furnished	chaast-ech-nye	*částečně*
	zarzh-ee-ze-nee	*zařízený*
unfurnished	ne-zarzh-ee-ze-nee	*nezařízený*

VE MĚSTE   AROUND TOWN

There are towns every few kilometres. Each town is quite unique, with its own character and history.

LOOKING FOR ...

Where's a/the ...?	gde-ye ...?	*Kde je ...?*
art gallery	ga-le-ri-ye	*galerie*
bank	ban-ka	*banka*
cinema	ki-no	*kino*
city centre	tsen-trum	*centrum*
... consulate	... kon-zu-laat	*... konzulát*
... embassy	... vel-vi-sla-nets-tvee	*... velvyslanectví*
... hotel	... ho-tel	*... hotel*
main square	hlav-nyee	*hlavní*
	naa-myes-tyee	*náměstí*
market	trzh-ni-tse	*tržnice*
police	po-li-tsi-ye	*policie*
post office	posh-ta	*pošta*
public toilet	ve-rzhey-neh	*veřejné*
	zaa-kho-di	*záchody*
telephone centre	te-le-fon-nyee	*telefonní*
	oo-strzhe-dna	*ústředna*
tourist office	tu-ri-sti-tskaa	*turistická*
	in-for-ma-chnyee	*informační*
	kan-tse-laarzh	*kancelář*
town square	naa-mye-styee	*náměstí*

AT THE BANK   V BANCE

I want to change (a) ...	khtyel/-a bikh vi-mnye-nyit ...	*Chtěl/a bych vyměnit ... (m/f)*
cash/money	pe-nyee-ze	*peníze*
(travellers) cheque	(tses-tov-nyee) shek	*(cestovní) šek*

Can I use my credit card to
withdraw money?
   mo-hu si vi-brat pe-nyee-ze s
   kre-dit-nyee kar-toh?

*Mohu si vybrat peníze s
kreditní kartou?*

Can I exchange money here?
   mo-hu si ta-di vi-mye-nyit
   pe-nyee-ze?

*Mohu si tady
vyměnit peníze?*

What's the exchange rate?
   ya-kee ye kurz?

Jaký je kurz?

What's your commission?
   ya-keh si ooch-tu-ye-te
   pop-lat-ki?

*Jaké si účtujete
poplatky?*

How many crowns per dollar?
   ko-lik ko-run do-sta-nu za
   ye-den do-lar?

*Kolik korun dostanu
za jeden dolar?*

Can I have smaller notes?
   moo-zhe-te mi daat
   men-shee bank-ov-ki?

*Můžete mi dát
menší bankovky?*

What time does the bank open?
   v ko-lik ho-dyin o-te-vee-raa
   ban-ka?

*V kolik hodin otevírá
banka?*

Where can I cash a
travellers cheque?
   gde mo-hu vi-mye-nyit
   tses-tov-nyee she-ki?

*Kde mohu vyměnit
cestovní šeky?*

Can I transfer money here
from my bank?
   mo-hu si sem przhe-vehst
   pe-nyee-ze ze sveh ban-ki?

*Mohu si sem převést
peníze ze své banky?*

How long will it take to arrive?
   yakh dloh-h o bu-de trvat
   nezh ta-di bu-doh?

*Jak dlouho bude trvat
než tady budou?*

Has my money arrived yet?
   przhi-shli mi uzh pe-nyee-ze?

Přišly mi už peníze?

Can I transfer money overseas?
   mo-hu u-dye-lat ban-ko-vnyee
   przhe-vod do za-hra-nyi-chee?

*Mohu udělat bankovní
převod do zahraničí?*

The automatic teller
swallowed my card.
   **ban-ko-mat mi
   ne-vraa-tyil kar-tu**

*Bankomat mi
nevrátil kartu.*

Please write it down.
   na-pish-te mi to pro-seem

Napište mi to prosím.

Where do I sign?
   gde to maam po-de-psat?

Kde to mám podepsat?

AT THE POST OFFICE   NA POŠTĚ

Larger post offices *(pošta)* have fax, telegram, telex and telephone services. Stamps *(známky)* can be purchased also at many
newspaper stalls, tobacconists and in hotels.

I want to buy ...	**raad/-a bikh koh-pil/-a ...**	*Rád/a bych koupil/a ...* (m/f)
postcards	**po-hled-nyi-tse**	*pohlednice*
stamps	**znaam-ki**	*známky*
I want to send a ...	**khtyel/-a bikh pos-lat ...**	*Chtěl/a bych poslat ...* (m/f)
fax	**faks**	*fax*
letter	**do-pis**	*dopis*
parcel	**ba-leek**	*balík*
postcard	**po-hled**	*pohled*

Please send it by air/surface.
   **po-shle-te to le-tets-ki/
   o-bi-chey-nye**

*Pošlete to letecky/
obyčejně.*

How much does it cost to send
this to ...?
   **ko-lik ye posh-tov-neh
   za to-hle do ...?**

*Kolik je poštovné
za tohle do ...?*

Where's the poste restante section?
   **gde ye od-dye-le-nyee po-ste
   re-stan-te?**

*Kde je oddělení poste
restante?*

Is there any mail for me?
   maam ta-di nye-ya-koh posh-tu?

Mám tady nějakou poštu?

AROUND TOWN

air mail	le-te-tski	*letecky*
express mail	eks-pres	*expres*
mail box	po-shto-vnyee	*poštovní*
	skhraan-ka	*schránka*
parcel	ba-leek	*balík*
postcode	posh-tov-nyee	*poštovní*
	smye-ro-va-tsee chee-slo	*směrovací číslo*
registered mail	do-po-ru-che-nye	*doporučeně*
surface mail	o-bi-chey-noh	*obyčejnou*
	posh-toh	*poštou*

TELECOMMUNICATIONS   TELEKOMUNIKACE

Where's the nearest public phone?
  gde ye ney-blizh-shee
  ve-rzhey-nee te-le-fon?

*Kde je nejbližší
veřejný telefon?*

Could I please use the telephone?
  mo-hu si za-te-le-fon-o-vat?

Mohu si zatelefonovat?

I want to call ...
  khtsi za-vo-lat ...

Chci zavolat ...

How much does a
three-minute call cost?
  ko-lik sto-yee trzhee-
  mi-nu-to-vee ho-vor?

*Kolik stojí tří-
minutový hovor?*

How much does each
extra minute cost?
  ko-lik sto-yee
  kazh-daa dal-shee mi-nu-ta?

*Kolik stojí
každá další minuta?*

The number is ...
  chees-lo ye ...

Číslo je ...

What's the area code for ...?
  ya-kaa ye przhed-vo-lba do ...?

Jaká je předvolba do ...?

I want to make a long-distance call
to (Australia).
  khtyel/-a bikh vo-lat do
  (ow-straa-li-ye)

*Chtěl/a bych volat do
(Austrálie).* (m/f)

I want to make a
reverse-charges/collect call.
  khtyel/-a bikh za-vo-lat na   *Chtěl/a bych zavolat na*
  oo-chet vo-la-neh-ho   *účet volaného.*

It's engaged.
  ye op-sa-ze-no   *Je obsazeno.*

I've been cut off.
  bil/-a ysem prze-ru-shen/-a   *Byl/a jsem přerušen/a.* (m/f)

area code/ telephone prefix	przhed-vol-ba	*předvolba*
direct	przhee-maa vol-ba	*přímá volba*
faulty line	po-ru-kha	*porucha*
long distance/ overseas call	me-zi-naa-rod-nyee-ho-vor	*mezinárodní hovor*
operator assisted calls	oo-strzhed-na	*ústředna*
operator	sbo-yo-va-tel-ka	*spojovatelka*
phone book	te-le-fon-nyee sez-nam	*telefonní seznam*
phone box	te-le-fon-nyee bu-tka/ka-bi-na	*telefonní budka/kabina*
phonecard	te-le-fon-nyee kar-ta	*telefonní karta*
STD call	me-zi-myes-tskee ho-vor	*meziměstský hovor*
urgent	ur-gen-tnyee	*urgentní*

The Internet   Internet

Is there a local Internet café?
  ye ta-di in-ter-net   *Je tady Internet*
  ka-vaar-na?   *kavárna?* (m/f)

I'd like to get Internet access.
  khtyel/-a bikh se przhi-po-yit *Chtěl/a bych se připojit*
  na in-ter-net   *na Internet.* (m/f)

I'd like to check my email.
  khtyel/-a bikh si skon-tro-lo-vat *Chtěl/a bych si skontrolovat*
  mooy e-meyl   *můj email.* (m/f)

I'd like to send an email.
  khtyel/-a bikh   *Chtěl/a bych*
  po-slat e-meyl   *poslat email.* (m/f)

AROUND TOWN

Making a Call   Telefonování

Hello, is (Peter) there?
  ha-law ye tam (petr)?   *Haló, je tam (Petr)?*

May I speak to (Jana)?
  mo-hu mlu-vit s (ya-noh)?   *Mohu mluvit s (Janou)?*

Who's calling?	gdo vo-laa?	*Kdo volá?*
It's (Joseph).	ta-di ye (yo-sef)	*Tady je (Josef).*
Yes, (he/she) is here.	yo ye ta-di	*Jo, je tady.*

One moment please.
  poch-key-te pro-seem   *Počkejte, prosím.*

I'm sorry, he's not here.
  ne-nyee ta-di   *Není tady.*

What time will she be back?
  gdi se vraa-tyee?   *Kdy se vrátí?*

Can I leave a message?
  mooh-zhu pro nyey/nyee   *Můžu pro něj/ní*
  ne-khat vzkaz?   *nechat vzkaz?*

Please tell (Carl) I called.
  pro-sim rzhek-nye-te (kar-lo-vi)   *Prosím řekněte (Karlovi),*
  ze ysem vo-lal/-a   *že jsem volal/a.* (m/f)

My number is ...
  meh chee-slo ye ...   *Mé číslo je ...*

I don't have a contact number.
  ne-maam te-le-fon   *Nemám telefon.*

I'll call back later.
  za-vo-laahm poz-dye-yi   *Zavolám později.*

What time should I call?
  fko-lik ho-din   *V kolik hodin*
  maam za-vo-lat?   *mám zavolat?*

THEY MAY SAY ...

to ye o-mil	You have the wrong number.
przhe-po-yeem	I'll transfer you.
ne-za-vye-shuy-te!	Don't hang up!
nyi-gdo to tam ne-be-re	Nobody is answering.

SIGHTSEEING

PROHLÍDKA MĚSTA

Where's the tourist office?
gde ye tu-ris-tits-kaa
kan-tse-laarzh?

*Kde je turistická
kancelář?*

Do you have a local map?
maa-te ma-pu o-ko-lee?

Máte mapu okolí?

Do you have a guidebook
in English?
maa-te proo-vot-tse v
an-glich-tyi-nye?

*Máte průvodce v
angličtině?*

What are the main attractions?
ya-keh ysoh zdey-shee
po-zo-ru-ho-dno-styi?

*Jaké jsou zdejší
pozoruhodnosti?*

We only have one day/two days.
maa-me ye-nom
ye-den/dva dni

*Máme jenom
jeden/dva dny.*

I'd like to see ...
khtyel/-a bikh vi-dyet ...

Chtěl/a bych vidět ... (m/f)

May we take photographs?
smee se tad-di fo-to-gra-fo-vat?

Smí se tady fotografovat?

I'll send you the photograph.
po-shlu vaam fot-ku

Pošlu vám fotku.

Could you take a
photograph of us?
moo-zhe-te naas
vi-fo-to-gra-fo-vat?

*Můžete nás
vyfotografovat?*

AROUND TOWN

Getting In

U Pokladny

What time does it open/close?
fko-lik ho-dyin o-te-vee-ra-yee/
za-vee-ra-yee?

*V kolik hodin otevírají/
zavírají?*

Is there an admission charge?
pla-tyee se tam fstu-pneh?

Platí se tam vstupné?

Is there a discount for ...?	ye tam sle-va pro ...?	*Je tam sleva pro ...?*
children	dye-tyi	*děti*
students	stu-den-ti	*studenty*
pensioners	pen-zi-sti	*penzisty*

The Sights   Památky

What is that building?
ya-kaa ye to bu-do-va?   *Jaká je to budova?*

What is this monument?
ya-kee ye to po-mnyeek?   *Jaký je to pomník?*

What is that?
tso ye to?   *Co je to?*

How old is it?
yak ye to zta-reh?   *Jak je to staré?*

castle	hrad/zaa-mekh	*hrad/zámek*
church/cathedral	ko-stel	*kostel*
cinema	ki-no	*kino*
concert hall	kon-tsert-nyee see-nye	*koncertní síň*
museum	muh-ze-um	*muzeum*
park	park	*park*
statue	so-kha	*socha*
university	u-ni-ver-zi-ta	*univerzita*

Tours

Prohlídka Města

Are there regular
tours we can join?
  po-rzhaa-da-yee se ta-di
  pra-vi-del-neh pro-hlee-dki?

*Pořádají se tady
pravidelné prohlídky?*

Can we hire a guide?
  moo-zhe-me si za-pla-tyit
  proo-vot-tse?

*Můžeme si zaplatit
průvodce?*

How much is the tour/a guide?
  ko-lik sto-yee zaa-yezd/
  proo-vod-tse?

*Kolik stojí zájezd/
průvodce?*

How long is the tour?
  yak dloh-ho trvaa zaa-yezd/
  pro-hleed-ka?

*Jak dlouho trvá zájezd/
prohlídka?*

Will we have free time?
  bu-de-me meet vol-nee chas?

Budeme mít volný čas?

How long are we here for?
  yak dloh-ho ta-di
  zoo-sta-ne-me?

*Jak dlouho tady
zůstaneme?*

What time should we be back?
  fko-lik ho-dyin se maa-me
  vraa-tyit?

*V kolik hodin se máme
vrátit?*

The guide has paid/will pay.
  proo-vod-tse za-pla-tyil/
  za-pla-tyee

*Průvodce zaplatil/
zaplatí.*

I'm with them.
  yaa ysem snyi-mi

Já jsem s nimi.

I've lost my group.
  stra-til/-a ysem svoh
  sku-pi-nu

*Ztratil/a jsem svou
skupinu.* (m/f)

Have you seen a group of
(Australians)?
  hle-daam sku-pi-nu
  (ow-stra-la-noo)?

*Hledám skupinu
(Australanů)?*

ARCHITECTURAL TERMS

When visiting Czechia, you'll inevitably be confronted with buildings of diverse architectural styles and periods. The oldest will be ruins of castles built as early as 800 AD, like Prague Castle, which was founded between 880 and 890 AD. Below is some useful terminology:

Románský styl   **Romanesque style**
This style dates from the 9th to 12th centuries and during that time Bohemia was incorporated into the Holy Roman Empire. The Romanesque style is characterised by massive walls, heavy rounded arches and cross vaults.

Gotika   **Gothic**
The Gothic style predominated in the Czech lands from the 13th to 16th centuries when Bohemia entered its so-called Golden Age. The Gothic style is characterised by high lofty cathedrals, castles built on top of hills and narrow towers guarding town gates. Broken arches were also a typical feature. Late Gothic is also known as 'ornamental Gothic'. Outstanding examples of Gothic architecture are St Vitus Cathedral (*Katedrála sv. Víta*) at Prague castle, the famous Charles Bridge (*Karlův most*), Charles University (*Carolinum*), Powder Tower and Karlstejn castle.

Renesance   **Renaissance**
During the Renaissance (1350-1650), numerous foreigners, mainly Italians, worked in Bohemia. Renaissance architecture is typified by classical forms, an obsession with grace and symmetry, and exterior walls covered with ornamental facades. Spacious majestic constructions are light, and equipped with decorative furniture.

Baroko   **Baroque**
The Baroque style (late 16th to early 18th centuries) is characterised by extensive ornamentation with movement and emotive sculptures and frescoes.

AROUND TOWN

Rokoko **Rococo**
Rococo became a part of the late Baroque architecture (18th century) and developed into a lifestyle. Rococo required a three-dimensional balance, drawing-room intimacy and decorative gentleness. A great example of the style is the Archbishop's Palace in Prague.

Romantismus/Historismus **Romantic/Historic**
The 19th century was known for the establishment of parks with exotic constructions, and the focus was on the countryside. Mountain cottages and look-out towers were built and castle ruins were popular garden features.

Klasicismus/Secese **Art Nouveau**
Art Nouveau was popular at the turn of the 19th Century. It's characterised by the use of natural forms, such as flowers and leaves. The Czech painter Alfons Mucha in particular made the style famous all over the world. Mass building of houses had begun and spa towns were established during this period.

Moderní architektura/Kubismus **Cubism**
Rich decoration was replaced by simplicity in the early 20th century and interiors focused on functionality. Cubist architecture is completely unique to Prague and many functionalist buildings are also of great artistic value. The triangle surfaces and broken edges, which create a plastic effect on the material, were typical features. In Prague, there are many important buildings from this period, notably *U Černé Matky* (The House at the Black Virgin), many villas under the Vyšehrad Rock as well as the Spa House in Bohdanec.

In 1920, the avant-garde *Devětsil* movement was established. *Devětsil* became a platform for functional Modernism, forming a program for a new approach to architecture, design, photography, film, literature and music.

AROUND TOWN

AT THE HAIRDRESSER OR BARBER   HOLIČ – KADEŘNÍK

I'd like my hair cut.
  khtyel/-a bikh
  o-stree-hat vla-si
Chtěl/a bych
ostříhat vlasy. (m/f)

Don't cut it too short.
  ne-khtsi to mots kraa-tkeh
Nechci to moc krátké.

I'd like my hair in the style of ...
  khteyl/-a bikh
  oo-ches po-dle ...
Chtěl/a bych
účes podle ... (m/f)

Shave it all off!
  khtsi to fse-khno vi-ho-lit!
Chci to všechno vyholit!

I'd like my hair dyed ...
(see page 117 for colours).
  khyel/-a bikh
  na-bar-vit vla-si na ...
Chtěl/a bych
nabarvit vlasy na ... (m/f)

I'd like a shave.
  pro-seem o-ho-lit
Prosím oholit.

I'd like my beard/moustache
trimmed please.
  pro-seem za-strzhi-noht
  voh-zi/kneer
Prosím zastřihnout
vousy/knír.

cut and blow wave	o-strzhi-at a vi-foh-kat	*ostříhat a vyfoukat*
haircut/trim	o-strzhee-hat	*ostříhat*
hairdressing salon	ho-lich-stvee-ka-derzh-nyits-tvee	*holičství-kadeřnictví*
perm	trva-loh	*trvalou*
trim	za-strzhih-noht	*zastřihnout*
wash and dry	u-meet u-su-shit	*umýt a usušit*
a little more off ...	tro-khu veets	*trochu víc ...*
the back/front	vzda-vu/vprzhe-du	*vzadu/vpředu*
around the neck	na krku	*na krku*
on the sides	po stra-naakh	*po stranách*
at the top	na-ho-rzhe	*nahoře*

SIGNS

KOUŘENÍ ZAKÁZÁNO	NO SMOKING
NEPŘETRŽITÝ PROVOZ	OPEN 24 HOURS
OTEVŘENO	OPEN
SEM	PULL
TAM	PUSH
TEPLÉ/STUDENÉ	HOT/COLD
UMÝVÁRNY/TOALETY/WC	TOILETS
DÁMY/ŽENY	LADIES/WOMEN
PÁNI/MUŽI	GENTLEMEN/MEN
VCHOD	ENTRANCE
VSTUP VOLNÝ	FREE ENTRY
VSTUP ZAKÁZÁN	NO ENTRY
VSTUPNÉ	ENTRY FEE
VÝCHOD	EXIT
ZÁKAZ	PROHIBITED
ZAVŘENO	CLOSED

AROUND TOWN

PAPERWORK / DOKLADY

name	ymeh-no	*jméno*
address	a-dre-sa	*adresa*
date of birth	da-toom na-ro-ze-nyee	*datum narození*
place of birth	mee-sto na-ro-ze-nyee	*místo narození*
age	vyek	*věk*
sex	po-la-vee	*pohlaví*
nationality	naa-rod-nost	*národnost*
religion	naa-bo-zhen-stvee	*náboženství*
profession/work	za-mye-stnaa-nyee	*zaměstnání*
reason for travel	doo-vod tse-sti	*důvod cesty*
marital status	staf	*stav*
single	svo-bo-dnee/-aa	*svobodný/á* (m/f)
married	zhe-na-tee/vda-naa	*ženatý/udaná* (m/f)
divorced	roz-ve-den/-a	*rozveden/a* (m/f)
widow/widower	vdo-vets/vdo-va	*vdovec/vdova* (m/f)

identification	proo-kas to-to-zhno-styi	*průkaz totožnosti*
passport number	chee-slo pa-su	*číslo pasu*
visa	vi-zum	*vizum*
baptismal certificate/ birth certificate	krzhe-stnyee list/ rod-nee list	*křestní list/ rodny list*
driver's licence	rzhi-dyich-skee proo-kaz	*řidičský průkaz*
customs	tsel-nyi-tse	*celnice*
immigration	e-mi-gra-tse	*emigrace*
purpose of visit	doo-vod naa-vshtye-vi	*důvod návštěvy*
holiday	do-vo-le-naa	*dovolená*
business	slu-zheb-nye	*služebně*
visiting relatives	naa-fshtye-va przee-buz-neekh	*návštěva příbuzných*
visiting the homeland	naa-fshtye-va vla-styi	*návštěva vlasti*

AROUND TOWN

KULTURA, ZÁBAVA

GOING OUT

It's common for Czech men to help a woman on with her coat, offer her a seat, let her enter first and open the door for her. Women usually accept these expressions of politeness.

GOING OUT
Where to Go

KULTURA, ZÁBAVA
Kam Jít

What's there to do in the evenings?
    kam-se ta-di daa ve-cher yeet?   *Kam se tady dá večer jít?*

Where can I find out what's on?
    yak se daa zyi-styit tso   *Jak se dá zjistit co*
    ye na pro-gra-mu?   *je na programu?*

What's on tonight?
    tso ye dnes ve-cher   *Co je dnes večer*
    na pro-gra-mu?   *na programu?*

Which paper are
the concerts listed in?
    fkte-reekh no-vi-naakh ye   *V kterých novinách je*
    pro-gram kon-tser-too?   *program koncertů?*

In the entertainment guide.
    v kul-tur-nyeem pro-gra-mu   *V kulturním programu.*

I feel like going to a/an/the ...	maam khuty jeet ...	*Mám chuť jít ...*
bar	do ba-ru	*do baru*
café	do ka-vaar-ni	*do kavárny*
cinema	do ki-na	*do kina*
concert	na kon-tsert	*na koncert*
disco	na di-sko-teh-ku	*na diskotéku*
opera	na o-pe-ru	*na operu*
restaurant	do re-stow-ra-tse	*do restaurace*
theatre	do dyi-vad-la	*do divadla*

I feel like ...	maam khooty ...	*Mám chuť...*
a stroll	na pro-khaa-sku	*na procházku*
dancing	za-tan-tso-vat si	*zatancovat si*
going for a	na ka-feh/	*na kafe/*
coffee/drink	na skle-nich-ku	*na skleničku*

Invitations   Pozvání

What are you doing this evening/
this weekend?
    tso dyeh-laash dnes
    ve-cher/ten-to vee-kend?   *Co děláš dnes*
                                    večer/tento víkend?

Would you like to go out somewhere?
    khtse se ti nye-kam yeet?   *Chce se ti někam jít?*

Do you know a good restaurant
(that's cheap)?
    znaash nye-ya-koh do-broh
    res-tow-rat-si (le-vnoh)?   *Znáš nejakou dobrou*
                                      restauraci (levnou)?

Would you like to go for a drink/meal?
    ne-maash khu-tye na
    skle-nich-ku/na yeed-lo?   *Nemáš chuť na*
                                      skleničku/na jídlo?

My shout. (I'll buy.)
    yaa pla-teem   *Já platím.*

Do you want to come to the ...
concert with me?
    khtyel/-a bi-ste jeet se
    mnoh na ... kon-tsert?   *Chtěl/a byste jít se*
                                      mnou na ... koncert? (m/f)

Responding to Invitations   Odpověď na Pozvání

Yes, I'd love to.
    yo mots raad/-a   *Jo, moc rád/a.* (m/f)

That's very kind of you.
    to ye od vaas mots hes-keh   *To je od vás moc hezké.*

Yes. Where shall we go?
    yo. kam pooy-de-me?   *Jo, kam půjdeme?*

No, I'm afraid I can't.
    ne ye mi lee-to a-le ne-mo-hu   *Ne, je mi líto, ale nemohu.*

What about tomorrow?
    a tso tak zee-tra?   *A co tak zítra?*

Nightclubs & Bars

Are there any good nightclubs?
  ysoh ta-di nye-ya-keh
  do-breh noch-nyee pod-ni-ki?
How do you get to this club?
  yak se ye-de do to-ho klu-bu?
Shall we dance?
  smeem pro-sit?
I'm sorry, I'm a terrible dancer.
  pro-miny-te a-le ney-sem
  do-bree ta-nech-nyeek
What type of music do you prefer?
  ya-koh hud-bu maa-te raad/-a?
I really like (polka).
  lee-bee se mi (pol-ka)
Where can we dance some (salsa)?
  gde si moo-zhe-me za-tan-chit
  (sal-su)?
Do you have to pay to enter?
  pla-tyee se tam fstup-neh?
Yes, it's ...
  yo pla-tyee se ...

Noční Kluby a Bary

*Jsou tady nějaké
dobré noční podniky?*

Jak se jede do toho klubu?

Smím prosit?

*Promiňte, ale nejsem
dobrý tanečník.*

Jakou hudbu máte rád/a? (m/f)

Líbí se mi (polka).

*Kde si můžeme zatančit
(salsu)?*

Platí se tam vstupné?

Jo, platí se ...

This place is great!
   to-le ye baa-ye-chneh mee-sto!   *Tohle je báječné místo!*
I'm having a great time!
   maam se fan-ta-sti-tski!   *Mám se fantasticky!*
I don't like the music here.
   ta-le hud-ba se mi ne-lee-bee   *Tahle hudba se mi nelíbí.*
Shall we go somewhere else?
   poo-yde-me nye-kam yi-nam?   *Půjdeme někam jinam?*

Arranging to Meet   Setkání
What time/Where shall we meet?
   kdi/gde se set-kaa-me?   *Kdy/Kde se setkáme?*
Let's meet at (eight o'clock) at the ...
   set-kaa-me se v (osm) przed ...   *Setkáme se v (osm) před ...*
OK. I'll see you then.
   za-tyeem a-hoy   *Zatím ahoj.*
I'll come over at (six).
   przhi-ye-du v (shest)   *Přijedu v (šest).*
I'll pick you up at (nine).
   przhi-ye-du pro te-be f (de-vyet)   *Přijedu pro tebe v (devět).*
I'll try to make it.
   bu-du se sna-zhit beet na-chas   *Budu se snažit být načas.*
If I'm not there by (nine),
don't wait for me.
   gdizh tam ne-bu-du do   *Když tam nebudu do*
   (de-vaa-teh) tak na mne   *(deváté) tak na mne*
   ne-che-key-te   *nečekejte.*
I'll be along later. Where will you be?
   przhi-ye-du po-zdye-yi.   *Přijedu později.*
   gde vaas nai-du?   *Kde vás najdu?*
See you later/tomorrow.
   na skhle-da-noh   *Na shledanou*
   po-zdye-yi/zeet-ra   *později/zítra.*
Sorry I'm late.
   pro-miny-te spoz-dyil ysem se   *Promiňte, zpozdil jsem se.*
Never mind.
   ne-va-dyee   *Nevadí.*

DATING & ROMANCE
The Date

Would you like to do something ...?	khtyel/-a bis nye-tso dye-lat ...?	
tomorrow	zeet-ra	
tonight	ve-cher	
at the weekend	o vee-ken-du	

Yes, I'd love to.
yo mots raad/-a

Thanks, but I'd rather not.
dye-ku-yi ra-dye-yi ne

I'm afraid I'm busy.
ye mi lee-to a-le ne-maam chas

Where would you like to go?
kam bikh-om shli?

Will you take me home?
vez-mesh mye do-moo?

Do you want to come inside for a while?
khtsesh jeet na khvee-li do-vnyitrzh?

Can I see you again?
moo-zhe-me se za-se nye-kdi strzhe-tnoht?

I'll call you tomorrow.
zee-tra tyi za-vo-laam

RANDE A ROMANCE
Rande

Chtěl/a bys něco dělat ...? (m/f)
zítra
večer
o víkendu

Jo, moc rád/a. (m/f)

Děkuji, raději ne.

Je mi líto, ale nemám čas.

Kam bychom šli?

Vezmeš mě domů?

Chceš jít na chvíli dovnitř?

Můžeme se zase někdy střetnout?

Zítra ti zavolám.

Classic Pick-Up Lines

Would you like a drink?
khtsesh se na-peet?

Do you have a light?
maash o-heny?

Do you mind if I sit here?
mo-hu si przhi-sed-noht?

Shall we get some fresh air?
pooy-dem se pro-vye-trat?

Do you have a girlfriend?
maash przhee-tel-ki-nyi?

Klasické Namlouvání

Chceš se napít?

Máš oheň?

Mohu si přisednout?

Půjdem se provětrat?

Máš přítelkyni?

Do you have a boyfriend?
   maash przhee-te-le?   *Máš přítele?*
He's/She's just a friend.
   to ye ye-nom ka-ma-raat/-ka   *To je jenom kamarád/ka.* (m/f)
Can I take you home?
   mo-hu tye vzeet do-moo?   *Mohu tě vzít domů?*

Classic Rejections

Klasické Odmítnutí

No, thank you.
   ne dye-ku-yi   *Ne, děkuji.*
I'd rather not.
   ra-dye-yi ne   *Raději ne.*
I'm here with my girlfriend.
   ysem ta-di se svoh   *Jsem tady se svou*
   przhee-tel-ki-nye   *přítelkyní.*
I'm here with my boyfriend.
   ysem ta-di se sveem   *Jsem tady se svým*
   przhee-te-lem   *přítelem.*
I'm sorry, I've got
better things to do.
   ye mi lee-to a-le maam   *Je mi líto, ale mám*
   yi-nee pro-gram   *jiný program.*
Stop hassling me!
   dey mi po-koy!   *Dej mi pokoj!*
Leave me alone!
   nekh mye beet!   *Nech mě být!*
Excuse me, I have to go now.
   pro-mi-ny a-le mu-seem yeet *Promiň, ale musím jít.*
Get lost!
   zmiz!   *Zmiz!*
I'm not interested!
   ne-maam zaa-yem!   *Nemám zájem!*

Making Love

I want you.
    khtsi tye

Do you like this?
    lee-bee se tyi to?

I (don't) like that.
    to se mi (ne-)lee-bee

Please (don't) stop!
    pro-seem (ne-)przhe-staa-vey!

I think we should stop now.
    mi-sleem zhe bi-khom yizh
    mye-li przhe-stat

Kiss me!
    lee-bey mye!

Take this off.
    sun-dey-to

Touch me here.
    po-hla-dye mye ta-di

I want to make love to you.
    khtsi se ste-boh mi-lo-vat

Let's go to bed!
    poy-dyme do po-ste-le!

Do you have a condom?
    maash kon-dom?

Afterwards

That was amazing!
    to bi-lo baa-yech-nee!

Would you like a cigarette?
    khtsesh tsi-ga-re-tu?

Can I stay over?
    mo-hu ta-di zoos-tat?
    przhez nots?

You can't sleep here tonight.
    dnes ta-di ne-moo-zhes spaat

When can I see you again?
    gdi tye za-se u-vi-dyeem?

Milování

Chci tě.

Líbí se ti to?

To se mi (ne)líbí.

Prosím (ne)přestávej!

*Myslím, že bychom již
měli přestat.*

Líbej mě!

Sundej to.

Pohlaď mě tady.

Chci se s tebou milovat.

Pojďme do postele!

Máš kondom?

Potom

To bylo báječný!

Chceš cigaretu?

*Mohu tady zůstat
pře noc?*

Dnes tady nemůžeš spát.

Kdy tě zase uvidím?

Love

I love you.
  mi-loo-yi tye
I'm really happy with you.
  ysem ste-boh sku-te-chnye
  stya-stnee/-aa
Do you love me?
  mi-loo-yesh mye?
Do you want to go out with me?
  khtsesh se mnoh kho-dyit?
Let's move in together.
  mo-hli bi-khom spo-lu zheet
Will you marry me?
  khtsesh si mye vzeet?

Leaving & Breaking Up

I have to leave tomorrow.
  zeet-ra mu-seem o-de-yeet
I'll miss you.
  bu-de se mi po to-bye stee-skat
I'll come and visit you.
  przhi-ye-du za te-boh
I really want us to keep in touch.
  khtyel/-a bikh a-bi-khom
  zoo-sta-li fkon-takt-u
I don't think it's working out.
  ne-mi-sleem zhe naam to
  kla-pe
I want to stay friends.
  khtyel/-a bikh a-bi-khom
  zoo-sta-li przhaa-te-leh

Láska

Miluji tě.

*Jsem s tebou skutečně
šťastný/á.* (m/f)

Miluješ mě?

Chceš se mnou chodit?

Mohli bychom spolu žít.

Chceš si mě vzít?

Odchod a Rozchod

Zítra musím odejít.

Bude se mi po tobě stýskat.

Přijedu za tebou.

*Chtěl/a bych, abychom
zůstali v kontaktu.* (m/f)

*Nemyslím, že nám to
klape.*

*Chtěl/a bych, abychom
zůstali přátelé.* (m/f)

RODINA

FAMILY

Family is very important to Czechs. Even distant relatives are considered as part of the close family circle.

QUESTIONS

OTÁZKY

Are you married?
  yste zhe-na-tee?
  yste vda-naa?

Jste ženatý? (m)
Jste vdaná? (f)

Do you have a
girlfriend/boyfriend?
  maash przhee-tel-ki-nyi/
  przee-te-le?

Máš přítelkyni/
přítele?

How many children do you have?
  ko-lik maa-te dye-tyee?

Kolik máte dětí?

How many brothers/
sisters do you have?
  ko-lik maa-te bra-troo/se-ster?

Kolik máte bratrů/sester?

How old are they?
  yak jsoh sta-rzhee?

Jak jsou staří?

Do you live with your family?
  bid-leesh se-svoh ro-dyi-noh?

Bydlíš se svou rodinou?

Do you get along with your family?
  vi-khaa-zeesh se-svoh
  ro-dyi-noh?

Vycházíš se svou
rodinou?

REPLIES

ODPOVĚDI

I'm ...	ysem ...	Jsem ...
single	svo-bod-nee/ svo-bod-naa	*svobodný/ svobodná* (m/f)
married	zhe-na-tee/ vda-naa	*ženatý/ vdaná* (m/f)
separated	ne-zhi-ye-me spo-lu	*nežijeme spolu*
divorced	roz-ve-de-nee/ roz-ve-de-naa	*rozvedený/ rozvedená* (m/f)
a widower/ widow	vdo-vets/ vdo-va	*vdovc/ vdova*

FAMILY

I have a partner.
maam part-ne-rzha/
part-ner-ku
Mám partneřa/
partnerku. (m/f)

We live together but
we're not married.
zhi-ye-me spo-lu a-le
ney-sme od-daa-ni
Žijeme spolu ale
nejsme oddáni.

I don't have any children.
ne-maam zhaa-dneh dye-tyi
Nemám žádné děti.

I have a daughter/son.
maam tse-ru/si-na
Mám dceru/syna.

I live with my family.
bid-leem sro-dyi-chi
Bydlím s rodiči.

FAMILY MEMBERS   ČLENOVÉ RODINY

baby	dyee-tye/mi-min-ko	*dítě/miminko*
boy	kluk	*kluk*
brother	bra-tr	*bratr*
children	dye-tyi	*děti*
daughter	tse-ra	*dcera*
family	ro-dyi-na	*rodina*
father/dad	taa-ta	*táta*
father-in-law	tkhaan	*tchán*
girl	hol-ka	*holka*
grandfather	dye-de-chekh	*dědeček*
grandmother	ba-bi-chka	*babička*
husband	man-zhel	*manžel*
mother/mum	mat-ka/maa-ma	*matka/máma*
mother-in-law	tkhee-nye	*tchýně*
sister	ses-tra	*sestra*
son	sin	*syn*
wife	man-zhel-ka	*manželka*

TALKING WITH PARENTS

KONVERZACE S RODIČI

FAMILY

When is the baby due?
  gdi to che-kaa-te?

Kdy to čekáte?

What are you going to call the baby?
  yak se boo-de yme-no-vat?

Jak se bude jmenovat?

Is this your first child?
  ye to va-she prvnyee dyee-tye?

Je to vaše první dítě?

How many children do you have?
  ko-lik maa-te dye-tyee?

Kolik máte dětí?

How old are your children?
  yak sta-reh ysoh va-she dye-tyi?

Jak staré jsou vaše děti?

I can't believe it! You look too young.
  to ne-nyee mo-zhneh!
  vi-pa-daa-te mots mla-dye

To není možné!
Vypadáte moc mladě.

Does he/she attend school?
  kho-dyee do shko-lee?

Chodí do školy?

Who looks after the children?
  gdo hlee-da dye-tyi?

Kdo hlídá děti?

Do you have grandchildren?
  maa-te vnoh-cha-ta?

Máte vnoučata?

What's the baby's name?
  yak se to dyee-tye yme-nu-ye?

Jak se to dítě jmenuje?

Is it a boy or a girl?
  ye to kluk ne-bo hol-ka?

Je to kluk nebo holka?

Is he/she well-behaved?
  ye ho-dnee/hod-naa?

Je hodný/hodná? (m/f)

Does he/she let you sleep at night?
  ne-khaa vaas vno-tsi spaat?

Nechá vás v noci spát?

He's/She's very big for his/her age!
  ye mots ve-li-kee/ve-li-kaa
  na svooy vyek!

Je moc veliký/veliká
na svůj věk! (m/f)

What a beautiful child!
  to ye he-skeh dye-tyaa-tko!

To ye hezké děťátko!

He/She looks like you.
  po-do-baa se na-vaas

Podobá se na vás.

FAMILY

He/She has your eyes.
maa va-she o-chi

Má vaše oči.

Who does he/she look like,
Mum or Dad?
po-do-baa se na maa-mu
ne-bo na taa-tu?

*Podobá se na mámu
nebo na tátu?*

TALKING WITH CHILDREN

KONVERZACE S DĚTMI

What's your name?
yak se yme-nu-yesh?

Jak se jmenuješ?

How old are you?
ko-lik ye tyi let?

Kolik je ti let?

When's your birthday?
gdi maash na-ro-ze-nyi-ni?

Kdy máš narozeniny?

Have you got brothers and sisters?
maash soh-ro-zen-tse?

Máš sourozence?

Do you have a pet at home?
maash do-ma nye-ya-keh
zvee-rzhaat-ko?

*Máš doma nějaké
zvířátko?*

Do you go to school or kinder?
kho-dyeesh do shko-li ne-bo
do shko-lki?

*Chodíš do školy nebo
do školky?*

Do you like school?
lee-bee se tyi ve shko-le?

Líbí se ti ve škole?

Do you play sport?
dye-laash nye-ya-kee sport?

Děláš nějaký sport?

What sport do you play?
ya-kee dye-laash sport?

Jaký děláš sport?

What do you do after school?
tso dye-laash po shko-le?

Co děláš po škole?

We speak a different language in
my country so I don't understand
you very well.
mi mlu-vyee-me u naas yi-neem
ya-zi-kem a pro-to ti
shpat-nye ro-zu-meem

*My mluvíme u nás jiným
jazykem a proto ti
špatně rozumím.*

FAMILY

Do you want to play a game?
    khtsesh si za-hraat
    nye-ya-koh hru?

*Chceš si zahrát
nějakou hru?*

What shall we play?
    yak si bu-de-me hraat?

Jak si budeme hrát?

Have you lost your parents?
    stra-tyi-li se tyi ro-dyi-che?

Ztratili se ti rodiče?

PETS

DOMÁCÍ ZVÍŘATA

Do you like animals?
    maash raad/-a zvee-rzha-ta?

Máš ráda zvířata? (m/f)

What a cute (puppy)!
    to ye hez-kee (pey-sek)!

To je hezký (pejsek)!

What's he/she called?
    yak se yme-nu-ye?

Jak se jmenuje?

What breed is he/she?
    ya-kaa ye to ra-sa?

Jaká je to rasa?

SMALL THINGS

The use of diminutive suffixes is common in Czech. These are additions to nouns and adjectives to express smallness or affection; for example, when expressing the smallness and cuteness of a puppy. The most common suffixes are *-ek* (m); *-ka* (f); *-ko* (neut).

rabbit	*zajíc*	little rabbit	*zajíček*
turtle	*želva*	little turtle	*želvička*
animal	*zvíře*	little animal	*zvířátko*

Diminutives aren't found in dictionaries. They're not only used when speaking with children, but also used in familiar communication between friends and family members, eg, *Haničko, pojď na kafíčko!*, 'Hanna, let's go for a coffee!'.

FAMILY

Does he/she bite?
koh-she?

Kouše?

Do you have any pets?
maash nye-ya-kaa zvee-rzha-ta?

Máš nějaká zvířata?

I have a ...	maam ...	*Mám ...*
bird	ptaa-chka	*ptáčka*
canary	ka-naa-ra	*kanára*
cat	ko-chi-chku	*kočičku*
dog	pey-ska	*pejska*
fish	ri-bi-chku	*rybičku*
guinea pig	mor-che	*morče*
hamster	krzhe-chka	*křečka*
mouse	mish	*myš*
rabbit	za-yee-tse	*zajíce*
tortoise	zhe-lvu	*želvu*

ZÁLIBY

INTERESTS

COMMON INTERESTS

SPOLEČNÉ ZÁLIBY

What do you do in
your spare time?
  yak traa-vi-te vol-nee chas?

Jak trávíte volný čas?

Do you like ...?   maa-te raad/-a ...?/   *Máte rád/a ...?*
                                          (m/f)/

                   lee-bee se vaam ...?   *Líbí se vám ...?*
I (don't) like ... (ne-)maam raad/-a .../ *(Ne)mám rád/a ...*
                                          (m/f)/

                   (ne-)lee-bee se mi ... *(Ne)líbí se mi ...*
  dancing   tunts-o-vaa-nee   *tancování*
  films   fil-mi   *filmy*
  food   yeed-lo   *jídlo*
  hiking   tu-ris-ti-ka   *turistika*
  music   hud-ba   *hudba*
  photography   fo-to-gra-fi-e   *fotografie*
  reading   chtye-nee/kni-hi   *čtění/knihy*
  shopping   na-ku-po-vaa-nee   *nakupování*
  talking   mlu-ve-nee   *mluvení*
  travelling   tses-to-vaa-nee   *cestování*

STAYING IN TOUCH

UDRŽOVÁNÍ KONTAKTŮ

Tomorrow is my last day here.
  zee-tra ye mooy pos-led-nee
  den ta-di

Zítra je můj posledný den tady.

Do you have a pen and paper?
  maa-te pe-ro a pa-peer?

Máte pero a papír?

Can I have your address?
  daa-te mi va-shi ad-re-su?

Dáte mi vaši adresu?

Here's my address.
  ta-di ye mo-ye ad-re-sa

Tady je moje adresa.

If you ever visit (Scotland) you
must come and visit us.
   gdizh przhi-de-te do
   (skot-ska) mu-see-te naas
   nav-shtee-vit

*Když přijedete do
(Skotska) musíte nás
navštívit.*

Do you have access to a fax machine?
   maa-te przhi-stup gfaks-u?

Máte přístup k faxu?

I'll send you copies of the photos.
   posh-lem vaam fot-ki

Pošlem vám fotky.

It's been great meeting you.
   ysem raad/-a zhe sme se
   se-znaa-mi-li

*Jsem rád/a, že sme se
seznámili. (m/f)*

Keep in touch!
   oz-vi-te se!

Ozvite se!

INTERESTS

ART
Seeing Art

UMĚNÍ
Návštěva Výstav

When is the gallery open?
   gdi ye ga-le-ri-e o-tev-rzhe-na?

Kdy je galerie otevřena?

What kind of art are you interested in?
   o yak-ee druh u-mye-nee
   maa-te zaa-yem?

*O jaký druh umění
máte zájem?*

I'm interested in ...	za-yee-mam se o ...	*Zajímam se o ...*
animation	a-ni-ma-tse	*animace*
cyber art	ki-ber-ne-ti-tskeh u-mye-nyee	*kybernetické umění*
design	di-zain	*dizajn*
graphic art	gra-fi-ku	*grafiku*
painting	mal-eerzh-stvee	*malířství*
performance art	re-pro-duk-chnyee u-mye-nyee	*reprodukční umění*
renaissance art	re-ne-san-chnyee u-mye-nyee	*renesanční umění*
romanesque art	ro-maan-skeh	*románské*
sculpture	so-kharzh-stvee	*sochařství*

What's in the collection?
  tso maa-te v zbeer-ke?

Co máte v zbírke?

There is a good collection of ...
  tam ye pye-knaa zbeer-ka ...

Tam je pěkná zbírka ...

altarpiece	ol-taar-nyee przhed-mye-ti	*oltární předměty*
building	bu-do-va	*budova*
church	kos-tel	*kostel*
curator	ku-raa-tor/spraav-tse	*kurátor/správce*
epoch	e-pokh-a/ob-dob-ee	*epocha/období*
etching	lept	*lept*
gardens	zaa-hrud-i	*záhrady*
permanent collection	staa-la vi-sta-va	*stálá výstava*
a print	re-pro-duk-tse/tisk	*reprodukce/tisk*
slide	di-a-poz-i-tiv	*diapozitiv*
statue	so-kha	*socha*

Doing Art

Umělecká Tvorba

artwork	u-mye-lets-keh dee-lo	*umělecké dílo*
canvas	plaat-no	*plátno*
exhibit	ex-po-naaht	*exponát*
exhibition	vee-sta-va	*výstava*
installation	in-stal-a-tse	*instalace*
opening	vern-i-saazh	*vernisáž*
painter	mul-eerzh	*malíř*
photographer	fo-to-graf	*fotograf*
sculptor	sokh-arzh	*sochař*
studio	stu-di-o	*studio*
style	stil	*styl*
technique	tekh-ni-ka	*technika*

MUSIC

HUDBA

Do you like ...?	raad/raa-da ...?	*Rád/Ráda ...?* (m/f)
listening	po-sloh-khaa-te	*posloucháte*
to music	hud-bu	*hudbu*
to dance	tun-chee-te	*tančíte*

Do you play an instrument?
hra-ye-te na nye-ya-kee
hu-dob-nee naa-stroy?

Hrajete na nějaký hudobní nástroj?

Do you sing?
spee-va-te?

Spívate?

What music do you like?
ya-kee dru hud-bi maa-te
raad/-a?

Jaký druh hudby máte rád/a? (m/f)

Which bands do you like?
kte-reh sku-pi-ni maa-te
raad/-a?

Které skupiny máte rád/a? (m/f)

I like (the) ...
lee-bi se mi ...

Líbi se mi ...

Have you heard the
latest record by ...?
sli-shel/-a ste po-sled-nyee
sklad-bu od ...?

Slyšel/a ste poslední skladbu od ...? (m/f)

Which station plays
(electronic) music?
na kte-reh sta-ni-tsi daa-va-yee
(e-lek-tro-nits-koh) hud-bu?

Na které stanici dávají (elektronickou) hudbu?

What frequency is it on?
na kte-reekh vlnaakh to ye?

Na kterých vlnách to je?

Where can you hear
traditional music around here?
gde se daa po-sloh-khat
tra-dich-nee hud-ba?

Kde se dá poslouchat tradiční hudba?

Shall we sit or stand?
khtse-te se-dyet ne-bo staat?

Chcete sedět nebo stát?

Where shall we sit?
gde si sed-ne-me?

Kde si sedneme?

INTERESTS

What a fantastic concert!
    fan-tas-tits-kee kon-tsert!

Fantastický koncert!

It's terrible!
    to ye strash-neh!

To je strašné!

This singer is brilliant.
    ten spye-vaak ye o-hrom-nee

Ten spěvák je ohromný.

See also On Tour, page 193.

INTERESTS

Useful Words

Užitečné Výrazy

band	sku-pi-na/ka-pe-la	*skupina/kapela*
bar with music	bar s hud-boh	*bar s hudbou*
booking office	przhed-pro-dey	*předprodej*
	v-stu-pen-ek	*vstupenek*
concert hall	kon-tsert-nyee seeny	*koncertní síň*
concert	kon-tsert	*koncert*
famous	slaa-vni	*slávny*
gig	vi-stoh-pye-nyee/	*vystoupění/*
	kon-tsert	*koncert*
musician	mu-zi-kant	*muzikant*
opera (house)	o-pe-ra	*opera*
orchestra	or-khes-tr	*orchestr*
performance	vi-stoh-pye-nyee	*vystoupění*
rock group	rok-o-vaa sku-pi-na	*rocková skupina*
show	shoh/przhed-sta-ve-nyee	*show/představení*
singer	spye-vaak	*spěvák*
song	pee-se-nye	*píseň*
stage	ye-vish-tye	*jeviště*
ticket office	po-klad-na	*pokladna*
tickets	lee-stki	*lístky*
venue	mee-sto	*místo*

CINEMA & THEATRE   KINO A DIVADLO

People dress formally to go to the theatre and concerts. Tickets are bought for assigned seats in movie theatres. When passing in front of people to move to your seat in a row, it is polite to face them and say *dovolíte?* 'do you mind?', *děkuji* 'thank you', or bow your head slightly. If you're running late for a theatre performance, you'll have to wait for the next break before entering.

I feel like going to a ...	khtyel/-a bykh vi-dyet ...	*Chtěl/a bych vidět ... (m/f)*
ballet	ba-let	*balet*
comedy	ko-meh-di-i	*komédii*
film	film	*film*
play	hru	*hru*

What's on at the cinema tonight?
tso daa-va-yee dnes v ki-nye?   *Co dávají dnes v kině?*

Where can I find a cinema guide?
gde nai-de-me pro-gram ki-na?   *Kde najdeme program kina?*

Are there any tickets for ...?
maa-te lee-stky na ...?   *Máte lístky na ...?*

Sorry, we're sold out.
li-tu-yi ye vi-pro-daa-no   *Lituji, je vyprodáno.*

Is it in English?
ye to v an-glich-ti-nye?   *Je to v angličtině?*

Does it have English subtitles?
ye to san-glits-kee-mi pod-ti-tul-ki?   *Je to s anglickými podtitulky?*

Are those seats taken?
ysoh ti-to mee-sta vol-neh?   *Jsou tyto místa volné?*

Have you seen ...?
vid-yel/-a ste ...?   *Viděl/a ste ...? (m/f)*

Have you seen the latest film by (Forman)?
vih-dyel/-a ste po-sled-nee film od (for-ma-na)?   *Viděl/a ste poslední film od (Forman)? (m/f)*

INTERESTS

Who's in it?
    gdo v nyem hra-ye?   *Kdo v něm hraje?*
It's directed by ...
    re-zhee-ro-val ho ...   *Režíroval ho ...*
It's been really well reviewed.
    maa dob-roh kri-ti-ku   *Má dobrou kritiku.*

I (don't) like ...	(ne-)maam raad/-a ...	(Ne)mám rád/a ... (m/f)
action movies	ak-chnee film	*akční film*
amateur film	a-ma-tyehr-ski film	*amatérsky film*
animated films	an-i-mo-va-neh fil-mi	*animované filmy*
art films	u-mye-lets-ke fil-mi	*umělecké filmy*
black comedy	cher-noh ko-me-di-i	*černou komedii*
classical theatre	klas-its-keh di-vad-lo	*klasické divadlo*
comedy	ko-me-di-e	*komedie*
documentary	do-ku-men-taar-nee film	*dokumentární film*
drama	draa-mu	*drámu*
horror movies	ho-ror	*horor*
period dramas	hi-sto-rits-keh fil-mi	*historické filmy*
realism	re-a-liz-mus	*realizmus*
sci-fi movies	stsi-fi	*sci-fi*
short films	kraa-tke fil-mi	*krátke filmy*
thrillers	thri-ler	*thriller*
war films	vaa-lech-neh fil-mi	*válečné filmy*

LITERATURE

LITERATURA

Who's your favourite author?
  gdo ye vaash ob-lee-be-nee spis-oh-va-tel?

Kdo je váš oblíbený spisovatel?

I read (Kundera).
  ch-tu (kun-de-ru)

Čtu (Kunderu).

I prefer the works of (Hrabal).
  ra-dye-yi maam (hra-ba-la)

Raději mám (Hrabala).

What kind of books do you read?
  ya-kee druh li-ter-a-tu-ri chte-tye?

Jaký druh literatury čtetě?

I (don't) like ...	(ne-)maam raad/a ...	*(Ne)mám rád/a ... (m/f)*
anthologies	an-to-lo-gi-e	*antologie*
biography	bi-o-gra-fi-e	*biografie*
the classics	kla-si-ki	*klasiky*
comics	ko-mi-ksi	*komiksy*
contemporary literature	soh-chaas-nyee li-ter-a-tu-ru	*součásní literaturu*
crime/detective novels	krih-mih-nahl-ky/ deh-tek-tiv-ky	*kriminálky/ detektivky*
erotic literature	e-ro-tits-koh li-ter-a-tu-ru	*erotickou literaturu*
fantasy literature	fan-tas-tits koh li-ter-a-tu-ru	*fantastickou literaturu*
fiction	be-le-tri-i	*beletrii*
non-fiction	li-ter-a-tu-ru fak-tu	*literaturu faktu*
novels	ro-ma-ni	*romány*
poetry	po-e-zi-i	*poezii*
romance	mi-lost-nyeeh ro-maa-ni	*milostní román*
science-fiction	stsi-fi	*sci-fi*
short stories	kraa-tke po-veed-ki	*krátke povídky*
travel writing	tse-sto-pi-si	*cestopisy*

Have you read ...?
chetl/-a ste ...?   *Četl/a ste ...?* (m/f)
I like the works of ...
lee-bi ze mi dee laa od ...   *Líbí se mi díla od ...*
Can you recommend a book for me?
moo-zhe-te mi od-po-ru-chit   *Můžete mi odporučit*
nye-ya-koh kni-hu?   *nějakou knihu?*

OPINIONS   HODNOCENÍ – NÁZORY

What did you think of ...?
tso si mi-slee-te o ...?   *Co si myslíte o ...?*
I liked it very much.
mots se mi to lee-bi-lo   *Moc se mi to líbilo.*
I didn't like it very much.
mne se to mots ne-lee-bi-lo   *Mne se to moc nelíbilo.*

I thought it was ...	z-da-lo se mi to ...	*Zdalo se mi to ...*
boring	nu-dneh	*nudné*
entertaining	za-yee-ma-veh	*zajímavé*

I thought	mi-sleem zhe	*Myslím, že*
it was ...	to bi-lo ...	*to bylo ...*
excellent	baa-yech-neh	*báječné*
OK	dob-reh	*dobré*

I had a few problems
with the language.
ne-ro-zu-myel/-a   *Nerozuměl/a*
sem to-mu dob-reh   *jsem tomu dobře.* (m/f)

It's ...	ye to ...	*Je to ...*
awful	hroz-neh	*hrozné*
beautiful	kraa-sneh	*krásné*
dramatic	draah-ma-tits-keh	*dramatické*
incomprehensible	ne-po-kho-pi-tel-neh	*nepochopitelné*
interesting	za-yee-ma-veh	*zajímavé*
marvellous	o-hrom-neh	*ohromné*
unusual	ne-ob-vi-kleh	*neobvyklé*

INTERESTS

It's not as good as ...
ne-nyee to azh tak
do-breh ya-ko ...   *Není to až tak*
                                       dobré jako ...
It's reminiscent of ...
przhi-po-mee-na mi to .../   *Připomíná mi to/*
vi-pa-daa to ya-ko ...   *vypadá to jako ...*

HOBBIES   ## KONÍČKY

Do you have any hobbies?	maa-te nye-ya-keh ko-nee-chki?	*Máte nějaké koníčky?*
I like ...	raad/-a ...	*Rád/a ... (m/f)*
gardening	dye-laam v zaa-hrad-tse	*dělám v zahradce*
travelling	tse-stu-yi	*cestuji*
I like to ...	raad/-a ...	*Rád/a ... (m/f)*
cook	va-rzheem	*vařím*
draw	kre-sleem	*kreslím*
paint	ma-lu-yi	*maluji*
sew	shi-yu	*šiju*
take photographs	fo-teem	*fotím*
I make ...	dye-laam ...	*Dělám ...*
pottery	hrn-cheerzh-stvee	*hrnčířství*
jewellery	shper-ki	*šperky*
I collect ...	zbee-ram	*Zbírám...*
books	kni-hi	*knihy*
coins	min-tse	*mince*
comics	kom-iks-si	*komiksy*
dolls	pa-nen-ki	*panenky*
miniature cars	mi-ni-a-tur-nye ow-tee-chka	*miniaturní autíčka*
stamps	znaam-ki	*známky*

INTERESTS

TALKING ABOUT TRAVELLING

KONVERZACE O CESTOVÁNÍ

Have you travelled much?
    tses-to-val yste ho-dnye?

Cestoval jste hodně?

How long have you been travelling?
    yak dloh-ho yste uzh
    na tses-taakh?

*Jak dlouho jste už
na cestách?*

I've been travelling for (two) months.
    uzh sem na tses-taakh (dva)
    mye-see-tse

*Už jsem na cestách (dva)
měsíce.*

Where have you been?
    gde ste vshu-de bil/-a?

Kde ste všude byl/a? (m/f)

I've been to ...
bil ysemv ...

Byl jsem v ...

What did you think of
(Cesky Krumlov)?
yak se vaam lee-bil (che-skee
kru-mlov)?

*Jak se vám líbil (Český
Krumlov)?*

I thought it was ...	bi-lo tam ...	*Bylo tam ...*
boring	nud-nye	*nudně*
great	baa-yech-nye	*báječně*
OK	dob-rzhe	*dobře*
too expensive	przhee-lish dra-ho	*příliš draho*
horrible	hroz-nye/strash-nye	*hrozně/strašně*

There are too many tourists there.
ye tam przhee-lish mno-ho
tu-ris-too

*Je tam příliš mnoho
turistů.*

Not many people speak (English).
ye-nom maa-lo li-di
mlu-vee (an-glits-ki)

*Jenom málo lidi
mluví (anglicky).*

I was ripped off in (Prague).
v (pra-ze) mye o-kra-dli

V (Praze) mě okradli.

People are really friendly there.
li-deh ysoh tam sku-tech-nye
przhaa-tel-skee

*Lidé jsou tam skutečně
přátelští.*

What's there to do in (Brno)?
tso se daa dye-lat v (br-nye)?

Co se dá dělat v (Brně)?

There's a really good
restaurant/hotel there.
ye tam sku-tech-nye dob-raa
res-tow-ra-tse/ho-tel

*Je tam skutečně dobrá
restaurace/hotel.*

I'll write down the details for you.
na-pi-shu tyi meh-no a ud-re-su

Napíšu ti jméno a adresu.

The best time to go is in (December).
ney-le-pshee do-ba na
tses-tu ye v (pro-sin-tsi)

*Nejlepší doba na
cestu je v (prosinci).*

Is it expensive?
ye tam dra-ho?

Je tam draho?

Did you go alone?
  shel si saam?   *Šel si sám?*

Is it safe for women travellers
on their own?
  ye to bez-pech-neh pro zhe-ny   *Je to bezpečné pro ženy*
  kte-reh tse-stu-yee sa-mo-tneh?   *které cestují samotné?*

Is it safe to hitch?
  ye to bez-pech-neh yeet sto-pem?   *Je to bezpečné jít stopem?*

STARS   ## HVĚZDY
Astrology   ### Astrologie

When's your birthday?
  gdy maash na-ro-ze-ni-ni?   *Kdy máš narozeniny?*

What star sign are you?
  vyak-ehm zna-myen-yee si   *V jakém znamení si*
  se na-ro-dil/-a?   *se narodil/a? (m/f)*

I don't believe in astrology.
  ne-vye-rzheem v as-tro-lo-gi-i   *Nevěřím v astrologii.*

I'm ...	sem ...	*Jsem ...*
Aries	be-ran	*beran*
Taurus	beek	*býk*
Gemini	blee-zhe-nets	*blíženec*
Cancer	rak	*rak*
Leo	lev	*lev*
Virgo	pan-na	*panna*
Libra	vaa-ha	*váha*
Scorpio	shteer	*štír*
Sagittarius	strzhe-lets	*střelec*
Capricorn	ko-zo-ro	*kozoroh*
Aquarius	vod-narzh	*vodnař*
Pisces	ri-ba	*ryba*

INTERESTS

Astronomy   **Astronomie**

Are you interested in astronomy?
    za-yee-ma vaas
    as-tron-o-mi-e?   *Zajíma vás astronomie?*

I'm interested in astronomy.
    za-yee-mam se o
    as-tron-o-mi-i   *Zajímam se o astronomii.*

Where's the best place near here
to see the night sky?
    gde ye ta-dee dob-reh mee-sto   *Kde je tady dobré místo*
    na po-zo-ro-vaa-nyee noch-nee   *na pozorování noční*
    ob-lo-hee?   *oblohy?*

Will it be cloudy tonight?
    bu-de dnes za-mrach-e-no?   *Bude dnes zamračeno?*

THE SOKOL MOVEMENT

Sokol (falcon) was a gymnastic society founded in Prague in 1862 to promote Czech culture and social life, and to cultivate physical, cultural and intellectual development among its members. It was a free family program that aimed to uphold the motto – 'A sound mind in a healthy body'. Because of its ideals, *Sokol* was always banned in times of restrictions: first under the Hapsburg dynasty, for supporting the Czech national revival, then during the Nazi occupation, and again for 40 years under communism. The movement was reborn after the decline of communist influence in the early 1990s. A national Assembly of *Sokols*, *slet*, is held every four years where events include gymnastic and sports competitions as well as the opportunity to socialise with *Sokols* from other units. The first *slet* was held in 1879 and the most recent was the 2000 Prague *Slet* which had many thousands of participants.

INTERESTS

When can I see ...?	gdi se daa vi-dyet ...?	*Kdy se dá vidět ...?*
Mercury	mer-koor	*Merkúr*
Mars	mars	*Mars*
Uranus	u-ran	*Uran*
Pluto	plu-to	*Pluto*
Venus	ve-nu-she	*Venuše*
Jupiter	yu-pi-ter	*Jupiter*
Saturn	sa-turn	*Saturn*

What time does it rise?
    gdi vi-khaa-zee?   *Kdy vychází?*

What time will it set?
    gdi za-pa-daa?   *Kdy zapadá?*

Which way is north?
    gde ye se-ver?   *Kde je sever?*

comet	ko-me-ta	*kometa*
Earth	zem	*Zem*
full moon	spln	*spln*
galaxy	gal-aks-i-e	*galaxie*
meteor	met-e-or	*meteor*
moon	myes-eets	*měsíc*
planet	pla-net-a	*planeta*
sky	ne-be/ob-lo-ha	*nebe/obloha*
space	ves-meer	*vesmír*
stars	hvye-zdi	*hvězdy*
sun	slun-tse	*slunce*
universe	ves-meer	*vesmír*

SOCIÁLNÍ PROBLÉMY

SOCIAL ISSUES

Czechs love to talk politics and very often express that they are not satisfied with things as they are.

POLITICS

POLITIKA

What do you think of the current government?

	tso si mi-slee-te o soh-cha-sneh vlaa-dye?	*Co si myslíte o současné vládě?*

I don't agree with their policy on ...	ne-soh-hla-seem sye-yikh przhee-stu-pem k/ke ...	*Nesouhlasím s jejich přístupem k/ke ...*
drugs	dro-gaam	*drogám*
the economy	ho-spo-daa-rzh-stvee	*hospodářství*
education	shko-lstvee	*školství*
the environment	zhi-vot-nyee-mu pro-strzhe-dyee	*životnímu prostředí*
military service	vo-ye-nskeh slu-zhbye	*vojenské službě*
privatisation	pri-va-ti-za-tsi	*privatizaci*
social welfare	so-tsi-aal-nyee peh-chi	*sociální péči*

Who do you vote for?

	ko-ho vo-leesh?	*Koho volíš?*

I support the ... party.	pot-po-ru-yi stra-nu ...	*Podporuji stranu ...*
communist	ko-mu-ni-sti-tskeh	*komunistické*
conservative	kon-zer-va-ti-vnyee	*konzervativní*
green	ze-le-neekh	*zelených*
social democratic	so-tsi-aal-nye de-mo-kra-ti-tskeh	*sociálně demokratické*
socialist	so-tsi-aa-lis-ti-tskeh	*socialistické*

I'm an anarchist.
 ysem a-nar-khi-sta *Jsem anarchista.*
I'm an abstainer.
 yaa se vo-leb ne-oo-chas-nyeem *Já se voleb neúčasním.*
In my country we have a
(socialist) government.
 u naas maa-me *U nás máme*
 (so-tsi-a-lis-ti-tskoh) vlaa-du *(socialistickou) vládu.*

corrupt	ko-ru-ptse	*korupce*
counting of votes	schee-taa-nyee	*sčítání*
	vo-leb-nyeekh lee-stkoo	*volebních lístků*
democracy	de-mo-kra-tsi-ye	*demokracie*
demonstration	de-mon-stra-tse	*demonstrace*
dole	pot-po-rav	*podpora v*
	ne-za-myest-na-no-sti	*nezaměstnanosti*
... elections	... vol-bi	*... volby*
local council	mee-stnyee oo-rzhad	*místní úřad*
regional	o-kre-snyee	*okresní*
general/	o-bets-nyee/	*obecní/*
national	naa-rod-nyee	*národní*
European	e-vro-pskee	*evropský*
electorate	vo-le-bnyee o-krs-ek	*volební okrsek*
exploitation	vi-u-zhee-vaa-nyee	*využívání*
legislation	zaa-ko-no-daar-stvee	*zákonodařství*
legalisation	le-ga-li-za-tse	*legalizace*
parliament	pa-rla-ment	*parlament*
policy	po-li-tits-kaa li-ni-ye	*politická linie*
polls	vo-leb-nyee mee-stnost/	*volební místnost/*
	ur-na	*urna*
president	pre-zi-dent	*prezident*
prime minister	mi-ni-ster-skee	*ministerský*
	przhe-dse-da	*předseda*
unemployment	ne-za-myest-na-nost	*nezaměstnanost*
vote	vo-le-bnyee hlas	*volební hlas*

ENVIRONMENT   ŽIVOTNÍ PROSTŘEDÍ

Where do you stand on ...?	ya-kee ye vaash naa-zor na ...?	*Jaký je váš názor na ...?*
deforestation	od-les-nyo-vaa-nye	*odlesňování*
nuclear testing	te-sto-vaa-nye nu-kle-aar-nyeekh zbra-nye	*testování nukleárních zbraní*
pollution	zne-chi-shtye-nye zhi-vo-tnyee-ho pro-strzhe-dyee	*znečištění životního prostředí*
antinuclear group	an-ti-nu-kle-aar-nye sku-pi-na	*antinukleární skupina*
biodegradable	skhop-nee ro-zkla-du	*schopný rozkladu*
conservation	o-khra-na przhee-ro-di	*ochrana přírody*
disposable	ye-dno-raa-zo-vee	*jednorázový*
drought	su-kho	*sucho*
ecosystem	e-ko-si-stehm	*ekosystém*
endangered species	oh-ro-zhe-neh dru-hi	*ohrožené druhy*
hunting	lov	*lov*
hydroelectricity	e-le-ktrzhi-naz vo-dnyeekh e-lek-traa-ren	*elekřina z vodních elektráren*
industrial pollution	zne-chi-stye-nye proo-mi-slem	*znečištění průmyslem*
irrigation	za-vla-zho-vaa-nye	*zavlažování*
nuclear energy	nu-kle-aar-nye e-ner-gi-e	*nukleární energie*
ozone layer	o-zo-no-vaa vrst-va	*ozonová vrstva*
pesticides	pe-sti-tsee-di	*pesticídy*
recyclable	vhod-neeh na re-tsi-klo-vaa-nye	*vhodný na recyklování*
recycling	re-tsih-kla-ce	*recyklace*
reservoir	naa-drzh	*nádrž*
toxic waste	to-ksi-tskee ot-pad	*toxický odpad*
water supply	zaa-so-bo-vaa-nye vo-doh	*zásobování vodou*

SOCIAL ISSUES   SOCIÁLNÍ PROBLÉMY

What do you think about ...?	tso si mi-slee-te o ...?	*Co si myslíte o ...?*
I'm in favour of ...	ysem pro ...	*Jsem pro ...*
I'm against ...	ysem pro-tyi ...	*Jsem proti ...*
abortion	po-tra-t	*potrat*
animal rights	zvee-rzhe-tsee praa-va	*zvířecí práva*
equal opportunity	ro-vno-praav-nost	*rovnoprávnost*
euthanasia	e-oo-ta-naa-zi-ye	*eutanázie*
immigration	e-mi-gra-tse	*emigrace*
party politics	stra-nyi-tskaa po-li-ti-ka	*stranická politika*
racism	ra-si-zhmus	*rasizmus*
sexism	di-skri-mi-na-tse zhen	*diskriminace žen*
tax	da-nye	*daň*
unions	od-bo-ri	*odbory*

What's the current policy on (immigration)?
ya-kaa ye soh-chah-snaa (e-mi-gra-chnee) po-li-ti-ka?
Jaká je současná (emigrační) politika?

Is there an (unemployment) problem here?
ye zde pro-blehms (ne-za-myest-na-nos-tee)?
Je zde problém s (nezaměstnaností)?

What assistance is there for ...?	ya-kaa ye vee-po-mots pro ...?	*Jaká je výpomoc pro ...?*
the aged	sta-reh li-dyi	*staré lidi*
homeless	bez-do-mo-vtse	*bezdomovce*
street kids	bez-pri-zor-neh dye-tyi/dye-tyi u-li-tse	*bezprizorné děti/děti ulice*

DRUGS

DROGY

I don't take drugs.
ne-be-ru zhaa-dneh-dro-gi

Neberu žádné drogy.

I take (cocaine) occasionally.
przhee-le-zhi-to-stne si
daam (ko-ka-in)

*Příležitostně si
dám (kokain).*

I'm a heroin addict.
ye-duv he-ro-i-nu

Jedu v heroinu.

Where can I find clean syringes?
kde mo-hu do-stat chi-steh
strzhe-ka-chki/yeh-li?

*Kde mohu dostat čisté
stříkačky/jehly?*

I'm out of it.
przhe-stal ysem sma-zhit

Přestal sem smažit.

My friend has taken an overdose.
mooy przhee-tehl to
przhe-shlehl

*Můj přítel to
přešlehl.*

This drug is for personal use.
ti-to dro-gi ysoh na
o-so-bnyee poh-zhi-tyee

*Tyto drogy jsou na
osobní použití.*

I'm trying to get off it.
khtsi przhe-stat sma-zhit

Chci přestat smažit.

Where can I get help
with a drug problem?
gde mo-hu se-hnat po-mots
s nar-ko-ma-ni-ee?

*Kde mohu sehnat pomoc
s narkomanií?*

I'm on a methadone program.
ysem na su-psti-tu-chnyeem
me-ta-do-no-vehm pro-gra-mu

*Jsem na substitučním
metadonovém programu.*

SOCIAL ISSUES

THEY MAY SAY ...

ney-rad-shi bikh si shleh-nul hu-le-nyee	I would love to get stoned

acid	ki-se-li-na (LSD)	*kyselina (LSD)*
addiction	nar-ko-ma-ni-e	*narkomanie*
cocaine	ko-ka-in	*kokain*
cocaine addict	zaa-vi-slee na	*závislý na*
	ko-ka-i-nu	*kokainu*
cold turkey	ab-sti-nen-chnyee	*abstinenční*
	przheeh-zna-ki	*příznaky*
drug addiction	zaa-vi-slost	*závislost*
drug dealer	di-la/dee-ler	*dyla/dealer*
heroin addict	zaa-vi-slost na	*závislost na*
	he-ro-i-nu	*heroinu*
to inject	shle-hnoht si	*šlehnout si*
overdose	przhe-shle-hnu-tyee	*přešlehnutí*
syringe	bu-khna	*buchna*
syringe disposal	naa-do-ba na bu-khni	*nádoba na buchny*

NAKUPOVÁNÍ SHOPPING

Expect shops (especially outside Prague) to close for lunch. Not many shops are open on Saturday afternoons or Sundays.

LOOKING FOR ...   HLEDÁM ...

Where can I buy ...?
  gde mo-hu koh-pit ...?   *Kde mohu koupit ...?*

Where's the nearest ...?	gde ye ney-blizh-shee ...?	*Kde je nejbližší ...?*
bookshop	knyih-ku-pets-tsvee	*knihkupectví*
cosmetics shop	dro-ge-ri-e	*drogerie*
clothing store	o-dye-vi	*oděvy*
department store	op-khod-nyee doom	*obchodní dům*
general store	smee-she-neh sbo-zhee	*smíšené zboží*
market	trzhi-tse	*tržnice*
newsagency	no-vi-ni	*noviny*
chemist/pharmacy	leh-kaa-rna	*lékárna*
souvenir shop	su-ve-nee-ri	*suvenýry*
stationers	pa-peer-nyi-tstvee	*papírnictví*
supermarket	sa-mo-ops-lu-ha	*samoobsluha*
travel agency	tses-tov-nyee kan-tse-laarzh	*cestovní kancelář*

MAKING A PURCHASE   PŘI NAKUPOVÁNÍ

I'm just looking.
  ye-nom se dyee-vaam   *Jenom se dívám.*
How much is this?
  ko-lik to sto-yee?   *Kolik to stojí?*
Can you write down the price?
  moo-zhe-te mi na-psat tse-nu?   *Můžete mi napsat cenu?*
I'd like to buy ...
  khtyel/-a bikh koh-pit ...   *Chtěl/a bych koupit ... (m/f)*
Do you have others?
  maa-te ye-shtye yi-neh?   *Máte ještě jiné?*

Can I look at it?
  mo-hu se na to po-dyee-vat?   *Mohu se na to podívat?*
I don't like it.
  to se mi ne-lee-bee   *To se mi nelíbí.*
Can you lower the price?
  moo-zhe-te mi nye-tso slev-it?   *Můžete mi něco slevit?*
Do you have something cheaper?
  maa-te nye-tso lev-nyey-shee-ho?   *Máte něco levnějšího?*
Do you accept credit cards?
  daa se pla-tyit kre-dit-nye   *Dá se platit kreditní*
  kar-toh?   *kartou?*
Could I have a receipt please?
  moo-zhe-te mi daat oo-chet   *Můžete mi dát účet,*
  pro-seem?   *prosím?*
Does it have a guarantee?
  ye na-to zaa-ru-ka?   *Je na to záruka?*
Can I have it sent overseas/abroad?
  moo-zhe-te mi to pos-lat   *Můžete mi to poslat*
  do zah-ra-nyi-chee?   *do zahraničí?*
Please wrap it.
  moo-zhe-te mi to   *Můžete mi to,*
  pro-seem za-ba-lit   *prosím, zabalit.*
I'd like to return this please.
  khtyel/-a bikh to vraa-tyit   *Chtěl/a bych to vrátit.* (m/f)
It's faulty.
  ye to va-dneh   *Je to vadné.*
I'd like my money back.
  khtyel/-a bikh spaa-tki   *Chtěl/a bych zpátky*
  pe-nyee-ze   *peníze.* (m/f)

| DID YOU KNOW... | *Antikvariát* in Czechia is usually a second-hand bookshop, and not an antique shop. |

ESSENTIAL GROCERIES

ZÁKLADNÍ POTRAVINY

Where can I find the ...?	gde nai-du ...?	*Kde najdu ...?*
I'd like ...	khtyel/-a bikh ...	*Chtěl/a bych ... (m/f)*
batteries	ba-ter-ki	*baterky*
bread	khlehb	*chléb*
butter	maa-slo	*máslo*
candles	sveech-ki	*svíčky*
cereal	tse-re-aa-li-e	*cereálie*
cheese	seer	*sýr*
chocolate	cho-ko-laa-du	*čokoládu*
eggs	vey-tse	*vejce*
flour	moh-ku	*mouku*
gas cylinder	pli-no-voh bom-bu	*plynovou bombu*
ham	shun-ku	*šunku*
honey	med	*med*
margarine	mar-ga-reen	*margarín*
marmalade	mar-me-laa-du/ dzhem	*marmeládu/ džem*
matches	sir-ki	*sirky*
milk	mleh-ko	*mléko*
mosquito coil	pro-strzhe-dek pro-tyi ko-maa-room	*prostředek proti komárům*
olive oil	o-li-vo-vee o-le-ye	*olivový olej*
pepper	peprzh/korzhe-nyee	*pepř/koření*
salt	sool	*sůl*
shampoo	sham-pawn	*šampón*
soap	mee-dlo	*mýdlo*
sugar	tsukr	*cukr*
toilet paper	to-a-le-tnyee pa-peer	*toaletní papír*
toothpaste	zu-bnyee pas-tu	*zubní pastu*
washing powder	pra-tsee praa-shek	*prací prášek*
yogurt	yo-gurt	*jogurt*

SOUVENIRS

carved wooden figure	drzhe-vye-naa fi-gur-ka	*dřevěná figurka*
embroidery	vee-shi-fka	*výšivka*
figurines	so-shki	*sošky*
handicraft	li-do-veh u-mye-nyee	*lidové umění*
porcelain	por-tse-laan	*porcelán*
pottery	ke-ra-mi-ka	*keramika*
souvenirs made of glass	su-ve-nee-ri ze skla	*suvenýry ze skla*

SUVENÝRY

CLOTHING

boots	tu-ris-tits-keh-bo-ti	*turistické-boty*
coat	ka-baat	*kabát*
dress	sha-ti	*šaty*
jacket	sa-ko	*sako*
jeans	jeen-si	*džínsy*
jumper (sweater)	sve-tr	*svetr*
pants	kal-ho-ti	*kalhoty*
raincoat	prshi-plaash-ty	*pršiplášť*
shirt	ko-shi-le	*košile*
shoes	bo-ti	*boty*
socks	po-no-zhki	*ponožky*
swimsuit	plaf-ki	*plavky*
T-shirt	tri-chko	*tričko*
underwear	spod-nyee praa-dlo	*spodní prádlo*

OBLEČENÍ

TAKE HOME A MONSTER

Popular souvenirs include Czech crystal glass (*krystal*), Czech garnet (*granát*) and puppets (*loutky*). Among the puppets is a legendary creature native to Czech rivers called *vodník*, 'water man'. This amphibious monster resembles a man with webbed fingers and is usually green. They lurk underwater near riverbanks, often close to mills or docks. *Vodník*s have a particularly bad temperament, and have been known to drag unsuspecting swimmers and fishermen under the water, holding them in their slimy embrace until they drown. Then they place their souls into separate containers where they live trapped in the *vodník's* underwater kingdom. If you want to see a water man, one appears in *Rusalka*, ('A water nymph') – the most famous of Dvořák's operas.

SHOPPING

Can I try it on?
  mo-hu si to sku-sit?   *Mohu si to zkusit?*
It doesn't fit.
  ne-se-dyee mi to   *Nesedí mi to.*

It's too ...	ye to mots ...	*Je to moc ...*
big	ve-li-keh	*veliké*
long	dloh-heh	*dlouhé*
loose	vol-neh	*volné*
short	kraat-keh	*krátké*
small	ma-leh	*malé*
tight	tye-sneh	*těsné*

MATERIALS   MATERIÁLY

brass	mo-saz	*mosaz*
ceramic	ke-ra-mi-ka	*keramika*
cotton	bavl-na	*bavlna*
glass	sklo	*sklo*
gold	zla-to	*zlato*
leather	koo-zhe	*kůže*
metal	kof	*kov*
plastic	umye-laa hmo-ta	*umělá hmota*
silk	hed-vaa-bee	*hedvábí*
silver	strzhree-bro	*stříbro*
stainless steel	ne-rez/ne-re-za-vye-yee-tsi o-tsel	*nerez/nerezavějící ocel*
synthetic	u-mye-leh vlak-no	*umělé vlákno*
wood	drzhe-vo	*dřevo*
wool	vl-na	*vlna*

COLOURS

dark ...	tma-vee ...	*tmavý ...*
light ...	svyet-lee ...	*světlý ...*
black	cher-nee	*černý*
blue	mo-dree	*modrý*
brown	hnye-dee	*hnědý*
green	ze-le-nee	*zelený*
grey	she-dee	*šedý*
orange	o-ran-zho-vee	*oranžový*
pink	roo-zho-vee	*růžový*
purple	fi-ya-lohvee	*fialový*
red	cher-ve-nee/roo-dee	*červený/rudý*
white	bee-lee	*bílý*
yellow	zhlu-tee	*žlutý*

DON'T FORGET YOUR WOOLLIES

If you travel just before Christmas, don't forget to pack a lined raincoat and buy a fur or woollen hat in Czechia. The temperature can plunge to minus 20 degrees Celsius. In summer, however, the temperature can be over 30 degrees Celsius for a fortnight and the Czechs love to expose their bodies to the sun. You'll see men in the streets with no tops on and at some lakeside beaches there are special areas for nude sunbathing.

TOILETRIES

aftershave	vo-da po ho-le-nyee	*voda po holení*
comb	hrzhe-ben	*hřeben*
condoms	pre-zer-va-ti-vi	*prezervativy*
dental floss	den-taal-nyee nyit	*dentální nit*
deodorant	de-zo-do-rant	*dezodorant*
hairbrush	kar-taach na-vla-si	*kartáč na vlasy*
moisturising cream	ple-tyo-vee krehm	*pleťový krém*
pregnancy test kit	tye-ho-ten-skee test	*těhotenský test*

razor	brzhi-tva	*břitva*
razor blades	zhi-le-tka	*žiletka*
sanitary napkins	vlozh-ki	*vložky*
shampoo	sham-pawn	*šampón*
shaving cream	krehm na ho-le-nyee	*krém na holení*
soap	meed-lo	*mýdlo*
sunblock	krehm na o-pa-lo-vaa-nyee	*krém na opalování*
tampons	tam-paw-ni	*tampóny*
tissues	pa-pee-ro-veh ka-pes-nyee-ki	*papírové kapesníky*
toilet paper	to-a-let-nyee pa-peer	*toaletní papír*
toothbrush	kar-taa-chek na zu-bi	*kartáček na zuby*
toothpaste	zub-nyee pas-ta	*zubní pasta*

FOR THE BABY

PRO DĚŤÁTKO

baby powder	dyet-skee poodr	*dětský pudr*
bib	slin-taa-chek/ brin-daa-chek	*slintáček/ bryndáček*
disposable nappies	pa-peer-o-veh plen-ki	*papírové plenky*
dummy/pacifier	dud-leek/shi-dyeet-ko	*dudlík/šidítko*
feeding bottle	ko-ye-net-skaa laa-hef	*kojenecká láhev*
nappies	plen-ki	*plenky*
nappy rash cream	dye-tskee krehm	*dětský krém*
powdered milk	ko-ye-net-skeh mleh-ko	*kojenecké mléko*
teat	dud-leek na lah-vi-chku	*dudlík na lahvičku*
tinned baby food	ko-ye-ne-tskaa vee-zhi-va	*kojenecká výživa*

STATIONERY & PUBLICATIONS

PAPÍRNICTVÍ KNIHKUPECTVÍ NOVINY

Is there a foreign-language bookshop nearby?

ye ta-di na blee-sku
tsi-zo-ya-zi-chneh
knyih-kupet-stvee?

Je tady nablízku cizojazyčné knihkupectví?

Have they got English-language books there?

ma-yee tam an-gli-tskeh knyi-hi?

Mají tam anglické knihy?

Is there a local entertainment guide in English?

maa-te proo-vo-tse po
kul-tur-nyeekh a spor-tov-nyeekh
a-ktseekh v an-glich-tyi-nye?

Máte průvodce po kulturních a sportovních akcích v angličtině?

Do you have any books in English by (Hrabal)?

maa-te nye-ya-keh an-glit-skeh
knyi-hi ot (hra-ba-la)?

Máte nějaké anglické knihy od (Hrabala?)

Do you sell ...?	pro-daa-vaa-te ...?	*Prodáváte...?*
magazines	cha-so-pi-si	*časopisy*
newspapers	no-vi-ni	*noviny*
postcards	po-let-ni-tse	*pohlednice*

dictionary	slov-nyeek	*slovník*
maps	ma-pi	*mapy*
newspaper in English	no-vi-ni v an-glich-tyi-nye	*noviny v angličtině*
paper	pa-peer	*papír*
pen (ballpoint)	pe-ro	*pero*
stamps	znaam-ki	*známky*

SHOPPING

MUSIC

I'm looking for a ... CD.
   hle-daam tse-de-chko ot ...
Do you have any ...?
   maa-te nye-ya-keh ...?
What is his/her best recording?
   kte-raa ye ye-ho/ye-yee
   ney-lep-shee nah-raaf-ka?
Can I listen to this CD here?
   mo-hu si ta-di po-sle-khnoht
   to-hle tse-de?
I need a blank tape.
   po-trzhe-bu-yi praaz-dnoh
   ka-ze-tu

HUDBA

Hledám CDčko od ...

Máte nějaké ...?

*Která je jeho/její
nejlepší nahrávka?*

*Mohu si tady poslechnout
tohle CD?*

*Potřebuji prázdnou
kazetu.*

PHOTOGRAPHY

How much is it to process
this film?
   ko-lik sto-yee vi-voh-laa-nyee
   fil-mu?
When will it be ready?
   gdi to bu-de ho-to-veh?
I'd like a film for this camera.
   khtyel/-a bikh film do
   fo-tyaa-ku

FOTOPOTŘEBY

*Kolik stojí vyvolání
filmu?*

Kdy to bude hotové?

*Chtěl/a bych film do
fotíku.* (m/f)

battery	ba-te-ri-e	*baterie*
B&W film	cher-no-bee-lee film	*černobílý film*
camera	fo-to-ah-pa-raat	*fotoaparát*
colour film	ba-re-vnee film	*barevný film*
flash/flash bulb	blesk	*blesk*
lens	ob-ye-ktif	*objektiv*
light meter	eks-po-zi-metr	*expozimetr*
slides	di-ya-po-zi-ti-vi	*diapozitivy*
videotape	vi-de-o ka-ze-ta	*video kazeta*

SMOKING

A packet of cigarettes, please.
 ba-lee-chek tsi-ga-ret pro-seem   *Balíček cigaret, prosím.*
Are these cigarettes strong or mild?
 ysoh ti-to tsi-ga-re-ti   *Jsou tyto cigarety*
 si-lneh ne-bo sla-beh?   *silné nebo slabé?*
Do you have a light?
 maa-teh o-henye?   *Máte oheň?*
Do you mind if I smoke?
 bu-de vaam va-dyit   *Bude vám vadit,*
 gdizh si za-paa-leem?   *když si zapálím?*
I'm trying to give up.
 po-koh-sheem se przhe-stat   *Pokouším se přestat.*

cigarettes	tsi-ga-re-ti	*cigarety*
cigarette papers	tsi-ga-re-to-vee pa-peer	*cigaretový papír*
filtered	sfil-trem	*s filtrem*
lighter	slap-shee	*slabší*
matches	sir-ki	*sirky*
pipe	deem-ka	*dýmka*
tobacco	ta-baak	*tabák*

TABÁK

SIZES & COMPARISONS

VELIKOSTI A SROVNÁVÁNÍ

heavy	tyezh-keh	*těžké*
light	le-hkeh	*lehké*
more	veets	*víc*
little (amount)	maa-lo	*málo*
too much/many	pzrhee-lish mots	*příliš moc*
many	mots	*moc*
enough	dost	*dost*
also	ta-keh	*také*
a little bit	tro-khuh	*trochu*

POTRAVINY   FOOD

Breakfast in the Czech Republic is usually a very quick meal eaten quite early in the morning (schools start before 8 am and work usually even earlier). Bread and rolls with butter accompanied by tea and coffee make up a basic breakfast. Lunch is the main meal of the day. It consists of more than one course, generally starting with soup, and is eaten between 12 and 2 pm. A light, often cold, evening meal is eaten between 6 and 8 pm.

breakfast	snyee-da-nye	*snídaně*
lunch	o-byed	*oběd*
dinner	ve-che-rzhe	*večeře*

| I'm hungry. | maam hlad | *Mám hlad.* |
| I'm (not) thirsty. | (ne-)maam zhee-zeny | *(Ne)mám žízeň.* |

BEFORE YOU EAT ... DOBROU CHUT'!

Czechs don't start eating until all say *Dobrou chut!* do-broh khu-tye! (bon appetit!) and they don't start drinking before they wish each other *Na zdraví!* na zdra-vee! (to health!).

BREAKFAST   SNÍDANĚ

Czechs tend to eat breakfast on the run. It usually consists of tea or coffee and bread with butter and jam or salami. The tea is usually served with sugar or honey and lemon. There are many eateries – *mléčne bary* and *bufety* – that serve hot or cold *snídaně* (snyee-da-nye).

housky/chléb, máslo a džem nebo med
   hohs-ki/khlehb maa-slo   bread rolls/bread with
   a dzhem ne-bo met   butter, jam or honey
míchaná vejce se slaninou
   mee-kha-naa vey-tse ze   scrambled eggs with
   sla-nyi-noh   bacon

FOOD

pečivo
  pe-chi-vo   bread rolls
topinka
  to-pin-ka   toast
vejce se šunkou
  ve-ye-tse ze shun-koh   ham and egg
vejce na měkko
  ve-ye-tse na myek-ko   soft-boiled eggs
vejce na tvrdo
  ve-ye-tse na tvrdo   hard-boiled eggs

VEGETARIAN & SPECIAL MEALS
VEGETARIÁNSKE A SPECIÁLNÍ DIETY

Vegetarians will probably find the range of vegetarian dishes limited. Even dishes that sound vegetarian are often served up with ham (*šunka*) unless you specifically demand otherwise.

I'm a vegetarian.
  ysem ve-ge-ta-ri-aan   *Jsem vegetarián.*
I don't eat meat.
  ne-yeem ma-so   *Nejím maso.*
I don't eat chicken, fish or ham.
  ne-yeem ku-rzhe anyi   *Nejím kuře, ani*
  ri-bu anyi shun-ku   *rybu ani šunku.*
I can't eat dairy products.
  ne-mo-hu yeest zhaad-neh   *Nemohu jíst žádné*
  mleh-chneh vee-rop-ki   *mléčné výrobky.*

TOP TIPS

Though the price includes service, it is customary to give a tip (*spropitné*), ranging from 5-10 percent of the price of the meal. Tips are not left on the table but are added to the amount to be paid and given to the waiter when paying the bill.

Do you have any
vegetarian dishes?
   maa-te ve-ge-ta-ri-aan-skaa/
   bez-ma-saa yeed-la?

*Máte vegetariánská/
bezmasá jídla?*

Does this dish have meat?
   yeh ftom-hle yeed-le ma-so?

Je v tomhle jídle maso?

Can I get this without meat?
   mo-hu do-stat to-hle
   bes ma-sa?

*Mohu dostat tohle
bez masa?*

Does it contain eggs?
   op-sa-hu-ye to vey-tse?

Obsahuje to vejce?

I'm allergic to (peanuts).
   ysem a-ler-gits-kee/-aa
   na (bu-raa-ki)

*Jsem alergický/á
na (buráky). (m/f)*

Is there a kosher restaurant here?
   ye tah-di ko-sher
   res-ta-u-ra-tse?

*Je tady košer
restaurace?*

Is this kosher?
   ye to ko-sher?

Je to košer?

Is this organic?
   ye to o-rga-nits-keh?

Je to organické?

CUTLERY SIGN LANGUAGE

When you have finished eating, put the cutlery together
on the right side of the plate. Your knife and fork left
crossed on the plate is a sign that you want to continue
eating and the waiter should not take your plate away.

SNACKS   OBČERSTVENÍ

As breakfast is eaten quite early in the morning, snack bars are
quite popular for *obložené chlebíčky* (open faced sandwiches) or
zákusky (cakes), usually with an espresso coffee. Popular dishes
are tripe soup (*dršťková polévka*) and goulash soup (*gulášová
polévka*) with beer.

FOOD

AT THE RESTAURANT

V RESTAURACI

Table for (five), please.
  stool pro (pyet) pro-seem

Stůl pro (pět), prosím.

May we see the menu?
  yee-del-nyee lee-stek pro-seem

Jídelní lístek, prosím?

Could you recommend something?
  tso naam moo-zhe-te
  do-po-ru-chit?

*Co nám můžete
doporučit?*

What's in that dish?
  tso ye ftom yeed-le?

Co je v tom jídle?

Do I get it myself or do they
bring it to us?
  mu-seem si jeet pro to saam
  ne-boh naam to do-ne-soh?

*Musím si jít pro to sám
nebo nám to donesou?*

MENU MATTERS

The menu is divided into two. *Hotová jídla* means
that the meal has been prepared already and will be
brought to you quite quickly. Meals from *Hotová jídla*
are usually a bit cheaper than the meals from *Jídla na
objednávku,* which are specially prepared according to
your order and also appear much more slowly. When
ordering from the *jídelní lístek* (menu), you choose and
pay for your side dishes – *přílohy* – separately.

At restaurants, expect to sit with other people. If
there's space at your table, others will sit with you.

Please bring a/an/the ...	przhi-ne-ste pro-seem ...	*Přineste prosím ...*
ashtray	po-pel-nyeek	*popelník*
bill	oo-chet	*účet*
fork	vi-dlich-ku	*vidličku*
glass of water (with/without ice)	skle-nyi-tsi vo-di (sle-dem; bes le-du)	*sklenici vody (s ledem; bez ledu)*
knife	noozh	*nůž*
plate	ta-leerzh	*talíř*

That was delicious!
  to bi-lo baa-ye-chneh! *To bylo báječné!*
Is service included in the bill?
  ye to fche-tnye op-slu-hi? *Je to včetně obsluhy?*

FOOD

Useful Words Užitečná Slovíčka

cold meals	stu-de-naa yee-dla	*studená jídla*
cup	shaa-lek/hrnek	*šálek/hrnek*
cutlery	przhee-bor	*příbor*
diet meals	di-et-nyee yee-dla	*dietní jídla*
dish	mi-ska	*miska*
fresh	cherst-veh	*čerstvé*
hot meals	teplaa yee-dla	*teplá jídla*
menu	yee-del-nyee lee-stek	*jídelní lístek*
side dishes	przhee-lo-hi	*přílohy*
stale/spoiled	ska-zhe-nee	*skažený*
sweet	slat-kee	*sladký*
toothpick	paa-rat-ko	*párátko*
tablespoon	lzhee-tse	*lžíce*
teaspoon	lzhi-chka	*lžička*
today's special	spe-tsi-a-li-ta dne	*specialita dne*
vegetarian	bez-ma-saa yee-dla	*bezmasá jídla*

FOOD

MENU DECODER

Starters		Předkrmy
bramborák	bram-bo-raak	potato cake
bramborová kaše	bram-bo-ro-vaa ka-she	mashed potatoes
hranolky	hra-nol-ki	chips
jelito	ye-li-to	black pudding
jitrnice	yi-trnyi-tse	white pudding
křenová rolka	krzhe-no-vaa rol-ka	ham and horse-radish roll
majonézový salát	ma-yo-neh-zo-vee sa-laat	potato salad with mayonnaise
ruské vejce	ru-skeh vey-tse	egg mayonnaise
šunka v aspiku	shun-ka fa-spi-ku	ham in aspic
tlačenka s cibulí	tla-chen-ka stsi-bu-lee	presswurst – pieces of pork pressed together with additional ingredients into a patty, served with brown onion
utopenci	u-to-pen-tsi	pickled sausages
uzené koleno	u-ze-neh ko-le-no	smoked hock
uzený jazyk	u-ze-nee ya-zik	smoked tongue
zavináč	za-vi-naach	rolled pickled herring

Soups		Polévky
bramborová polévka	bram-bo-ro-vaa po-lehf-ka	potato soup
bramboračka	bram-bo-rach-ka	thick soup of potatoes and mushrooms with a touch of garlic and marjoram
cibulačka	tsi-bu-lach-ka	onion soup
česneková polévka	ches-ne-ko-vaa po-lehf-ka	garlic soup

dršťková polévka	drsh-ty-ko-vaa po-lehf-ka	spicy tripe soup
fazolová polévka	fa-zo-lo-vaa po-lehf-ka	bean soup
gulášová polévka	gu-laash-o-vaa po-lehf-ka	beef goulash soup
hovězí vývar s játrovými knedlíčky	ho-vye-zee vee-var zyaa-tro-vee-mi kned-leech-ki	beef broth with little dumplings of seasoned liver
hrachová polévka s uzeným	hra-kho-vaa po-lehf-ka su-ze-neem	pea soup with smoked pork
zeleninová polévka	ze-le-nyi-no-vaa po-lehf-ka	vegetable soup
zelňačka	zel-nyach-ka	thick sauerkraut, potato and cream soup

FOOD

Main Course:
Menu meals   Hlavní jídla

lečo
   le-cho
   stewed onion, capsicum, tomatoes and eggs with or
   without sausage
plněná paprika
   plnye-naa pap-ri-ka
   stuffed capsicums in tomato sauce
svíčková na smetaně
   sveech-ko-vaa na-sme-ta-nye
   beef in cream sauce with dumplings and lemon
   or cranberries
hovězí guláš
   ho-vye-zee gu-laash
   beef stew served with dumplings
vepřová pečeně s knedlíky a zelím
   vep-rzho-vaa pe-che-nye skned-lee-ki a ze-leem
   roast pork with dumplings and cooked sauerkraut
uzené se zelím a knedlíky
   u-ze-neh se ze-leem a kned-lee-ki
   smoked pork with cooked sauerkraut and dumplings

FOOD

smažený květák s bramborem
   sma-zhe-nee kvye-taak s-bram-bo-rem
   popular dish made from cauliflower rosettes fried in
   breadcrumbs, served with boiled potatoes and tartar
   sauce. A favourite vegetarian dish.
smažený sýr
   sma-zhe-nee seer
   fried cheese in breadcrumbs
sekaná
   se-ka-naa
   meatloaf
těstoviny
   tye-sto-vi-ni
   pasta
španělský ptáček
   shpa-nyel-skee ptaa-chek
   stuffed beef

Meals prepared to order   Jídla na objednávku

dušená roštěnka
   du-she-naa ro-shtyen-ka
   roast beef with rice
smažený vepřový řízek
   sma-zhe-nee vep-rzho-vee rzhee-zek
   Wiener schnitzel with potatoes (*s bramborem*) or potato
   salad (*bramborovým salátem*)
přírodní řízek
   przhee-ro-dnyee rzhee-zek
   natural/stewed pork steak
pečená kachna
   pe-che-naa kakh-na
   roasted duck served with cabbage or sauerkraut
   and dumplings
smažený kapr
   sma-zhe-nee kapr
   pieces of carp fried in breadcrumbs
pstruh na másle
   pstru na-maa-sle
   grilled trout with butter

Desktops **Moučníky/Zákusky**

Desserts		**Moučníky/Zákusky**
dort/koláč	dort/ko-laach	cake
jablečný závin/	ya-ble-chnee zaa-vin/	apple strudel
štrúdl	shtroodl	
koblihy	ko-bli-hi	doughnuts
makový koláč	ma-ko-vee ko-laach	poppy seed roll
palačinky	pa-la-chin-ki	pancakes/ crepes with jam and cream
pudink	pu-dink	custard
šlehačka	shle-hach-ka	whipped cream
švestkové knedlíky	shvest-ko-veh kned-lee-ki	sweet dump- lings filled with fresh plums and sprinkled with sugar and melted butter
zmrzlina	zmrzli-na	ice cream

FOOD

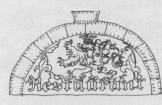

Salads		**Salát**
okurkový salát	o-kur-ko-vee sa-laat	cucumber salad
šopský salát	shop-skee sa-laat	Greek salad
vlašský salát	vlash-skee	salami/meat salad with mayonnaise
zeleninový míchaný salát	ze-le-ni-no-vee mee-cha-nee sa-laat	mixed vegetable salad

FOOD

SELF-CATERING
In the Delicatessen

How much is 100 g of (cheese)?
ko-lik sto-yee de-set
de-ka (see-ru)?

Do you have anything cheaper?
maa-te nye-tso lev-nye-ysheeho?

What's the local speciality?
tso ye mee-stnyee spe-tsi-a-li-ta?

Give me (half) a kilo please.
dey-te mi (pool) ki-la pro-seem.

I'd like 200 g of ham.
khtyel/-a bikh dva-tset de-ka
shun-ki

Can I taste it?
mo-hu to o-khu-tnat?

STRAVOVÁNÍ
Lahůdky/Bufet

*Kolik stojí deset
deka (sýru)?*

Máte něco levnějšího?

Co je místní specialita?

Dejte mi (půl) kila, prosím.

*Chtěl/a bych dvacet deka
šunky.* (m/f)

Mohu to ochutnat?

Making Your Own Meals   Příprava jídel

See Essential Groceries page 113 for words and phrases on making your own meals.

BUFET THE ENTRÉE SLAYER

There are several shops called *bufet* (bu-fet), *mléčný bar* (mleh-chnee bar) or *lahůdky* (la-hoo-dki) that sell delicatessen foods. Prices are calculated according to weight and the food is asked for in decagrams, not grams (100 grams equals 10 decagrams).

AT THE MARKET
Meat & Poultry

FOOD

bacon/speck	sla-nyi-na	*slanina*
beef	ho-vye-zee	*hovězí*
chicken	ku-rzhe	*kuře*
cutlet/chop	kot-le-ta	*kotleta*
duck	kakh-na	*kachna*
frankfurters	paar-ki	*párky*
game	zvye-rzhi-na	*zvěřina*
goat	ko-zee	*kozí*
goose	hoo-sa	*husa*
hamburger	kar-ba-naa-tek	*karbanátek*
innards	vni-trzho-sti	*vnitřostyi*
lamb	yeh-nye-chee	*jehněčí*
kidneys	le-dvi-nki	*ledvinky*
leg	kee-ta	*kýta*
liver	yaa-tra	*játra*
liverwurst	yaa-tro-vaa pa-shti-ka	*játrová paštika*
loin	ve-przho-veh ka-reh	*vepřové karé*
meat	ma-soh	*maso*
meatballs	che-vap-chi-chi	*čevapčiči*
mutton	sko-po-veh	*skopové*
neck	kr-ko-vi-tse	*krkovice*
pheasant	ba-zhant	*bažant*
pork	vep-rzho-veh	*vepřové*
rabbit	za-yeets	*zajíc*
ribs	zhe-beer-ka	*žebírka*
salami	sa-laam	*salám*
sausage	klo-baa-ska	*klobása*
schnitzel	rzhee-zek	*řízek*
steak	bif-tek	*biftek*
turkey	kroo-ta	*krůta*
veal	te-le-tsee	*telecí*
venison	zvye-rzhi-na	*zvěřina*

Seafood

Ryby

Common and traditional varieties of freshwater fish are carp and trout. Saltwater fish is rare, as is seafood.

FOOD

carp	ka-pr	*kapr*
cod	tres-ka	*treska*
cod liver	tres-chee yaa-tra	*tresčí játra*
lobster	hu-mr	*humr*
mussels	mu-shle	*mušle*
oysters	oo-strzhi-tse	*ústřice*
shrimp	gar-naat	*garnát*
trout	pstruh	*pstruh*
tuna	tu-nyaak	*tuňák*
salmon	lo-sos	*losos*
smoked herring	u-ze-naach	*uzenáč*

Vegetables		**Zelenina**
artichoke	ar-ti-chok	*artyčok*
asparagus	shpa-rgle	*špargle*
aubergine/ eggplant	li-lek/ba-kla-zhaan	*lilek/baklažán*
(green) beans	fa-zo-lo-veh lus-ki	*fazolové lusky*
bean sprouts	klee-chki	*klíčky*
beetroot	cher-ve-naa rzhe-pa	*červená řepa*
Brussels sprouts	ka-pu-styi-chki	*kapustičky*
cabbage	ze-lee	*zelí*
carrot	mrkef	*mrkev*
red/green capsicum	cher-ve-naa/ze-le-naa pap-ri-ka	*červená/zelená paprika*
cauliflower	kvye-taak	*květák*
celery	tse-ler	*celer*
courgette/ zucchini	tsu-ke-ti	*cukety*
cucumber	o-ku-rek	*okurek*
garlic	ches-nek	*česnek*
leeks	paw-rek	*pórek*
lettuce	ze-le-nee sa-laat	*zelený salát*
mushrooms	hoh-bi/zham-pi-o-ni	*houby/žampiony*
onion	tsi-bu-le	*cibule*
peas	hraa-shek	*hrášek*
potato	bram-bo-ri	*brambory*
radish	rzhed-kvi-chka/ rzhed-kev	*ředkvička/ ředkev*
savoy cabbage	ka-pu-sta	*kapusta*
spinach	shpe-naat	*špenát*
spring onion	yar-nyee tsi-bul-kaa	*jarní cibulka*
tomatoes	rai-cha-ta/rai-sk ya-blee-chka	*rajčata/rajská jablíčka*
vegetables	ze-le-nyi-na	*zelenina*

FOOD

FOOD

Fruit & Nuts

		Ovoce a Ořechy
apple	yab-ko	*jabko*
apricot	me-ru-nye-ka	*meruňka*
avocado	a-vo-ka-do	*avokado*
banana	ba-naan	*banán*
blueberries	bo-roof-ki	*borůvky*
cherries	trzhe-shnye	*třešně*
morello cherries	vish-nye	*višně*
fig	fee-ki	*fíky*
grapes	hro-zna	*hrozna*
lemon	tsi-tron	*citrón*
melon	tsoo-kro-vee me-lohn	*cukrový meloun*
orange	po-me-ranch	*pomeranč*
peach	bros-kef	*broskev*
pear	hroosh-ka	*hruška*
pineapple	a-na-nas	*ananas*
plum	shvest-ka	*švestka*
strawberries	ya-ho-di	*jahody*
watermelon	me-lohn	*meloun*
raspberries	ma-li-ni	*maliny*
almonds	man-dle	*mandle*
blanched	loh-pa-neh	*loupané*
raw	cher-stveh	*čerstvé*
roasted	pra-zhe-neh	*pražené*
hazelnut	lee-sko-veh	*lískové*
	or-zheesh-ki	*oříšky*
mixed nuts	or-zhee-shki	*oříšky*
peanut	a-ra-shee-di/bu-raa-ki	*arašídy/buráky*

DID YOU KNOW... *Gastro* in Czech is short for gastronomy or gastrology (gourmet foods and eateries) not gastric disorders or stomach problems, and *Gastrocentrum* is like a food court.

FOOD

Pulses   Luštěniny

broad beans	bob	*bob*
kidney beans	fa-zo-le	*fazole*
lentils	choch-ka	*čočka*
rice	ree-zhe	*rýže*

SCRUMPTIOUS DUMPLIN'S

knedlíky	dumplings
bramborové knedlíky	potato dumplings
houskové knedlíky	bread dumplings
ovocné knedlíky	dumplings with fruit
špekové knedlíky	bacon dumplings

Spices & Condiments   Koření

black pepper	pe-przh	*pepř*
carraway seed	kmeen	*kmín*
chillies	fe-fe-raw-ni	*feferóny*
chives	pa-zhit-ka	*pažitka*
cranberry sauce	bru-sin-ki	*brusinky*
dill	kopr	*kopr*
garlic	ches-nek	*česnek*
garnish	ob-lo-ha	*obloha*
ginger	zaaz-vor	*zázvor*
horseradish	krzhen	*křen*
Hungarian	cher-ve-naa	*červená*
paprika	pa-pri-ka	*paprika*
mustard	ho-rzhchi-tse	*hořčice*
parsley	pe-trzhel	*petržel*
salt	sool	*sůl*
sauce	o-maa-chka	*omáčka*
soy sauce	so-yo-vaa o-maa-chka	*sojová omáčka*
tartar sauce	ta-tar-skaa o-maa-chka	*tatarská omáčka*
tomato sauce	ke-chup	*kečup*
vinegar	o-tset	*ocet*

FOOD

Cooking Methods

boiled	va-rzhe-neh	*vařené*
fried	sma-zhe-nee	*smažený*
grilled	gri-lo-va-neh	*grilované*
smoked	u-ze-neh	*uzené*
in (beer) batter	v (piv-neem)	*v (pivním)*
	tye-styee-chku	*těstíčku*

Návod na Připrav

TEA WITH A TWIST OF *CITRÓN*

Tea is seldom drunk with milk. It is more usual to have it with lemon.

DRINKS
Non-Alcoholic

NÁPOJE
Nealkoholické

There are many different varieties of excellent genuine local mineral waters available, some are flavoured and bottled with carbon dioxide to increase their fizz.

coffee	kaa-va	*káva*
fruit cordials	o-vo-tsneh shtyaa-vi	*ovocné šťtĭvy*
lemonade	li-mon-aa-da	*limonáda*
orange juice	po-me-ran-cho-vee	*pomerančový*
	dzhus	*džus*
(cup of) tea	chay	*čaj*
with/without	smleh-kem/	*s mlékem/*
milk	bez mlee-ka	*bez mlíka*
with/without	s tsuk-rem/	*s cukrem/*
sugar	bes tsu-kru	*bez cukru*
water	vo-da	*voda*
mineral water	mi-ner-aal-ka	*minerálka*
boiled water	przhe-var-zhe-naa vo-da	*převařená voda*

Alcoholic		**Alkoholické**
beer	pi-vo	*pivo*
brandy	bran-di	*brandy*
champagne	sham-pa-nye-skeh	*šampaňské*
cocktail	kok-tayl	*koktajl*
mulled wine	sva-rzhaak	*svařák*
rum	rum	*rum*
whisky	wis-ki	*whisky*
shot of whisky	ma-laa wis-ki/ panaak	*malá whisky/ panák*
a bottle/glass/ carafe of ... wine	laa-hef/skle-nyi-tsi/ dzhbaa-nek ... vee-na	*láhev/sklenici/ džbánek ... vína*
red	cher-ve-neh	*červené*
rosé	roo-zho-veh	*růžové*
sparkling	shu-mi-veh	*šumivé*
sweet	slad-keh	*sladké*
white	bee-leh	*bílé*
small glass	ma-laa skle-nyi-tse	*malá sklenice*
tall glass	vel-kaa skle-nyi-tse	*velká sklenice*
small bottle	ma-laa laa-hev	*malá láhev*
large bottle	vel-kaa laa-hev	*velká láhev*
jug	dzhbaan	*džbán*

FOOD

BEAUTIFUL BEER!

There are several Czech sayings that portray the beauty and magic of beer:

Pivo, buřt a špekáček, to je správný Čecháček.
Beer, kabana and sausages help create real Czechs.

Kde se pivo vaří, tam se dobře daří.
Life flourishes where beer is brewed.

Pivo dělá hezká těla.
Beer makes beautiful bodies.

Večer chutná, ráno pomáhá.
It tastes good at night and it heals in the morning.

FOOD

The following spirits are traditional drinks, unique to the Czechs:

borovička	bo-ro-vich-ka	(made from juniper berries)
slivovice	sli-vo-vits-e	plum brandy
Karlovarská	kar-lo-var-skaa	a famous herb
becherovka/	bekh-e-rof-ka/	liqueur from
Karlovy Vary	kar-lo-vi vari	Karlsbad believed to aid digestion

BURP !!!

Czechs are world leaders in the production and consumption of beer. Not only that but Czech beer is also recognised as one of the world's best. Not all Czech beers are lagers, some are light ales as well as stouts. But they are usually bitter and hoppy. *Pivo* is served by the half-litre – if you want a smaller one you must specifically ask for *malé pivo*, which is 300ml. There are many famous pubs and inns, *pivárna*, and each usually serves only one brand of beer. The most famous Czech beer is probably *Plzeňský prazdroj* brewed in Plzeň, a city 80 km southeast of Prague. The original *Budvar,* adopted and sold under its German name Budweiser by American brewers, is brewed in České Budějovice (Budweis). Another famous brewery and beer is *Staropramen* in Smíchov. The dark beer *Měšťan* is brewed in Holešovice. The two Moravian breweries, *Radegast* and *Velkopopovický kozel,* are getting more and more popular and both their *černé* (dark) and *světlé* (light) varieties are well worth trying. Beer served on tap is chilled with a large creamy head. Shops sell bottled and canned beer of many different brands.

FOOD

In the Bar

	V Baru
Excuse me!	
pro-mi-nye/-te!	*Promiň/te!* (inf/pol)
I'm next.	
tety ysem na rzha-dye yaa	*Teď jsem na řadě já.*
I'll buy you a drink.	
zvu tye na skle-nyich-ku	*Zvu tě na skleničku.*
What would you like?	
tso si daa-te?	*Co si dáte?*
I'll have ...	
khtyel/-a bikh ...	*Chtěl/a bych ...* (m/f)

No ice, please.	
bez le-du pro-seem	*Bez ledu, prosím.*
It's my round.	
tu-hle run-du pla-tyeem jaa	*Tuhle rundu platím já.*
You can get the next one.	
ti moo-zhesh za-pla-tyit	*Ty můžeš zaplatit*
dal-shee run-du	*další rundu.*
Same again, please.	
to sa-meh pro-seem	*To samé, prosím.*
How much is that?	
ko-lik to sto-yee?	*Kolik to stojí?*

FOOD

ONE TOO MANY?

I feel fantastic!
   ye mi baa-yech-nye!   *Je mi báječně!*

I really, really love you.
   yaa tye oprav-du a-le   *Já tě opravdu ale*
   opravdu mi-lu-yi   *opravdu miluji.*

I'm feeling drunk.
   ysem o-pi-lee/-aa;   *Jsem opilý/á;*
   stya-tee/-aa   *statý/á. (m/f)*

I think I've had one too many.
   myel sem dost   *Měl ysem dost.*

I feel ill.
   ye mi shpa-tnye   *Je mi špatně.*

NA VENKOVĚ

IN THE COUNTRY

Camping is extremely popular and many people have their own holiday houses – *chata* (kha-ta) or *chalupa* (kha-lu-pa) – which they visit as often as possible.

CAMPING

KEMPOVÁNÍ

camping	kem-pink	*kempink*
campsite	ow-to-kemp	*autokemp*
rope	la-no	*lano*
tent	stan	*stan*
torch (flashlight)	bat-er-ka	*baterka*

Where's the nearest campsite?
gde nay-du ney-blizh-shee
ow-to-kemp/sta-no-vee taa-bor?

Kde najdu nejbližší autokemp/ stanový tábor?

Do you have any sites available?
maa-te vol-naa mees-ta?

Máte volná místa?

How much is it ...?	ko-lik se pla-tyee za ...?	*Kolik se platí za ...?*
per person	o-so-bu	*osobu*
per tent	stan	*stan*
per vehicle	ow-to	*auto*

Where can I hire a tent?
gde se daa pooy-chit stan?

Kde se dá půjčit stan?

Are there shower facilities?
ysoh ta-di spr-khi?

Jsou tady sprchy?

Can we camp here?
moo-zhem ta-di sta-no-vat/
taa-borzh-it?

Můžem tady stanovat/ tábořit?

Who owns this land?
ko-mu pat-rzhee te-nto
po-ze-mek?

Komu patří tento pozemek?

Can I talk to him/her?
moo-zhu sneem/snyee mlu-vit?

Můžu s ním/s ní mluvit?

HIKING
Getting Information

TURISTIKA
Informace

Where can I find out about
hiking trails in the region?

gde moo-zhu se-hnat
in-for-ma-tse o tur-ist-its-keekh
stez-kaakh v teh-to ob-la-styi?

*Kde můžu sehnat
informace o turistických
stezkách v této oblasti?*

Where's the nearest village?

gde ye ney-blizh-shee
ve-snit-tse?

*Kde je nejbližší
vesnice?*

Is it safe to climb this mountain?

ye bez-pyech-neh lehzt na
tu-to ho-ru?

*Je bezpečné lézt na
tuto horu?*

Is there a hut up there?

ye tam na-ho-rzhe kha-ta?

Je tam nahoře chata?

Are there guided treks?

maa-te ta-di vee-stu-pi
sproo-vod-tsem/
or-ga-ni-zo-va-neh vee-stu-pi?

*Máte tady výstupy
s průvodcem/
organizované výstupy?*

I'd like to talk to someone who
knows this area.

khtyel/-a bikh mlu-viht z
nye-keem gdo znaa to-hle
o-ko-lee

*Chtěl/a bych mluvit s
někým kdo zná tohle
okolí.* (m/f)

How long is the trail?

yak dloh-haa ye ta tra-sa?

Jak dlouhá je ta trasa?

Is the track (well-)marked?

ye ta tra-sa (do-brzhe)
vi-zna-che-naa?

*Je ta trasa (dobře)
vyznačená?*

How high is the climb?

yak ye to vi-sok-o?

Jak je to vysoko?

Which is the shortest/easiest route?

kte-raa tra-sa ye ney-krat-shee/
ney-leh-chee?

*Která trasa je nejkratší/
nejlehčí?*

Is the path open?

ye ta tse-sta o-te-vrzhe-na?

Je ta cesta otevřena?

When does it get dark?
  gdi se stmee-vaa?

Kdy se stmívá?

Is it very scenic?
  ye tam he-zki?

Je tam hezky?

Where can I hire mountain gear?
  gde si mo-hu vi-pooy-chit
  ho-ro-lez-ets-koh veez-broy?

*Kde si mohu vypůjčit
horolezeckou výzbroj?*

Where can we buy supplies?
  gde moo-zhe-me na-koh-pit
  zaa-so-bi?

*Kde můžeme nakoupit
zásoby?*

On the Path

Na Turistické Stezce

Where have you come from?
  od-kud ste przhi-shel?

Odkud jste přišel?

How long did it take you?
  yak dloh-ho vaam to trva-lo?

Jak dlouho vám to trvalo?

Does this path go to ...?
  ve-de ten-hle khod-nyeek do ...?

Vede tenhle chodník do ...?

I'm lost.
  stra-til/-a ysem se

Ztratil/a jsem se. (m/f)

Where can we spend the night?
  gde moo-zhe-me
  przhe-no-tso-vat?

*Kde můžeme
přenocovat?*

Can we go through here?
  mu-zhe-me ta-di pro-yeet?

Můžeme tady projít?

Is the water OK to drink?
  ye to pit-naa vo-da?

Je to pitná voda?

SIGNS

KOUPÁNÍ ZAKÁZÁNO	NO SWIMMING
NEPITNÁ VODA	UNSUITABLE FOR DRINKING
PITNÁ VODA	DRINKING WATER
ZÁKAZ KEMPOVÁNÍ	NO CAMPING
ZÁKAZ ROZDĚLÁVÁNÍ OHNĚ	FIRE BAN

IN THE COUNTRY

compass	kom-pas	*kompas*
first-aid kit	leh-kar-nyich-ka	*lékarnička*
	prvnye po-mo-tsi	*první pomoci*
gloves	ru-ka-vi-tse	*rukavice*
guide	proo-vo-dtse	*průvodce*
guided trek	vee-stup	*výstup*
	sproo-vod-tsem	*s průvodcem*
hiking	tu-ri-sti-ka	*turistika*
hiking boots	tu-ri-stits-keh bo-ti	*turistické boty*
hunting	lov	*lov*
map	ma-pa	*mapa*
mountain climbing	ho-ro-le-ze-tstvee	*horolezectví*
pick	krum-paach	*krumpáč*
provisions	po-tra-vi-ni	*potraviny*
rock climbing	vee-stup na skaa-li	*výstup na skály*
rope	la-no	*lano*
signpost	zna-chka	*značka*
steep	str-mee	*strmý*
trek	tses-ta/stes-ka	*cesta/stezka*

AT THE BEACH   NA PLÁŽI

Can we swim here?
  moo-zhe se ta-di pla-vat?   *Může se tady plavat?*
Is it safe to swim here?
  daa se ta-di be-spech-nye   *Dá se tady bezpečně*
  pla-vat?   *plavat?*
Is there a (public) beach near here?
  ye ta-di pu-bleezh   *Je tady publíž*
  (ve-rzhey-naa) plaazh?   *(veřejná) pláž?*
Do we have to pay?
  pla-tyee se tu fstu-pneh?   *Platí se tu vstupné?*

How much for ...?	ko-lik sto-yee ...?	*Kolik stojí ...?*
a chair	le-haa-tko	*lehátko*
a hut	khat-ka	*chatka*
an umbrella	slu-nech-nyeek	*slunečník*

fishing	khi-tat ri-bi	*chytat ryby*
snorkelling	shnorkh-lo-vaa-nyee	*šnorchlování*
sunblock	krehm na	*krém na*
	o-pa-lo-vaa-nyee	*opalování*
sunglasses	slu-nech-nyee bree-le	*sluneční brýle*
swimming	pla-vaa-nyee	*plavání*
towel	ruch-nyeek	*ručník*
waterskiing	vo-dnyee li-zho-vaa-nyee	*vodní lyžování*
waves	vlni	*vlny*
windsurfing	vind-sur-fing	*windsurfing*

IN THE COUNTRY

Aquatic Creatures

Vodní Zvířata

crab	krap	*krab*
eel	oo-ho-rzh	*úhoř*
fish (pl)	ri-bi	*ryby*
lobster	humr	*humr*
seagull	ra-tsek	*racek*
shellfish	myek-keesh	*měkkýš*
turtle	zhel-va	*želva*

WEATHER

POČASÍ

What's the weather like?
  ya-keh bee-vaa po-cha-see?   *Jaké bývá počasí?*

Today it's ...	dnes ye ...	*Dnes je ...*
cloudy	za-ta-zhe-no	*zataženo*
cold	khlad-no/zi-ma	*chladno/zima*
hot	ho-rko	*horko*
warm	te-plo	*teplo*
windy	vye-tr-no	*větrno*

It's raining heavily.	li-ye	*Lije.*
It's raining lightly.	prshee	*Prší.*
It's flooding.	ye zaa-pla-va	*Je záplava.*
It's foggy.	ye za-ml-zhe-no	*Je zamlženo.*

IN THE COUNTRY

GEOGRAPHICAL TERMS

ZEMĚPISNÉ NÁZVY

beach	plaa-zh	*pláž*
bridge	most	*most*
creek	po-tok	*potok*
cave	yes-ki-nye	*jeskyně*
farm	sta-tek	*statek*
field	po-le	*pole*
footpath	kho-dnyeek	*chodník*
forest	les	*les*
hill	ko-pets	*kopec*
hot spring	te-rmaa-lnyee pra-men	*termální pramen*
island	o-strov	*ostrov*
lake	ye-ze-ro	*jezero*
mountain	ho-ra	*hora*
river	rzhe-ka	*řeka*
valley	oo-do-lee	*údolí*
waterfall	vo-do-paad	*vodopád*

FAUNA

FAUNA

| What animal is that? | ya-keh ye to zvee-rzhe? | *Jaké je to zvíře?* |

Domestic Creatures

Domácí Zvířata

cat	koch-ka	*kočka*
chicken	ku-rzhe	*kuře*
cow	kraa-va	*kráva*
dog	pes	*pes*
donkey	o-sel	*osel*
duck	ka-khna	*kachna*
goat	ko-za	*koza*
hen	sle-pi-tse	*slepice*
horse	koo-ny	*kůň*
pig	pra-se	*prase*
rooster	ko-hoht	*kohout*
sheep	of-tse	*ovce*

Wildlife

ant	mra-ven-ets	*mravenec*
bee	fche-la	*včela*
bird	ptaak	*pták*
butterfly	mo-teel	*motýl*
fly	moh-kha	*moucha*
frog	zhaa-ba	*žába*
game	dyi-vo-kaa zvy-erzh	*divoká zvěř*
leech	pi-ya-vi-tse	*pijavice*
mosquito	ko-maar	*komár*
mouse/mice	mish	*myš*
snake	had	*had*
spider	pa-vohk	*pavouk*
squirrel	ve-ver-ka	*veverka*

FLORA & AGRICULTURE

What plant is that?
   yak-aa ye to ro-stli-na?   *Jaká je to rostlina?*
Can you eat the fruit?
   moo-zhe se to o-vo-tse jeest?   *Může se to ovoce jíst?*

Herbs, Flowers Trees & Crops

agriculture	pol-no-ho-spo-daarzh-stvee	*polnohospo-dářství*
barley	yech-men	*ječmen*
clover	ye-tel	*jetel*
corn	kuk-urzh-i-tse	*kukuřice*
crops	plod-yi-ni	*plodiny*
hop	khmel	*chmel*
flax	len	*len*
flower	kvyet	*květ*
grapevine	hro-zno	*hrozno*
harvest (n)	skli-zeny	*sklizeň*
irrigation	za-vla-zho-vaa-nyee	*zavlažování*
leaf	list	*list*

linden tree	lee-pa	*lípa*
oat	o-ves	*oves*
oak	dub	*dub*
orchard	o-vo-tsnee sad	*ovocný sad*
pine	bo-ro-vi-tse	*borovice*
planting/sowing	saa-ze-nyee/se-tba	*sázení/setba*
poppy	maak	*mák*
rosemary	roz-mar-een	*rozmarýn*
rye	zhi-to	*žito*
sunflower	slu-nech-nyi-tse	*slunečnice*
thyme	ti-mi-aan	*tymián*
tree	strom	*strom*
vineyard	vi-ni-tse	*vinice*
wheat	pshen-i-tse	*pšenice*

AKTIVITY

ACTIVITIES

TYPES OF SPORT

DRUHY SPORTU

What sport do you play?
yak-ee dye-laa-te sport ?

Jaký děláte sport ?

I play/practise ...	dye-laam/hrayi ...	*Dělám/Hraji ...*
aerobics	e-ro-bik	*aerobik*
American	a-me-rits-kee	*americký*
football	fot-bal	*fotbal*
athletics	a-tle-ti-ku	*atletiku*
Australian	ow-straal-skee	*austrálský*
Rules football	fot-bal	*fotbal*
basketball	ko-shee-ko-voh	*košíkovou*
boxing	boks	*box*
cycling	tsi-klis-ti-ku	*cyklistiku*
diving	po-taa-pye-nyee	*potápění*
fencing	sherm	*šerm*
gymnastics	gim-nas-ti-ku	*gymnastiku*
handball	haa-ze-noh	*házenou*
hockey (field)	po-zem-nyee ho-key	*pozemní hokej*
hockey (ice)	led-nyee ho-key	*lední hokej*
rowing	ve-slo-vaa-nyee	*veslování*
rugby	rag-bi	*ragby*
skiing	li-zho-vaa-nyee	*lyžování*
swimming	pla-vaa-nyee	*plavání*
tennis	te-nis	*tenis*
volleyball	vo-ley-bal/	*volejbal/*
	od-bee-ye-noh	*odbíjenou*
weightlifting	fspee-raa-nyee	*vzpírání*

Calmer Activities

Relaxační Aktivity

These activities are increasing in popularity in the Czech Republic:

meditation	me-di-ta-tse	*meditace*
Tai Chi	tai-chi	*Tai Chi*
yoga	yaw-ga	*jóga*

TALKING ABOUT SPORT

DISKUSE O SPORTU

Do you like sports?
   maa-te raad/-a sport?   *Máte rád/a sport?* (m/f)
Yes, very much.
   yo yaa maam   *Jo, já mám.*
No, not at all.
   mye sport ne-za-yee-maa   *Mě sport nezajímá.*
I like watching it.
   raad se dee-vaam na sport   *Rád se dívám na sport.*
What sports do you follow?
   yak-eh spor-ti sle-du-ye-te?   *Jaké sporty sledujete?*

I follow ...	sle-du-yi ...	*Sleduji ...*
I support ...	fan-dyeem ...	*Fandím ...*

Who's your	gdo ye vaash	*Kdo je váš*
favourite ...?	ob-lee-be-nee ...?	*oblíbený ...?*
player	hraach	*hráč*
sportsperson	sport-o-vets	*sportovec*

What team do you support?
   kte-reh-mu tee-mu fan-dyeesh?   *Kterému týmu fandíš?*
How do you play (basketball)?
   yak hra-yesh (ba-sket-bal)?   *Jak hraješ (basketbal)?*

ACTIVITIES

Can you play (rugby)?
    u-meesh hraat (rag-bi)?   *Umíš hrát (ragby)?*
Yes, I know how to play.
    yo veem yak se to hra-ye   *Jo, vím jak se to hraje.*
No, I don't know how to play.
    ne ne-veem yak se to hra-ye   *Ne, nevím jak se to hraje.*
Do you feel like
(going for a run)?
    maash khu-ty si (za-bye-hat)?   *Máš chuť si (zaběhat)?*
Do you want to go
(skiing) this weekend?
    khtsesh si jeet o vee-kendu   *Chceš si jít o víkendu*
    (za-li-zho-vat)?   *(zalyžovat)?*
Come and watch us play.
    przhi-ye dy se na naas   *Přijeď se na nás*
    po-dyee-vat yak hraye-me   *podívat, jak hrajeme.*
Can I join in?
    mo-hu se przhi-dat?   *Mohu se přidat?*
Yes, that'd be great.
    yo pri-ma   *Jo, prima.*
Not at the moment, thanks.
    mo-men-tal-nye ne   *Momentálně ne,*
    dye-ku-yi   *děkuji.*
I'm sorry, I can't.
    li-tu-yi a-le ne-mo-hu   *Lituji, ale nemohu.*

ACTIVITIES

SOCCER IT TO ME

The most popular spectator sports are soccer in summer
and ice hockey in winter. The soccer season runs from
September to December and games pull in the crowds
on Sunday afternoons especially at big stadiums like
Dukla Praha and *Sparta Praha*.

GOING TO THE MATCH

JEDEME NA ZÁPAS

Would you like to go to a match?
  khsesh yeet snaa-mi na zaa-pas?   *Chceš jít s námi na zápas?*

Where is it being held?
  na kte-rehm hrzh-shtyi/
  stud-i-aw-nu se hra-ye?   *Na kterém hřišti/*
  stadiónu se hraje?

How much are the tickets?
  ko-lik sto-yee leest-ki?   *Kolik stojí lístky?*

What time does it start?
  fko-lik to za-chee-naa?   *V kolik to začíná?*

Who's playing?
  gdo hra-ye?   *Kdo hraje?*

Who do you think will win?
  na ko-ho tip-u-yesh   *Na koho tipuješ,*
  zhe vi-hra-ye?   *že vyhraje?*

Who are you supporting?
  ko-mu fand-yeesh?   *Komu fandíš?*

Which team is winning/losing?
  kte-reh muzh-stvo   *Které mužstvo*
  vi-hraa-va/pro-hraa-vaa?   *vyhrává/prohrává?*

What's the score?
  ya-kee ye stav?   *Jaký je stav?*

He's/She's good.
  on/-a ye do-bree/-aa   *On/a je dobrý/á. (m/f)*

He's/She's no good.
  on/-a ne-nyee do-bree/-aa   *On/a není dobrý/á. (m/f)*

What a ...!	ya-kee/-kaa ...!	*Jaký/á ...! (m/f)*
goal	gawl	*gól*
hit	raa-na/tre-fa	*rána/trefa*
kick	strzhe-la	*střela*
pass	po-daa-nyee/	*podání/*
	przhi-raa-fka	*přihrávka*

What a great performance!
  vi-nyi-kayee-tsi zaa-pas!   *Vynikající zápas!*

The referee has disallowed it.
  roz-hod-chee to ne-uz-nal   *Rozhodčí to neuznal.*

How much time is left?
  ko-lik cha-su zbee-vaa?   *Kolik času zbývá?*

That was a really good game!
  bil to sku-te-chnye
  do-bree zaa-pas!   *Byl to skutečně dobrý zápas!*

What a boring game!
  ye to nud-nee zaa-pas!   *Je to nudný zápas!*

What was the final score?
  yak to skon-chi-lo?   *Jak to skončilo?*

It was a draw.
  ne-roz-hod-nye   *Nerozhodně.*

international	me-zi-naa-roh-nyee	*mezinárodní*
championships	mi-strof-stveeh	*mistrovství*
national	naa-rod-nyee	*národní*
championships	mi-strof-stvee	*mistrovství*
Olympic Games	o-lim-piy-skeh hri	*olympijské hry*
referee	roz-hod-chee	*rozhodčí*
seat (actual seat)	se-dad-lo	*sedadlo*
seat (place)	mee-sto	*místo*

ACTIVITIES

SOCCER   FOTBAL

Do you follow soccer?
  sle-duy-esh fot-bal/ko-pa-noh?   *Sleduješ fotbal/kopanou?*

Who's at the top of the league?
  gdo ye na prvnyeem mee-stye?   *Kdo je na prvním místě?*

What a terrible team!
  to ye hroz-nee teem!   *To je hrozný tím!*

Who's the best team?
  kte-ree teem ye ney-lep-shee?   *Který tím je nejlepší?*

Who plays for (Real Madrid)?
  gdo hra-ye za (reel ma-drid)?   *Kdo hraje za (Real Madrid)?*

My favourite player is ...
   mooy ney-o-blee-be-nyey-shee
   hraach ye ...

Můj nejoblíbenější
hráč je ...

He played brilliantly in the match
against (Italy).
   hraal baa-yech-nye
   pro-tyi (i-taa-li-i)

Hrál báječně
proti Itálii.

coach	tre-ner/kohch	*trenér/kouč*
corner	roh	*roh*
cup	po-haar	*pohár*
fans	fa-noh-shtsi	*fanoušci*
free kick	vol-nee kop	*volný kop*
foul	fowl	*faul*
goal	bran-ka/gawl	*branka/gól*
goalkeeper	bran-kaarzh	*brankař*
kick off	vee-kop	*výkop*
league	li-ga	*liga*
manager	ma-na-zher	*manažer*
offside	of-said	*ofsajd*
penalty	po-ku-ta	*pokuta*
player	hraakch	*hráč*
to score	skaw-ro-vat	*skórovat*
to shoot	strzhee-let	*střílet*

ACTIVITIES

YOU MAY HEAR ...

to bil e-vi-dent-nyee fowl
   That was clearly a foul.
pro-hraa-li ysme nu-la yed-na
   We lost zero to one.
vi-hraa-li ysme o yed-nu bran-ku!
   We won by one goal!
yak skon-chil mi-nu-lee zaa-pas?
   How did the last match end?

FOOTBALL & RUGBY

English	Pronunciation	Czech
I play ...	yaa hra-yu ...	*Já hraju ...*
Have you ever seen ...?	vi-dyel si nye-gdi ...?	*Viděl ysi někdy ...?*
American football	a-me-rit-skee fot-bal	*americký fotbal*
Aussie Rules	ow-straa-lskee fot-bal	*australský fotbal*
rugby	rag-bi	*ragby*

It's a contact sport.	ye to do-ti-ko-vee sport	*Je to dotykový sport.*
Do you want me to teach you to play?	khtsesh a-bikh tye to now-chil hraat?	*Chceš abych tě to naučil hrát?*

English	Pronunciation	Czech
field goal	gawl ze hri	*gól ze hry*
forward	oo-to-chnyeek	*útočník*
fullback	o-braan-tse	*obránce*
to kick for touch	vee-kop za do-tik	*výkop za dotyk*
kick-off	vee-kop	*výkop*
pass	nahraaf-ka	*nahrávka*
scrum	za-daak	*zadák*
tackle	oo-toch-nyeek	*útočník*
to touch down	po-lo-zhit meech do bran-ko-veh-ho oo-ze-mee	*položit míč do brankového území*
winger	krzhee-dlo	*křídlo*

Typical Scoring — **Typické skórování**

English	Pronunciation	Czech
draw/even	re-mee-za	*remíza*
love (zero)	nu-la/bez bra-nek	*nula/bez branek*
match point	match-bawl	*mečból*
nil (zero)	nu-la	*nula*

ACTIVITIES

KEEPING FIT

UDRŽOVÁNÍ SE V KONDICI

Where's the best place to jog/
run around here?

  gde se ta-di do-brzhe
  bye-haa?

*Kde se tady dobře
běhá?*

Where's the nearest ...?	gde ye ta-di ney-blizh-shee ...?	*Kde je tady nejbližší ...?*
gym	po-si-lov-na	*posilovna*
swimming pool	ba-zehn	*bazén*
tennis court	te-ni-so-vee kurt	*tenisový kurt*

What's the charge per ...?	ko-lik se pla-tyee za ...?	*Kolik se platí za ...?*
day	den	*den*
game	hru	*hru*
hour	ho-dyi-nu	*hodinu*

ACTIVITIES

OH THOSE SPORTING CZECHS!

The Czech Republic is well known for excellence in
a number of sports, such as tennis, with players like
Navrátilová, Lendl and Korda. Another familiar name
is Emil Zátopek, who was the top runner of the 20th
century. He's world renowned for one of track's rarest
feats – winning the 5,000m, 10,000m and marathon in
a single Olympic Games (in Helsinki, 1952).
    Skiing is also a popular traditional sport. Walking
and mountaineering are equally popular and the Czech
Republic has some wonderfully beautiful mountain
ranges for these pursuits.
    The lakes, rivers and reservoirs are ideal not only for
swimming and water sports but for fishing too.

Can I hire ...?	moo-zhu si pooy-chit ...?	*Můžu si půjčit ...?*
a bicycle	ko-lo	*kolo*
a racquet	ra-ke-tu	*raketu*
shoes	bo-ti	*boty*

Do I have to be a member to attend?
    mu-seem beet chle-nem   *Musím být členem*
    a-bikh se mol zoo-cha-stnit?   *abych se mohl zúčastnit?*
Is there a women-only session/pool?
    ye to nye-gdi vi-hra-ze-no   *Je to někdy vyhrazeno*
    yen pro zhe-ni?   *jen pro ženy?*
Where are the changing rooms?
    gde ysoh sha-tni?   *Kde jsou šatny?*
May I see the gym?
    mo-hu se po-dee-vat na   *Mohu se podívat na*
    po-si-lov-nu?   *posilovnu?*
Is there a crêche (daycare)?
    ye tam shkol-ka pro dye-tyi?   *Je tam školka pro děti?*

exercise bicycle	shla-pa-tsee ko-lo	*šlapací kolo*
jogging	bye-haa-nyee	*běhání*
gym	tye-lo-tsvich-na	*tělocvična*
massage	ma-saazh	*masáž*
rowing machine	ve-slarzh-skee	*veslařský*
	przhee-stroy	*přístroj*
sauna	sow-na	*sauna*
shower	sprkha	*sprcha*
towel	ruch-nyeek	*ručník*
weights	chin-ki	*činky*
workout	po-si-lo-vaa-nyee	*posilování*

WALKING & MOUNTAINEERING

TURISTIKA A HOROLEZECTVÍ

See In the Country chapter, pages 144 to 146, for hiking terms.

> **DID YOU KNOW...**
>
> Gymnázium in Czech means 'secondary college' and not 'gym'. And remember – saunas are always single sex and always nude!

TENNIS

TENIS

Do you like tennis/table tennis?
    maash raad/-a te-nis/
    ping-pong?   *Máš rád/a tenis/*
                                   ping pong? (m/f)

Do you play tennis?
    hrayesh te-nis?   *Hraješ tenis?*

Would you like to play tennis?
    khtyel/-a bis
    hraat te-nis?   *Chtěl/a bys hrát*
                                   tenis? (m/f)

Is there a tennis court near here?
    ysoh ta-di blee-zko
    te-nis-o-veh kur-ti?   *Jsou tady blízko*
                                     tenisové kurty?

What type of surface
does the court have?
    ya-kee po-vrkh maa ten-to kurt?   *Jaký povrch má tento kurt?*

How much is it to hire the court?
    ko-lik se pla-tyee za kurt?   *Kolik se platí za kurt?*

Is there racquet and ball hire?
    ye tam pooy-chov-na
    ra-ket a mee-chkoo?   *Je tam půjčovna*
                                     raket a míčků?

Are there instructors?
    ysoh tam in-struk-to-rzhi/
    tre-nehr-zhi?   *Jsou tam instruktoři/*
                                   trenéři?

ACTIVITIES

ace	bod/e-so	*bod/eso*
advantage	vee-ho-da	*výhoda*
clay	an-tu-ka	*antuka*
deuce	sho-da	*shoda*
fault	khi-bneh po-daa-nyee	*chybné podání*
first serve	prvnyee po-daa-nyee	*první podání*
game, set, match	hra, sa-da, zaa-pas	*hra, sada, zápas*
game ball	geym-bawl	*gejmból*
grass court	trav-na-tee dvo-rets	*travnatý dvorec*
hard court	tvr-dee dvo-rets	*tvrdý dvorec*
line	chaa-ra	*čára*
love	nu-la	*nula*

to match	vi-ro-vnat	*vyrovnat*
match-point	match bawl	*mečból*
net	see-ty	*síť*
ping pong ball	ping-pong-o-vee	*ping-pongový*
	mee-chek	*míček*
to play doubles	chtirzh-hra	*čtyřhra*
point	bod	*bod*
racquet	ra-ke-ta	*raketa*
second service	dru-heh po-daa-nyee	*druhé podání*
serve	po-daa-nyee/ser-vis	*podání/servis*
set	set	*set*
table tennis	stol-nyee te-nis/	*stolní tenis/*
	ping-pong	*ping-pong*
table tennis table	ping-pong-o-vee stool	*ping-pongový stůl*
table tennis bat	ping-pong-o-vaa	*ping-pongová*
	ra-ke-ta/paal-ka	*raketa/pálka*
tennis court	te-ni-so-vee kurt	*tenisový kurt*

CYCLING   CYKLISTIKA

For terminology on cycling, see the Getting Around chapter, page 41.

Where does the race pass through?
  ku-di pro-yeezh-dyee zaa-vod?   *Kudy projíždí závod?*
Who's winning?
  gdo vi-hraa-vaa?   *Kdo vyhrává?*
How many kilometres is
today's race?
  ko-lik ki-lo-me-troo maa   *Kolik kilometrů má*
  dne-shnyee zaah-vod?   *dnešní závod?*
Where does it finish?
  gde kon-chee?   *Kde končí?*
My favourite cyclist is ...
  mooy o-blee-be-nee   *Můj oblíbený*
  tsi-kli-sta ye ...   *cyklista je ...*

cyclist	tsi-kli-sta	*cyklista*
hilly stage of the race	ko-ptso-vi-tee oo-sek	*kopcovitý úsek*
leg (in race)	e-ta-pa/oo-sek	*etapa/úsek*
(yellow) jersey	zhlu-teh trich-ko	*žluté tričko*
race against the clock	zaa-vod scha-sem	*závod s časem*
winner	vee-tyez	*vítěz*

ACTIVITIES

SKIING   LYŽOVÁNÍ

How much is a pass for these slopes?
  ko-lik sto-yee per-man-ent-ka?   *Kolik stojí permanentka?*
What are the skiing conditions
like at ...?
  yak-eh ysoh li-zarzh-skeh   *Jaké jsou lyžařské*
  pod-meen-ki na ...?   *podmínky na ...?*
Is it possible to go
cross-country skiing at ...?
  daa se yet na   *Dá se jet na*
  byezh-kaakh na ...?   *běžkách na ...?*

Where are the	gde ysoh	*Kde jsou*
slopes for ...?	sye-sdof-ki pro ...?	*sjezdovky pro...?*
beginners	za-chaa-te-chnyee-ki	*začátečníky*
intermediate	pok-ro-chi-leh	*pokročilé*
experienced	do-breh li-zha-rzhe	*dobré lyžaře*
Where are	gde ysoh	*Kde jsou*
the ski-lifts?	li-zharzh-skeh vle-ki?	*lyžařské vleky?*
chair lift	sed-ach-ko-vaa la-nof-ka	*sedačková lanovka*
cross-country	byezh-ki	*běžky*
downhill	syezd	*sjezd*
instructor	in-struk-tor	*instruktor*
safety binding	bez-pech-no-stnyee	*bezpečnostní*
	vaa-zaa-nyee	*vázání*
skis	li-zhe	*lyže*
ski-boots	li-zharzh-skeh bo-ti	*lyžařské boty*
ski-lift	li-zharzh skeh vle-ki	*lyžařské vleky*
ski slope	syez-dov-ka	*sjezdovka*
ski-suit	li-zharzh-skee	*lyžařský*
	ob-leche-nyee	*oblečeni*
sunblock	krehm na	*krém na*
	o-pa-lo-vaa-nyee	*opalování*
How is the snow?	yak-ee ye snyeeh?	*Jaký je sníh?*
wet	mok-ree	*mokrý*
sticky	lep-ka-vee	*lepkavý*
powdery	prash-an	*prašan*

ACTIVITIES

SIGNS

HORSKÁ SLUŽBA	MOUNTAIN RESCUE SERVICE
POZOR, NEBEZPEČÍ LAVIN!	WARNING! BEWARE OF AVALANCHES!

AQUATIC SPORTS

VODNÍ SPORTY

dinghy	gu-mo-vee chlun	*gumový člun*
fins	ploht-ve	*ploutve*
goggles	okh-ran-neh bree-le	*ochranné brýle*
mainsail	hluv-nyee plakh-ta	*hlavní plachta*
mask	po-taa-pyech-skaa mas-ka	*potápěčská maska*
mast	stye-zhe-ny	*stěžeň*
motorboat	mo-tor-o-vee chlun	*motorový člun*
oars	ve-sla	*vesla*
sail	pla-khta	*plachta*
sailing (the sport)	pla-khtye-nyee	*plachtění*
water-skiing	vod-nyee lizh-o-vaa-nyee	*vodní lyžování*
water-skis	vod-nyee li-zhe	*vodní lyže*
wave	vl-na	*vlna*
wetsuit	ne-o-pren	*neopren*
windsurfing	vind-sur-fing	*windsurfing*

HORSE RACING

DOSTIHY

Where are horse races held?
  gde ysoh do-styi-hi?   *Kde jsou dostihy?*
Where is the (horse) racetrack?
  gde ye do-styi-ho-vaa draa-ha?   *Kde je dostihová dráha?*
Shall we have a bet?
  vsa-dyee me si?   *Vsadíme si?*
How much do you want to put on?
  ko-lik khtse-te vsa-dyit?   *Kolik chcete vsadit?*

I'd like to have a bet on ...	khtyel bykh vsa-dit na ...	*Chtěl bych vsadit na ...*
for a place	na u-mee-stye-nyee	*na umístění*
for a win	na vee-hru	*na výhru*
both ways	na o-bo-yee	*na obojí*

Which horse is the favourite?
kte-ree koo-ny ye fa-vor-i-tem?   *Který kůň je favoritem?*

At what odds is this horse?
ya-koh prav-dye-po-dob-nost   *Jakou pravděpodobnost*
maa ten-hle koo-ny?   *má tenhle kůň?*

This horse is five to one.
pom-yer ye pyet ku yed-neh   *Poměr je pět ku jedné.*

What weight is the horse carrying?
ya-koh vaa-hu ne-se ten koo-ny?   *Jakou váhu nese ten kůň?*

bet	saa-zka	*sázka*
bookmaker	saaz-ko-vaa	*sázková*
	kan-tsel-aarzh	*kancelář*
horse	koo-ny	*kůň*
jockey	zho-key	*žokej*
photo finish	pro-ye-tyee tsee-lem	*projetí cílem*
	v tyes-nehm sle-du	*v těsném sledu*
race	do-stih	*dostih*
to ride (v)	yez-dit	*jezdit*

HORSE RIDING

JÍZDA NA KONI

Is there a horse-riding school
around here?
ye ta-di na-blee-zku   *Je tady nablízku*
yez-dets-kaa shko-la?   *jezdecká škola?*

Are there rides available?
daa se ta-di yez-dyit?   *Dá se tady jezdit?*

How long is the ride?
yak dloh-ho trvaa yeez-da?   *Jak dlouho trvá jízda?*

How much does it cost?
ko-lik to sto-yee?   *Kolik to stojí?*

Do you offer rides for beginners?
na-bee-zee-te yeez-di pro   *Nabízíte jízdy pro*
zach-aa-tech-nyee-ki?   *začátečníky?*

I'm an experienced rider.
ysem sku-she-nee yez-dets   *Jsem zkušený jezdec.*

ACTIVITIES

Can I rent a hat and boots?
  mo-hu si pooy-chit
  hel-mu a bo-ti?

*Mohu si půjčit
helmu a boty?*

canter	tsval/pok-lus	*cval/poklus*
crop	bi-cheek	*bičík*
mare	ko-bi-la	*kobyla*
gallop	trisk/ri-khlee bye-h	*trysk/rychlý běh*
stables	staa-ye	*stáje*
stallion	hrzhe-bets	*hřebec*
trot	klu-sat	*klusat*

CAR RACING

AUTOMOBILOVÉ ZÁVODY

a crash	ha-vaa-ri-ye/sraa-zhka	*havárie/srážka*
to crash/collide	na-ra-zit/ko-liz-e	*narazit/kolize*
driver	rzhi-dich	*řidič*
Formula One	form-u-le yed-na	*formule jedna*
... kilometres	... ki-lo-met-roo	*... kilometrů*
an hour	za ho-dyi-nu	*za hodinu*
lap	ko-lo	*kolo*
to overtake/pass	przhed-bye-hnoht	*předběhnout*
racetrack	zaa-vod-nyee draa-ha	*závodní dráha*
racing car	zaa-vod-nyee ow-to	*závodní auto*
to skid	smik/do-stat smik	*smyk/dostat smyk*
to take the lead	vi-hraa-vat/ beet na che-le	*vyhrávat/ být na čele*

GOLF

bunker	pee-sko-vaa przhe-kaa-zhka	*písková překážka*
flagstick	vlay-ka	*vlajka*
follow-through	pro-taa-hnoht	*protáhnout*
golfball	golf-o-vee mee-chek	*golfový míček*
golf course	golf-o-vee hrzhi-shtye	*golfové hřiště*
golf cart	golf-o-vee vo-zeek	*golfový vozík*
hole	yam-ka	*jamka*
iron	golf-o-vaa hool	*golfová hůl*
teeing ground	na-sa-dyit meech na ko-leek	*nasadit míč na kolík*
wood	drzhe-vye-naa golf-o-vaa hool	*dřevěná golfová hůl*

GAMES / HRY

Do you play ...?	hra-ye-te ...?	*Hrajete ...?*
billiards	ku-lech-nyeek	*kulečník*
cards	kar-ti	*karty*
chess	sha-khi	*šachy*
computer games	po-chee-tach-o-veh	*počítačové*
dominoes	do-mi-no	*domino*
draughts	daa-mu	*dámu*
ludo	chlo-vye-che ne-zlob se	*člověče nezlob se*
noughts and crosses	mlee-nek	*mlýnek*
pinball	ti-vo-li/hra-tsee ow-to-mat	*tivoli/hrací automat*
pool	ku-lech-nyeek	*kulečník*
roulette	ru-let-u	*ruletu*
table football	stol-nyee kop-a-noh	*stolní kopanou*

I'm sorry, I don't know
how to play (chess).
  li-tu-yi a-le ne-u-meem
  hraat (sha-khi)

*Lituji, ale neumím
hrát (šachy).*

How do you play (dominoes)?
  yak se hra-ye (do-mi-no)?

Jak se hraje (domino)?

What are the rules?
  ya-keh ysoh pra-vid-la?

Jaké jsou pravidla?

Whose turn is it?
  gdo ye na rzha-dye?

Kdo je na řadě?

It's my turn.
  yaa ysem na rzha-dye

Já jsem na řadě.

I'm winning/losing.
  vi-hraa-vaam/pro-hraa-vaam

Vyhrávám/prohrávám.

Stop cheating!
  ne-pod-vaa-dyey!

Nepodváděj!

Cards   Karty

Do you want	**khtsesh si**	*Chceš si*
to play ...?	**za-raat ...?**	*zahrát ...?*
cards	**kar-ti**	*karty*
bridge	**bridzh**	*bridž*
poker	**pok-er**	*poker*

I don't know how to play.
  ne-veem yak se to hra-ye

Nevím, jak se to hraje.

I'll teach you.
  now-cheem tye to

Naučím tě to.

It's your turn to pick up a card.
  si na rzha-dye

Jsi na řadě.

I can't go.
  ne-mo-hu yeet

Nemohu jít.

I'll bet (200).
  vsa-dyeem se o (dvye stof-ki)

Vsadím se o (dvě stovky).

I'll see you.
  przhi-yee maam saa-zku

Přijímám sázku.

I'll raise you (100).
  przhi-ho-deem (stof-ku)

Přihodím (stovku).

ace	e-so	*eso*
clubs	krzhee-zhe/tre-fi	*kříže/trefy*
to deal	rohz-daa-vat	*rozdávat*
deck	ba-lee-chek kar-et	*balíček karet*
diamonds	kaa-ro	*káro*
hand	hra/hraach	*hra/hráč*
hearts	srtse	*srdce*
jack	kluk/spo-dek	*kluk/spodek*
joker	zho-leek	*žolík*
king	kraal	*král*
knight	koo-ny	*kůň*
queen	daa-ma	*dáma*
to shuffle	(za)mee-khat	*(za)míchat*
spades	ze-le-neh/pi-ki	*zelené/piky*

ACTIVITIES

Poker   Poker

four of a kind	chtirzh-ka	*čtyřka*
full hand	kom-bin-a-tse z	*kombinace z*
	jed-neh dvoy-its-e a	*jedné dvojice a*
	jed-neh troy-its-e	*jedné trojice*
pair	dvoy-its-e	*dvojice*
royal flush	kraa-lov-skaa	*královská*
	sek-ven-tse	*sekvence*
	(chis-taa u-kon-chen-aa	*(čistá ukončená*
	e-sem)	*esem)*
straight	chis-taa sek-ven-tse	*čistá sekvence*
	(v yed-neh bar-vye)	*(v jedné barvě)*
three of a kind	troy-its-e	*trojice*
two pairs	dvye dvoy-its-e	*dvě dvojice*

Chess   Šachy

Shall we play chess?
   za-hraye-me si sha-khi?   *Zahrajme si šachy?*
White starts.
   bee-lee za-chee-naa   *Bílý začíná.*
It's my move.
   yaa ysem na ta-hu   *Já jsem na tahu.*
Hurry up and make a move!
   spye-khey/dyeley si na ta-hu!   *Spěchej/dělej, jsi na tahu!*
Check (to the king)!
   shakh (s kraa-lem)!   *Šach (s králem)!*
Checkmate!
   shakh-mat!   *Šachmat!*

bishop	strzh-e-lets	*střelec*
black/white pieces	cher-neh/bee-leh fig-ur-ki	*černé/bílé figurky*
castle/rook	vyezh	*věž*
chess board	shakh-ov-nits-e	*šachovnice*
king	kraal	*král*
knight	yez-dets/koo-ny	*jezdec/kůň*
pawn(s)	shakh-o-vaa fig-ur-ka	*šachová figurka*
queen	kraa-lov-naa	*královná*
stalemate	mat	*mat*

ACTIVITIES

THE LOTTERY   LOTERIE

I'd like a lottery ticket, please.
   khtyel/-a bykh si
   koh-pit lo-te-ri-i   *Chtěl/a bych si*
                  koupit loterii. (m/f)
Can I choose the numbers?
   mo-hu si vi-brat chees-la?   *Mohu si vybrat čísla?*

TV & VIDEO

Do you mind if I put the TV on?
  bu-de vaam va-dyit kdizh
  za-pnu tel-e-vi-zi?
Turn the TV off!
  vip-nyi tel-e-vi-zi!
Do you mind if I turn the
volume up/down?
  bu-de vaam va-dyit k-dyzh
  to ze-see-leem/styi-sheem?
Can I change the channel?
  mo-hu przhep-noht pro-gram?
Which channel do you
want to watch?
  yakee pro-gram khse-te?

TELEVIZE A VIDEO

*Bude vám vadit, když
zapnu televizi?*

Vypni telivizi!

*Bude vám vadit, když
to zesílím/ztiším?*

Mohu přepnout program?

Jaký program chcete?

I feel like watching ...	po-dydee-val/-a bykh se na ...	*Podívala bych se na ... (m/f)*
cartoons	kre-sle-nee film	*kreslený film*
current affairs	spraa-vi/ ko-men-taarzh	*zprávy/ komentář*
a documentary	do-ku-men-taar-nyee film	*dokumentární film*
a film	nye-ya-kee film	*nějaký film*
a game show	kvee-zo-vee po-rzhad	*kvízový pořad*
kids' programs	dyet-skee pro-gram	*dětský program*
news	spraa-vi	*zprávy*
a series	se-ri-aal	*seriál*
a soap opera	te-le-viz-nyee se-ri-aal	*televizní seriál*
sport	sport	*sport*
a variety program	zaa-bav-nee pro-gram	*zábavný program*
the weather	przhed-po-vyedy po-cha-see	*předpověď počasí*

ACTIVITIES

Can we watch the
English-language TV?
  moo-zhe-me se dyee-vat na   *Můžeme se dívat na*
  an-glits-kee pro-gram?   *anglický program?*
Where's the remote control?
  gde ye o-vlad-ach?   *Kde je ovladač?*
The TV isn't working.
  te-le-vi-ze ne-fun-gu-ye   *Televize nefunguje.*

antenna	an-tehn-a	*anténa*
buttons	knof-lee-ki	*knoflíky*
cable TV	ka-be-lo-vaa tel-e-vi-ze	*kabelová televize*
channel	pro-gram	*program*
remote control	daal-ko-veh	*dálkové*
	o-vlaad-aa-nyee	*ovládání*
satellite dish	sa-te-lit	*satelit*
television	te-le-viz-e	*televize*
TV set	te-le-vi-ze	*televize*
volume	hla-si-tost	*hlasitost*

Video   Video

Where can we hire videos?
  gde si moo-zhe-me   *Kde si můžeme*
  vi-pooy-chit vid-e-o ka-ze-ti?   *vypůjčit video kazety?*
Do I have to be a member to
borrow videos?
  mu-seem beet chle-nem   *Musím být členem,*
  a-bikh si mol pooy-chit vid-e-o?   *abych si mohl půjčit video?*
How much is it to hire this video?
  ko-lik sto-yee pooy-che-nyee   *Kolik stojí půjčení*
  teh-to ke-ze-ti?   *této o kezeti?*
Is this film for daily or weekly hire?
  ye ten-to film na den-nyee   *Je tento film na denní*
  ne-bo na tee-den-nyee   *nebo na týdenní*
  pooy-che-nyee?   *půjčení?*

ACTIVITIES

FESTIVALY A STÁTNÍ SVÁTKY   FESTIVALS & HOLIDAYS

PUBLIC HOLIDAYS

Nový rok	New Year's Day	January 1
Velikonoční pondělí	Easter Monday	March/April
Svátek práce	May Day	May 1
Den osvobození	Liberation Day	May 8
Svatého Cyrila a Metoděje	St Cyril's and St Methodius' Day	July 5
Mistr Jan Hus	Anniversary of Jan Hus' death	July 6
Den vzniku samostatného Československého státu	Independence Day	October 28
Štědrý den	Christmas Eve	December 24
První svátek vánoční	Christmas Day	December 25
Druhý svátek vánoční	Boxing Day	December 26

to celebrate (an event)	sla-vit	*slavit*
to celebrate (in general)	o-sla-vo-vat	*oslavovat*
champagne	sham-pa-nye-skeh	*šampaňské*
church	kos-tel	*kostel*
gift	daa-rek	*dárek*
holiday	svaa-tek	*svátek*
party	paar-ti	*párty*

BIRTHDAYS & SAINTS' DAYS

NAROZENINY A SVÁTKY

When's your ...?	gdi maash ...?	*Kdy máš ...?*
birthday	nar-o-zen-yi-ni	*narozeniny*
saint's day	svaat-ek	*svátek*

My (birthday) is on ...	maam (nar-o-zen-i-ni) ...	*Mám (narozeniny) ...*

Congratulations!	bla-ho-przhe-ye-me!	*Blahopřejeme!*
Happy Birthday!	vshekh-no ney-lep-shee kna-ro-ze-nyi-naam!	*Všechno nejlepší k narozeninám!*
Happy Saint's Day!	bla-ho-przhe-ye-me ksvaa-tku!	*Blahopřejeme k svátku!*
Blow out the candles!	sfohk-nyi svee-chki!	*Sfoukni svíčky!*

birthday cake	dort	*dort*
candles	svee-chki	*svíčky*

CHRISTMAS & NEW YEAR

VÁNOCE A NOVÝ ROK

Christmas is a family event to which friends are rarely invited. The highlight is Christmas Eve, when presents are found under the Christmas tree, typically after a dinner of fried carp and *bramborový salát* (potato salad).

Christmas Day	bo-zhee hod vaa-noch-nyee	*Boží hod vánoční*
Christmas Eve	shtyed-ree ve-cher	*Štědrý večer*
New Year's Eve	sil-ve-str	*Silvestr*
New Year's Day	no-vee rok	*Nový rok*
Epiphany	trzhee kraa-lo-veh	*Tří králové*

Happy Christmas!	ve-se-leh vaa-no-tse!	*Veselé Vánoce!*
Happy New Year!	shtya-snee no-vee rok!	*Šťastný Nový rok!*

EASTER   VELIKONOCE

On Easter Monday, women, young and old, have to look out for themselves. Once the men and boys find them, they are splashed with or even soaked in water and whipped around the ankles with plaited willow branches. Once upon a time, this was to rid the women of evil spirits, today it is simply romping! The women then are expected to give the beasts real eggs that are painted in glorious bright colours for Easter.

Happy Easter!	ve-se-leh ve-li-ko-no-tse!	*Veselé Velikonoce!*
chocolate eggs	cho-ko-laa-do-vaa va-yeech-ka	*čokoládová vajíčka*
chocolate bunny	cho-ko-laa-do-vee za-yee-chek	*čokoládový zajíček*
easter cake	ve-li-ko-noch-nyee dort	*velikonoční dort*
religious procession	pro-tse-see	*procesí*

CHRISTENINGS & WEDDINGS   KŘESTY A SVATBY

Congratulations!	bla-ho-przhe-ye-me!	*Blahopřejeme!*
To the bride and groom!	na zdra-vee ne-vye-stye a zhe-nyi-kho-vi!	*Na zdraví nevěstě a ženichovi!*
baptism	krzh-est	*křest*
engagement	zaa-snu-bi	*zásnuby*
honeymoon	sva-te-bnyee tse-sta	*svatební cesta*
wedding	svat-ba	*svatba*
wedding anniversary	vee-ro-chee svat-bi	*výročí svatby*
wedding cake	sva-teb-nyee dort	*svatební dort*
wedding present	sva-teb-nyee dar	*svatební dar*

TOASTS & CONDOLENCES

PŘÍPITKY A PROJEVY SOUSTRASTI

Bon appetit!	doh-broh khu-ty!	*Dobrou chuť!*
Bon voyage!	shtya-stnoh tse-stu!	*Šťastnou cestu!*
Cheers!	naz dra-vee!	*Na zdraví!*

Sickness

Nemoce

Get well soon!	brs-keh u-zdra-ve-nyee!	*Brzké uzdravení!*
Bless you!	naz dra-vee!	*Na zdraví!*
(after sneezing)		

The response to *na zdraví* is *děkuju* (thank you) – Czechs don't excuse themselves after sneezing.

Death

Úmrtí

I'm very sorry.
  ye mi ve-li-tse lee-to   *Je mi velice líto.*
My deepest sympathy.
  przhiy-mye-te u   *Přijměte*
  oo-preem-noh sohs-trast   *upřímnou soustrast.*
My thoughts are with you.
  ysem vdu-khus vaa-mi   *Jsem v duchu s vámi.*

Luck

Štěstí

Good luck!	hod-nye shteys-tyee!	*Hodně štěstí!*
Hope it goes well!	slom vaz!	*Zlom vaz!*
What bad luck!	to ye smoo-la!	*To je smůla!*
Never mind!	ne-va-dyee!	*Nevadí!*

FESTIVALS & HOLIDAYS

FESTIVALS
Mikuláš

FESTIVALY
St Nicholas Day

On the evening of December 6 – *Mikuláš* – after dark falls on towns and villages, the Saint Nicholas trio – *Mikuláš* accompanied by *anděl*, 'the angel' and *čert*, 'the Devil' – wander the streets and visit houses, bringing small gifts to the children. Before receiving a bag of goodies, wrapped in red cellophane, the children must recite a poem and say whether they've been good or bad in school and at home during the year. Good children receive a bag filled with fruit, nuts, and chocolates, while naughty children receive a sack of *uhlí*, 'coal' or *brambory*, 'potatoes'. Adults dress up as the trio: *Mikuláš*, the patron saint of children, wears a bishop's robe and a white mitre decorated with a cross, and carries a bishop's staff; the *anděl* is all in white with wings; and *čert* is dressed in black with horns on his head and carries chains to rattle.

St Nicholas Day is the beginning of pre-Christmas preparations. Live carp is sold on the streets for Christmas Eve dinner, Christmas trees are set up in town squares and cribs decorate the churches.

A DAY BY ANY OTHER NAME

Czechs have an old tradition of the name day –*svátek*. The name day is not *narozeniny*, a birthday, but rather a celebration for all people bearing the same name. All names have assigned their own day in the Czech calendar, for example, September 12th is Marie. A celebration of *svátek* is an opportunity for friends and acquaintances to get together and celebrate their very special name day without having to deal with their age: *Všechno nejlepší k svátku!* – 'Happy name day!'.

Pálení Čarodějnic   The Day of the Witches

The Day of the Witches, or The Burning of the Witches, known as *Pálení čarodějnic*, takes place on April 30. This was once a pre-Christian festival during which an old pagan ritual was enacted. Huge bonfires are still lit all over the country and old brooms are thrown out and burned to ward off evil spirits, especially witches, who, it was believed, rode off on broomsticks to a party with the Devil. Now it has also become an end of winter celebration, signifying the time for a spring cleaning in homes and around properties.

ZDRAVÍ   HEALTH

Emergency treatment is given at *Pohotovost* in hospitals. General practitioners and specialists usually work from *Poliklinika* (clinics). Medication has to be paid for and prescription drugs and other remedies are bought at the chemist. You always have to pay unless treatment is covered by an insurance policy.

AT THE DOCTOR   U LÉKAŘE

I'm sick.
  ysem ne-mo-tsnee/
  ne-mots-naa
*Jsem nemocný/
nemocná.* (m/f)

My friend is sick.
  mooy przhee-tel ye ne-mo-tsnee
Můj přítel je nemocný.

I need a doctor who speaks English.
  po-trzhe-bu-yi leh-kar-zhe
  kte-ree mlu-vee an-glits-ki
*Potřebuji lékaře,
který mluví anglicky.*

Could the doctor come here?
  mohl bi leh-karzh
  przhi-yee-t sem?
*Mohl by lékař
přijít sem?*

Where's the	gde ye	*Kde je*
nearest ...?	ney-blizh-shee ...?	*nejbližší ...?*
doctor	dok-tor/leh-karzh	*doktor/lékař*
hospital	ne-mots-nyi-tse	*nemocnice*
chemist	leh-kaar-na	*lékárna*
dentist	zoo-barzh	*zubař*

AILMENTS   ONEMOCNĚNÍ

I'm ill.
  ysem ne-mo-tsen
Jsem nemocen.

I've been vomiting.
  zvra-tsel/-a ysem
Zvracel/a jsem. (m/f)

I feel nauseous.
  ye mi ne-vol-no
Je mi nevolno.

I can't sleep.
  ne-mo-hu spaat
Nemohu spát.

HEALTH

I feel dizzy.	maam zaa-vra-tye	*Mám závratě.*
I feel shivery.	trzhe-su se	*Třesu se.*
I feel weak.	ysem sla-bee/-aa	*Jsem slabý/á.* (m/f)

THE DOCTOR MAY SAY...

tso vaam skhaa-zee?
  What's the matter?

bo-lee vaas nye-tso?
  Do you feel any pain?

gde to bo-lee?
  Where does it hurt?

maa-te men-stru-a-tsi?
  Are you menstruating?

maa-te ho-re-chku?
  Do you have a temperature?

yak dloh-ho uzh maa-te ti-to przhee-zna-ki?
  How long have you been like this?

myel/-a yste to yizh przhed-tyeem?
  Have you had this before?

u-zhee-vaa-te nye-ya-keh leh-ki?
  Are you on medication?

koh-rzhee-te?
  Do you smoke?

pi-ye-te?
  Do you drink?

be-re-te nye-ya-keh dro-gi?
  Do you take drugs?

yste a-ler-gits-kee/-aa na nye-tso?
  Are you allergic to anything?

yste tye-hot-naa?
  Are you pregnant?

HEALTH

I have (a/an) ...	maam ...	*Mám ...*
I've had (a/an) ...	myel/-a ysem ...	*Měl/a jsem ... (m/f)*
allergy	a-le-rgi-i	*alergii*
anaemia	a-neh-mi-i	*anémii*
bronchitis	zaa-pal proo-du-shek	*zápal průdušek*
burn	po-paa-le-ni-nu	*popáleninu*
cancer	ra-ko-vi-nu	*rakovinu*
chicken pox	pla-neh ne-shto-vi-tse	*plané neštovice*
cold	ree-mu	*rýmu*
constipation	zaa-tspu	*zácpu*
cough	ka-shel	*kašel*
cystic fibrosis	tsi-sti-tskaa fi-braw-za	*cystická fibróza*
cystitis	in-fe-ktsi	*infekci*
	mo-cho-veekh tsest	*močových cest*
diarrhoea	proo-yem	*průjem*
fever	ho-rech-ku	*horečku*
gastroenteritis	zaa-nyet zha-lu-de-chnyee sliz-ni-tse	*zánět žaludeční sliznice*
glandular fever	in-fek-chnyee mo-no-nu-kle-aw-zu	*infekční mononukleózu*
hayfever	sen-noh ree-mu	*sennou rýmu*
headache	bo-le-nyee hla-vi	*bolení hlavy*
heart condition	srde-chnyee ne-mots	*srdeční nemoc*
hepatitis	zhloh-ten-ku	*žloutenku*
indigestion	shpa-tneh traa-ve-nyee	*špatné trávení*
infection	in-fek-tsi	*infekci*
inflammation	zaa-nyet	*zánět*
influenza	khrzhip-ku	*chřipku*
pain	bo-lest	*bolest*
rash	vi-raazh-ki	*vyrážky*
sprain	pod-vrt-nu-tyee	*podvrtnutí*
sunstroke	oo-zhe/oo-pal	*úžeh/úpal*
urinary infection	in-feh-ktsi mo-cho-veekh tsest	*infekci močových cest*
venereal disease	poh-la-vnye o-ne-mots-nye-nyee	*pohlavní onemocnění*
worms	chyer-vi	*červy*

HEALTH

I have a ...	bo-lee mye ...	*Bolí mě ...*
sore throat	f krku	*v krku*
stomachache	brzhi-kho	*břicho*
toothache	zup	*zub*

| I have travel sickness. | maam tse-sto-vnyee ho-rech-ku | *Mám cestovní horečku.* |

Useful Phrases — Užitečné Fráze

It hurts there.
 ta-di to bo-lee — *Tady to bolí.*
I feel better/worse.
 ye mi leh-pe/hoorzh — *Je mi lépe/hůř.*
This is my usual medicine.
 nor-maal-nye be-ru tih-le leh-ki — *Normálně beru tyhle léky.*
I've been vaccinated.
 bil/-a ysem och-ko-vaan/-a — *Byl/a jsem očkován/a.* (m/f)
I don't want a
blood transfusion.
 nekh-tsi tran-sfu-zi — *Nechci transfuzi.*
Can I have a receipt
for my insurance?
 mo-hu do-stat po-tvr-ze-nyee pro po-yish-tyov-nu? — *Mohu dostat potvrzení pro pojišťovnu?*

WOMEN'S HEALTH — ŽENSKÉ NEMOCI

Could I see a female doctor?
 khtye-la bkhi dok-tor-ku? — *Chtěla bych doktorku?*
I'm pregnant.
 ysem tye-hot-naa — *Jsem těhotná.*
I think I'm pregnant.
 mi-sleem zhe ysem tye-hot-naa — *Myslím, že jsem těhotná.*
I'm on the Pill.
 be-ru an-ti-kon-tse-ptsi — *Beru antikoncepci.*

I haven't had my
period for ... weeks.
   ne-do-sta-la ysem
   men-stru-a-tsi ... tee-dnoo

*Nedostala jsem
menstruaci ... týdnů.*

I'd like to get the
morning-after pill.
   khtye-la bikh
   an-ti-kon-tse-pchnyee
   ta-blet-ku po sti-ku

*Chtěla bych
antikoncepční
tabletku po styku.*

I'd like to have a pregnancy test.
   moo-zhe-te mi u-dye-lat
   tye-ho-ten-skee test

*Můžete mi udělat
těhotenský test.*

abortion	po-trat	*potrat*
cystitis	zaa-nyet	*zánět*
	mo-cho-veekh tsest	*močových cest*
diaphragm	pe-sar	*pesar*
IUD	vni-tro-dye-lo-zhnye	*vnitroděložní*
	tye-lee-sko/da-na	*tělísko/dana*
mammogram	ma-mo-gram	*mamogram*
menstruation	men-stru-a-tse	*menstruace*
miscarriage	po-trat	*potrat*
pap smear	vee-tyer s pokh-vi	*výtěr z pochvy*
period pain	men-stru-a-chnyee	*menstruační*
	bo-le-styi	*bolesti*
the Pill	an-ti-kon-tse-pchnyee	*antikoncepční*
	ta-blet-ki	*tabletky*
premenstrual	przhed-men-stru-	*předmenstru-*
	a-chnyee	*ační*
tension	bo-le-styi	*bolesti*
thrush	plee-se-nye pokh-vi	*plíseň pochvy*
ultrasound	ul-tra-zvuk	*ultrazvuk*

HEALTH

SPECIAL HEALTH NEEDS

SPECIÁLNÍ ZDRAVOTNÍ POTŘEBY

I'm ...	ysem ...	*Jsem ...*
anaemic	khu-do-kre-vnee	*chudokrevný*
asthmatic	a-stma-tik	*astmatik*
diabetic	di-a-be-tik	*diabetik*

I'm allergic to ...	ysem a-ler-gi-tskee/-aa na ...	*Jsem alergický/á na ... (m/f)*
antibiotics	an-ti-bi-o-ti-ka	*antibiotika*
aspirin	a-spi-rin	*aspirin*
bees	fche-li	*včely*
codeine	ko-de-in	*kodein*
dairy products	mleh-chneh·vee-rob-ki	*mléčné výrobky*
penicillin	pe-nits-i-lin	*penicilin*
pollen	pil	*pyl*

I have high/low blood pressure.
maam vi-so-kee/nyee-skee kre-vnyee tlak
Mám vysoký/nízký krevní tlak.

I have a weak heart.
maam sla-beh srd-tse
Mám slabé srdce.

Is that a new syringe you're using?
po-u-zhee-vaa-te no-voh strzhee-ka-chku/ye-hlu?
Používáte novou stříkačku/jehlu?

I have my own syringe.
maam svoh vla-stnyee strzee-kach-ku
Mám svou vlastní stříkačku.

I'm on medication for ...
be-ru leh-ki pro-tyi/na ...
Beru léky proti/na ...

I'm on a special diet.
ysem na spe-tsi-aal-nyee di-e-tye
Jsem na speciální dietě.

addiction	zaa-vis-lost	*závislost*
bite	shtyee-pnu-tyee	*štípnutí*
blood test	kre-vnyee skoh-shka	*krevní zkouška*
inhaler	in-ha-laa-tor	*inhalátor*
injection	in-yek-tse	*injekce*
injury	zra-nye-nyee	*zranění*
pacemaker	kar-di-o-sti-mu-laa-tor	*kardiostimulátor*
wound	yi-zva	*jizva*

HEALTH

DID YOU KNOW...

In a *Lékárna* (pharmacy) you have to ask for everything over the counter. There are two different counters – the prescription counter and the regular counter.

ALTERNATIVE TREATMENTS

ALTERNATIVNÍ LÉČBA

acupuncture	a-ku-punk-tu-ra	*akupuntura*
aromatherapy	a-ro-ma-te-ra-pi-e	*aromaterapie*
chiropractor	khi-ro-pra-ktik	*chiropraktik*
faith healer	zaa-zra-chnee leh-karzh	*zázračný lékař*
herbalist	bi-lin-kaarzh	*bylinkář*
homeopathy	ho-me-o-pa-ti-e	*homeopatie*
massage	ma-saazh	*masáž*
meditation	me-dit-a-tse	*meditace*
naturopath	przhee-rod-nyee me-di-tsee-na	*přírodní medicína*
reflexology	re-fle-kso-lo-gi-e	*reflexologie*
reiki	rey-ki	*reiki*

HEALTH

PARTS OF THE BODY

My ... hurts.	bo-lee mye ...	*Bolí mě ...*
I have a pain in my ...	maam bo-les-tyi f ...	*Mám bolesti v ...*
I can't move my ...	ne-mo-hu hee-bat ...	*Nemohu hýbat ...*

ČÁSTI TĚLA

ankle	kot-nyeek	*kotník*
appendix	sle-peh strzhe-vo	*slepé střevo*
arm	pa-zhe	*paže*
back	zaa-da	*záda*
bladder	mo-cho-vee mye-kheerzh	*močový měchýř*
blood	kref	*krev*
bone	kost	*kost*
chest	hru-dy/prsa	*hruď/prsa*
ears	u-shi	*uši*
eye	o-chi	*oči*
finger	prst	*prst*
foot	no-ha/kho-dyi-dlo	*noha/chodidlo*
hand	ru-ka	*ruka*
head	hla-va	*hlava*
heart	srt-se	*srdce*
jaw	che-list	*čelist*
kidney	led-vi-na	*ledvina*
knee	ko-le-no	*koleno*
leg	no-ha	*noha*
liver	yaa-tra	*játra*
lungs	plee-tse	*plíce*
mouth	oo-sta	*ústa*
muscle	sva-li	*svaly*
nose	nos	*nos*
ribs	rzhe-bra	*žebra*
shoulders	ra-me-na	*ramena*
skin	koo-zhe	*kůže*
spine	paa-terzh	*páteř*
stomach	brzhi-kho	*břicho*
teeth	zu-bi	*zuby*
throat	krk/hrd-lo	*krk/hrdlo*
vein	zhee-la	*žíla*

HEALTH

AT THE DENTIST

U ZUBAŘE

I have a toothache.
  bo-lee mye zup

Bolí mě zub.

I have a hole.
  maam dee-ru vzu-bu

Mám díru v zubu.

I've lost a filling.
  vi-pa-dla mi plom-ba

Vypadla mi plomba.

I've broken my tooth.
  zlo-mil ysem si zup

Zlomil jsem si zub.

My gums hurt.
  bo-lee mye daa-sna

Bolí mě dásna.

I don't want it extracted.
  nekh-tsi ho vi-tr-hnoht

Nechci ho vytrhnout.

Please give me an anaesthetic.
  moo-zhe-te mi to
  umrt-vit pro-seem

*Můžete mi to
umrtvit, prosím.*

Ouch!
  aaaaaa!

au!

AT THE PHARMACY

V LÉKÁRNĚ

Is there an all-night
pharmacy nearby?
  gde ye ney-blizh-shee po-ho-
  to-vo-stnee leh-kaa-rna?

*Kde je nejbližší
pohotovostní lékárna?*

I need something against/for ...
  po-trzhe-bu-yi nye-tso
  pro-tyi/-na ...

*Potřebuji něco
proti/na ...*

Do I need a prescription for ...?
  po-trzhe-bu-yi re-tsept na ...?

Potřebuji recept na ...?

I have a prescription.
  maam re-tsept

Mám recept.

How many times a day?
  ko-lik-kraat den-nye?

Kolikrát denně?

twice a day	dva-kraat den-nye	*dvakrát denně*
with food	zyeed-lem	*s jídlem*

HEALTH

Can I drive on this medication?
  moo-zhu rzhee-dyit kdizh   *Můžu řídit, když*
  be-ru ten-to lehk?   *beru tento lék?*
Will it make me drowsy?
  bu-du po-tom os-pa-lee/-aa   *Budu potom ospalý/á?* (m/f)

antibiotics	**an-ti-bi-o-ti-ka**	*antibiotika*
antiseptic	**an-ti-sep-ti-tskee**	*antiseptický*
	pro-strzhe-dek	*prostředek*
aspirin	**as-pi-rin**	*aspirin*
bandage	**o-bi-na-dlo**	*obinadlo*
Band-aids	**naa-plast/**	*náplast/*
	le-oo-ko-plast	*leukoplast*
condoms	**kon-do-mi**	*kondomy*
contraceptives	**an-ti-kon-tsep-tse**	*antikoncepce*
cough medicine	**si-rup pro-tyi**	*sirup proti*
	ka-shli	*kašli*
gauze	**ob-vaz**	*obvaz*
laxatives	**pro-yee-ma-dlo**	*projímadlo*
painkillers	**praa-shki pro-tyi**	*prášky proti*
	bo-le-styi	*bolesti*
sleeping pills	**spa-tsee praa-shki**	*spací prášky*

For general pharmaceuticals, see the Shopping chapter, pages 117 to 118.

SPECIÁLNÍ POTŘEBY

SPECIFIC NEEDS

DISABLED TRAVELLERS

TĚLESNĚ POSTIŽENÍ CESTUJÍCÍ

There are few special facilities for disabled travellers in and around buildings and on public transport, although the situation is likely to improve.

I'm disabled/handicapped.
ysem in-va-lida/tye-le-snye
po-styi-zhe-nee/-aa

Jsem invalida/tělesně postižený/á. (m/f)

I need assistance.
po-trzhe-bu-yi po-mots

Potřebuji pomoc.

What services do you
have for disabled people?
ya-keh slu-zhbi pos-ki-tu-ye-te
in-va-li-doom/tye-le-snye
po-styi-zhe-neem?

Jaké služby poskytujete invalidům?/tělesně postiženým?

Is there wheelchair access?
ye tam ram-pa pro
in-va-lid-nyee vo-zeek?

Je tam rampa pro invalidní vozík?

I'm deaf.
ysem hlu-khee

Jsem hluchý.

I have a hearing aid.
maam slu-khaat-ko pro
ne-dos-lee-kha-veh

Mám sluchátko pro nedoslýchavé.

Speak more loudly, please.
mlu-vte pro-seem hla-snye-yi

Mluvte prosím hlasněji.

Are guide dogs permitted?
ysoh sle-pe-tskeh
psi po-vo-le-nyi?

Jsou slepecké psy povoleni?

braille library	knyi-hov-na se sle-pets-keem tyi-skem	*knihovna se slepeckým tiskem*
disabled person	in-va-lida	*invalida*
guide dog	sle-petskee pes	*slepecký pes*
wheelchair	in-va-li-dnyee vo-zeek	*invalidní vozík*

GAY TRAVELLERS — HOMOSEXUÁLOVÉ

Where are the gay hangouts?
gde se skhaa-ze-yee
ho-mo-se-ksu-aa-lo-veh?

*Kde se scházejí
homosexuálové?*

Is there a predominantly
gay street/district?
ye ta-di u-li-chka ne-bo
chtvrty gde se skhaa-ze-yee
ho-mo-se-ksu-aa-lo-veh?

*Je tady ulička nebo
čtvrť, kde se scházejí
homosexuálové?*

Are we/Am I likely
to be harassed here?
bu-doh naas/mye ta-di
pro-naa-sle-do-vat?

*Budou nás/Mě tady
pronásledovat?*

TRAVELLING WITH THE FAMILY — CESTOVÁNÍ S RODINOU

Are there facilities for babies?
maa-te ta-di zar-zhee-ze-nyee
pro ko-yen-tse?

*Máte tady zařízení
pro kojence?*

Do you have a
child-minding service?
maa-te ta-di shkol-ku pro dye-ti?

Máte tady školku pro děti?

Where can I find an
English-speaking babysitter?
gde moo-zu na-yeet an-glits-ki
mlu-vee-tsee pa-nyeek dee-tye-ti?

*Kde můžu najít anglicky
mluvící paní k dítěti?*

Can you put an extra
bed/cot in the room?
moo-zhe-te przhi-dat do
po-ko-ye po-steel-ku
ne-bo przhi-steel-ku?

*Můžete přidat do
pokoje postýlku
nebo přistýlku?*

I need a car with a child seat.
po-trzhe-bu-yi ow-tos
dyet-skeem se-daat-kem

*Potřebuji auto s
dětským sedátkem.*

Is it suitable for children?
ye to vhod-neh pro dye-tyi?

Je to vhodné pro děti?

Are children allowed?
ye fstup dye-tem po-vo-len?

Je vstup dětem povolen?

Do you have a children's menu?
maa-te yee-dla
pro dye-tyi?

*Máte jídla
pro děti?*

Are there any activities for children?
ysoh ta-di nye-ya-keh a-kti-vi-ti
pro dye-tyi?

*Jsou tady nějaké aktivity
pro děti?*

Is there a playground nearby?
ye na-bleez-ku dyet-skeh
hrzhi-shtye?

*Je nablízku dětské
hřiště?*

LOOKING FOR A JOB

PŘI HLEDÁNÍ ZAMĚSTNÁNÍ

Where can I find local
job advertisements?
gde nay-du in-ze-raa-ti
na praa-tsi?

*Kde najdu inzeráty
na práci?*

Do I need a work permit?
pot-rzhe-bu-yi pra-tsov-nyee
po-vo-le-nyee?

*Potřebuji pracovní
povolení?*

I've come about
the position advertised.
przhi-shel ysem kvoo-li teh
praa-tsi tso bi-la in-ze-ro-va-naa

*Přišel jsem kvůli té
práci co byla inzerovaná.*

I'm ringing about
the position advertised.
vo-laam o-le-dnye teh praa-tse
tso bi-la in-ze-ro-va-naa

*Volám ohledně té práce
co byla inzerovaná.*

I have experience.
maam pra-ksi

Mám praxi.

What is the wage?
ya-kee ye vee-dye-lek?

Jaký je výdělek?

SPECIFIC NEEDS

Do I have to pay tax?
  mu-seem pla-tyit da-nye?   *Musím platit daně?*

I can start ...	**mo-hu za-cheet ...**	*Mohu začít ...*
today	**dnes**	*dnes*
tomorrow	**zee-tra**	*zítra*
next week	**przhee-shtyee tee-den**	*příští týden*

Useful Words		**Užitečná Slovíčka**
casual	**przhee-le-zhi-tost-nye**	*příležitostní*
employee	**za-mye-stna-nets**	*zaměstnanec*
employer	**za-mye-stna-va-tel**	*zaměstnavatel*
full-time	**plnee oo-va-zek**	*plný úvazek*
job	**praa-tse/**	*práce/*
	za-myest-naa-nye	*zaměstnání*
part-time	**po-lo-vich-nye**	*poloviční*
	oo-va-zek	*úvazek*
resume/cv	**zhi-vo-to-pis**	*životopis*

ON BUSINESS   SLUŽEBNÍ CESTA

We're attending	**oo-chast-nyee-me**	*Účastníme*
a ...	**se ne ...**	*se ne ...*
conference	**kon-fe-ren-tse**	*konference*
meeting	**skhoo-ze**	*schůze*
trade fair	**ve-le-trhu**	*veletrhu*

I'm on a course.
  ysem na ku-rzu   *Jsem na kurzu.*
I have an appointment with ...
  maam zkhooz-kuz ...   *Mám schůzku s ...*
Here's my business card.
  ta-di ye maa vi-zit-ka   *Tady je má vizitka.*
I need an interpreter.
  po-trzhe-bu-yi tlu-moch-nye-ka   *Potřebuji tlumočníka.*
I'd like to use a computer.
  khtyel bikh poh-zheet   *Chtěl bych použít*
  po-chee-tach   *počítač.*

Useful Words | Užitečná Slovíčka

client	kli-ent	*klient*
colleague	ko-le-ga	*kolega*
distributor	dis-tri-bu-tor	*distributor*
exhibition	vee-sta-va	*výstava*
manager	ma-na-zhehr	*manažér*
proposal	naa-vrh	*návrh*

ON TOUR | NA ZÁJEZDU

We're part of a group.	ysme ta-di se sku-pi-noh	*Jsme tady se skupinou.*
We're on tour.	ysme na zaa-yez-dye	*Jsme na zájezdě.*

I'm with the ...	ysem ta-di se ...	*Jsem tady se ...*
crew	o-saad-koh	*osádkou*
band	ka-pe-loh	*kapelou*
group	sku-pi-noh	*skupinou*
team	tee-mem	*tímem*

Please speak with our manager.
ye-dney-te pro-seem s na-shim ma-na-zheh-rem
Jednejte prosím s naším manažérem.

We've lost our equipment.
stra-tyi-li ysme na-she za-rzhee-ze-nyee
Ztratili jsme naše zařízení.

We sent equipment on this ...	po-sla-li ysme za-rzhee-ze-nyee teem-to ...	*Poslali jsme zařízení tímto ...*
bus	ow-to-bu-sem	*autobusem*
flight	le-ta-dlem	*letadlem*
train	vla-kem	*vlakem*

We're taking a break of ... days.
be-re-me si do-vo-le-noh na ... dnoo
Bereme si dovolenou na ... dnů.

Film & TV Crews

Filmový a Televizní Štáb

We're on location.
   ysme na lo-ka-tsi/mees-tye
Jsme na lokaci/místě.
We're filming!
   fil-mu-ye-me!
Filmujeme!
May we film here?
   moo-zhe-me ta-di fil-mo-vat?
Můžeme tady filmovat?

We're making a ...	to-chee-me ...	*Točíme ...*
documentary	do-ku-men-taar-nyee film	*dokumentární film*
film	film	*film*
TV series	te-le-vi-znyee se-ri-aal	*televizní seriál*

PILGRIMAGE & RELIGION

POUTĚ A NÁBOŽENSTVÍ

What is your religion?
   ya-ke yste vee-ri?
Jaké jste víry?

I'm ...	yaa ysem ...	*Já jsem ...*
Buddhist	bud-hi-sta	*budhista*
Christian	krzhe-styan	*křesťan*
Hindu	hind	*hind*
Jewish	zhid	*žid*
Muslim	mu-slim	*muslim*

I'm not religious.
   ysem bez vi-znaa-nye
jsem bez vyznání.
I'm (Catholic), but not practising.
   ysem (ka-to-leek) a-le
   ne-kho-dyeem do ko-ste-la
Jsem (katolík), ale nechodím do kostela.
I believe in destiny/fate.
   vye-rzheem v o-sud
Věřím v osud.
I'm interested in astrology/philosophy.
   za-yee-maam se o
   a-stro-lo-gi-i/fi-loz-o-fi-i
Zajímám se o astrologii/filozofii.

I'm an atheist.
  ysem a-te-i-sta   *Jsem ateista.*
I'm agnostic.
  ysem a-gno-stik   *Jsem agnostik.*
Can I attend this service/mass?
  mo-hu se oo-chast-nyit   *Mohu se účastnit*
  teh-to bo-ho-slu-zhbi/mshe?   *této bohoslužby/mše?*
Where can I pray/worship?
  gde se ta-di moo-zhu   *Kde se tady můžu*
  po-mo-dlit?   *pomodlit?*
Where can I go to
confession (in English)?
  gde mo-hu yeet ke   *Kde mohu jít ke*
  spo-vye-dyi (v a-nglich-tyi-nye)?   *zpovědi (v angličtině)?*
Can I receive communion here?
  mo-hu yeet ta-di na   *Mohu jít tady na*
  przhi-yee-maa-nyee svaa-to-styi?   *přijímání svátosti?*

baptism/christening	krzhest	*křest*
church	ko-stel	*kostel*
communion	przhi-yee-maa-nyee	*přijímání*
	svaa-to-styi	*svátosti*
confession	spo-vye-dy	*zpověď*
funeral	poh-rzheb	*pohřeb*
god	booh	*bůh*
prayer	mot-lit-ba	*modlitba*
priest	knyez	*kněz*
relic	re-lik-vi-ye	*relikvie*
saint	sva-tee	*svatý*
shrine	re-li-kvi-aarzh	*relikviář*
temple	khraam	*chrám*

TRACING ROOTS & HISTORY

RODOKMEŇ A PÁTRÁNÍ PO RODINNÉ HISTORII

SPECIFIC NEEDS

I think my ancestors
came from this area.
  mi-sleem zhe mo-yi
  przhe-dko-veh po-khaa-zee z
  teh-to o-bla-styi

Myslím, že moji
předkové pochází z
této oblasti.

I'm looking for my relatives.
  hle-daam przhe-bu-zneh

Hledám příbuzné.

Is there anyone here by the name of ...?
  ye ta-di nye-gto gto se
  yme-nu-ye ...?

Je tady někdo kdo se
jmenuje ..?

I'd like to go to the cemetery.
  khtyel/-a bikh yeet na
  hrzh-bi-tof

Chtěl/la bych jít na
hřbitov. (m/f)

I think he fought/died near here.
  mi-sleem zhe ta-di
  bo-yo-val/ze-mrzhel

Myslím, že tady
bojoval/zemřel.

My (father) fought/died
here in WWI/II.
  mooy (taa-ta) ta-di bo-yo-val/
  ze-mrzhel v prvnyee/dru-heh
  svye-to-veh vaal-tse

Můj (táta) tady bojoval/
zemřel v první/druhé
světové válce.

My (grandmother)
nursed here in WWI/II.
  mo-ye (sta-raa mat-ka) bi-la
  ta-di zdra-vot-nyee se-stroh
  v prvnyee/dru-heh
  svye-to-veh vaal-tse

Moje (stará matka) byla
tady zdravotní sestrou
v první/druhé
světové válce.

ČAS & DATUM   TIME & DATES

TELLING THE TIME   ČAS

Czechs use a 24 hour clock, ie, 1.00pm becomes 1300 hours,
2.00pm becomes 1400 hours, etc. 'Half past' in Czech becomes
'half to' the next hour, so, they look ahead at the coming hour.
For example, 10:30 becomes *půl jedenácté*, ie, half an hour has
passed towards eleven o'clock.

What time is it?
  ko-lik ye ho-dyin?   *Kolik je hodin?*
(It's) one o'clock.
  ye yed-na ho-dyi-na   *Je jedna hodina.*
(It's) ten o'clock.
  ye de-set ho-dyin   *Je deset hodin.*
Half past one.
  ye pool dru-heh   *Je půl druhé.*
Quarter past one.
  ye chtvrt na dvye   *Je čtvrt na dvě.*
Quarter to one.
  ye trzhi-chtvr-tye na ye-dnu   *Je třičtvrtě na jednu.*
Twenty to one.
  za pyet mi-nut trzhi-chtvr-tye na ye-dnu   *Za pět minut třičtvrtě na jednu.*
Half past three.
  ye pool chtvr-teh   *Je půl čtvrté.*

DID YOU KNOW ...	The days of the week and the names of the months are always written in small letters.

DAYS OF THE WEEK   DNY V TÝDNU

Monday	pon-dye-lee	*pondělí*
Tuesday	oo-te-ree	*úterý*
Wednesday	strzhe-da	*středa*
Thursday	chtvr-tek	*čtvrtek*
Friday	paa-tek	*pátek*
Saturday	so-bo-ta	*sobota*
Sunday	ne-dye-le	*neděle*

MONTHS

MĚSÍCE

January	le-den	*leden*
February	oo-nor	*únor*
March	brzhe-zen	*březen*
April	du-ben	*duben*
May	kvye-ten	*květen*
June	cher-ven	*červen*
July	cher-ve-nets	*červenec*
August	sr-pen	*srpen*
September	zaa-rzhee	*září*
October	rzhee-yen	*říjen*
November	li-sto-pat	*listopad*
December	pro-si-nets	*prosinec*

SEASONS

ROČNÍ OBDOBÍ

summer	leh-to	*léto*
autumn	pod-zim	*podzim*
winter	zi-ma	*zima*
spring	ya-ro	*jaro*

DATES

DATUM

What date is it today?
   ko-li-kaa-teh-ho ye dnes?   *Kolikátého je dnes?*

It's 18 October.
   ye o-smnaa-tstee-ho rzhee-yna   *Je osmnáctýho října.*

TIME & DATES (side tab)

TIME ON YOUR HANDS

The Czech Republic uses Central European Time which is one hour ahead of Greenwich Mean Time. Daylight saving time is usually between March and October. When you see dates in written form, you may find that Czechs still use Roman numerals for months as opposed to Arabic numerals for days, ie, 15. IX. 68 stands for 15 September 1968. Remember, II stands for February (the second month) and not November (the eleventh month)!

PRESENT

today	dnes	*dnes*
this morning	dnes do-po-led-ne	*dnes dopoledne*
this afternoon	dnes ot-po-led-ne	*dnes odpoledne*
tonight	ve-cher	*večer*
this week	ten-to tee-den	*tento týden*
this month	ten-to mye-seets	*tento měsíc*
this year	le-tos	*letos*
(right) now	(praa-vye) tety	*(právě) teď*

PŘÍTOMNOST

LUCKY STARS

The foundation stone for the Charles Bridge was laid by Charles IV on the 9th of July 1357 at 5.31 am – precisely when a conjunction of the Sun with Saturn occurred. This particular time was selected, because according to medieval astrology, this was the luckiest moment of that year.

PAST

yesterday	fche-ra	*včera*
day before yesterday	przhe-de-fchee-rem	*předevčírem*
yesterday morning	fche-ra raa-no	*včera ráno*
yesterday afternoon/ evening	fche-ra ot-po-le-dne/ ve-cher	*včera odpoledne/ večer*
last night	fche-ra ve-cher	*včera večer*
last week	mi-nu-lee tee-den	*minulý týden*
last month	mi-nu-lee mye-seets	*minulý měsíc*
last year	lo-ni	*loni*
(half an hour) ago	przhed pool ho-dyi-noh	*před půl hodinou*
(three) days ago	przhed (trzhe-mi) dni	*před (třemi) dny*
(five) years ago	przhed (pye-tyi) leh-ti	*před (pěti) léty*
a while ago	ne-daa-vno	*nedávno*
since (May)	od (kvyet-na)	*od (května)*

MINULOST

TIME & DATES

FUTURE   BUDOUCNOST

tomorrow	zee-tra	*zítra*
day after tomorrow	po-zee-trzhee	*pozítří*
tomorrow morning	zee-tra raa-no	*zítra ráno*
tomorrow afternoon	zee-tra ot-po-le-dne	*zítra odpoledne*
tomorrow evening	zee-tra ve-cher	*zítra večer*
next week	przhe-shtyee tee-den	*příští týden*
next month	przhe-shtyee mye-seets	*příští měsíc*
next year	przhe-shtyee rok	*příští rok*
in (five) minutes	za (pyet) mi-nut	*za (pět) minut*
in (six) days	za (shest) dnoo	*za (šest) dnů*
within an hour/ month	za ho-dyi-nu/ mye-seets	*za hodinu/ měsíc*
until (June)	do (cher-vna)	*do (června)*

DURING THE DAY   BĚHEM DNE

It's early.	ye brzi	*Je brzy.*
It's late.	ye po-zdye	*Je pozdě.*
afternoon	ot-po-le-dne	*odpoledne*
dawn	svee-taa-nyee	*svítání*
day	den	*den*
evening	ve-cher	*večer*
lunchtime	o-byed	*oběd*
midnight	pool-nots	*půlnoc*
morning	raa-no/do-po-le-dne	*ráno/dopoledne*
night	nots	*noc*
noon/midday	po-led-ne	*poledne*
sunrise	vee-khod slun-tse	*východ slunce*
sunset	zaa-pat slun-tse	*západ slunce*

TIME & DATES

ČÍSLOVKY A MÍRY

NUMBERS & AMOUNTS

CARDINAL NUMBERS   ZÁKLADNÍ ČÍSLOVKY

In Czech, number 'one' and numbers ending in 'one' are followed by the nominative singular form of a word (see Grammar chapter, page 18), and 'one' agrees with the gender of the noun that follows:

jeden týden (m)	one week
jedna kniha (f)	one book

Number 'two' agrees with the gender of the noun as well, but the noun is naturally in plural.

dva měsíce (m pl)	two months
dvě děvčata (neut pl)	two girls

Other numbers are followed by the genitive (possessive) plural.

sedm knih (f pl)	seven books

0	**nu-la**	*nula*
1	**ye-den**	*jeden*
2	**dva**	*dva*
3	**trzhi**	*tři*
4	**chti-rzhi**	*čtyři*
5	**pyet**	*pět*
6	**shest**	*šest*
7	**sedm**	*sedm*
8	**osm**	*osm*
9	**de-vyet**	*devět*
10	**de-set**	*deset*
11	**ye-de-naatst**	*jedenáct*
12	**dva-naatst**	*dvanáct*

13	trzhi-naatst	*třináct*
14	chtr-naatst	*čtrnáct*
15	pa-tnaatst	*patnáct*
16	shest-naatst	*šestnáct*
17	sedm-naatst	*sedmnáct*
18	osm-naatst	*osmnáct*
19	de-va-te-naatst	*devatenáct*
20	dva-tset	*dvacet*
21	dva-tset ye-den/	*dvacet jeden/*
	ye-dna-dva-tset	*jednadvacet*
22	dva-a-dva-tset	*dvaadvacet*
30	trzhi-tset	*třicet*
40	chti-rzhi-tset	*čtyřicet*
50	pa-de-saat	*padesát*
60	she-de-saat	*šedesát*
70	sedm-de-saat	*sedmdesát*
80	osm-de-saat	*osmdesát*
90	de-va-de-saat	*devadesát*
100	sto	*sto*
1000	tyi-seets	*tisíc*
one million	mi-li-yawn	*milión*

NUMBERS & AMOUNTS

ORDINAL NUMBERS   ŘADOVÉ ČÍSLOVKY

1st	pr-vnyee	*první*
2nd	dru-hee	*druhý*
3rd	trzhe-tyee	*třetí*
4th	chtvr-tee	*čtvrtý*
5th	paa-tee	*pátý*

CURRENCY & DECIMALS

PENÍZE A DESÍTKOVÁ SOUSTAVA

You'll come across decimals on price tags displayed in shops. Czechs use commas where we would use a point, so that an article for 4 crowns 20 is written 4,20 Kč.

The currency is the Czech *Koruna* (crown) and *halíře*. There are 100 *halíř* in one *Koruna*. The coins go up to 20 Kč and notes begin at 20 Kč and go up to 5000,00 Kč.

FRACTIONS

ZLOMKY

a quarter	chtvr-tyi-na	*čtvrtina*
a half	po-lo-vi-na	*polovina*
a third	trzhe-tyi-na	*třetina*
three-quarters	trzhi-chtvr-tyi-ni	*třičtvrtiny*
all	fshi-khnyi/fshe-khno	*všichni/všechno*
none	nyi-gto/nyits	*nikdo/nic*

USEFUL AMOUNTS

UŽITEČNÉ VÁHY A MÍRY

(just) a little	tro-khu	*trochu*
some/a few	nye-ko-lik	*několik*
double	dvo-yi-tee	*dvojitý*
a dozen	tu-tset	*tucet*
enough	dost	*dost*
less	meh-nye	*méně*
many/much/a lot	mno-ho	*mnoho*
more	vee-tse	*více*
once	ye-dnoh	*jednou*
a pair	paar	*pár*
some	nye-kte-ree	*některý*
too many/much	przhee-lish/ho-dnye	*příliš/hodně*
twice	dva-kraat	*dvakrát*

A FEW THINGS ABOUT PAIRS

In spoken Czech, *pár* (couple) doesn't necessarily mean 'two' – rather it's used in the sense of 'a few, several', eg, *pár dnů* is 'a few days' (not strictly a couple of days).

Párek takes its name from a diminutive of *pár* (pair). *Párek v rohlíku* means 'hot dog', but *To je hezký párek!* means 'What a nice couple!'.

a bottle of	**laa-hev**	*láhev*
half a kg of	**pool ki-la**	*půl kila*
100 grams	**de-set de-ka**	*deset deka*
a jar	**skle-nyich-ka**	*sklenička*
a kg	**ki-lo**	*kilo*
a packet	**ba-lee-chek**	*balíček*
a slice of	**plaa-tek**	*plátek*
a tin	**ple-khof-ka**	*plechovka*

PRVNÍ POMOC
EMERGENCIES

GENERAL

Help!	**po-mots!**	*Pomoc!*
Stop!	**zas-tav!**	*Zastav!*
Go away!	**ydye-te prich!**	*Jděte pryč!*
Thief!	**zlo-dye-y!**	*Zloděj!*
Fire!	**ho-rzhee!**	*Hoří!*
Watch out!	**po-zor!**	*Pozor!*

BĚŽNÁ

It's an emergency!
   to-ye na-leh-ha-vee przhee-pad!   *To je naléhavý případ!*
Could you help us please?
   moo-zhe-te naam pro-seem   *Můžete nám prosím*
   po-mo-tsi?   *pomoci?*
Could I please use the telephone?
   mo-hu po-u-zheet te-le-fon?   *Mohu použít telefon?*
I'm lost.
   stra-tyil/-a ysem se   *Ztratil/a jsem se.* (m/f)
Where are the toilets?
   gde ysoh zaa-kho-di?   *Kde jsou záchody?*

PAYING FOR THE PRIVILEGE

Be prepared to pay 3 Kč to 5 Kč for using public toilets.

POLICE   POLICIE

Call the police!
zavoleyte po-li-tsi-yi!   *Zavolejte policii!*

Where's the police station?
gde ye po-li-tsey-nyee   *Kde je policejní*
sta-nyi-tse?   *stanice?*

We want to report an offence.
khtye-li bi-khom o-hlaa-sit   *Chtěli bychom ohlásit*
przhe-stu-pek   *přestupek.*

I've been raped/assaulted.
bi-la ysem znaa-sil-nye-na/   *Byla jsem znásilněna/*
przhe-pa-de-na   *přepadena.*

I've been robbed.
bil/-a ysem o-kra-den/-a   *Byl/a jsem okraden/a.*
                                                    (m/f)

My ... was/	oo-krad-li mi ...	*Ukradli mi ...*
were stolen.		
backpack	ba-toh	*batoh*
bags	za-va-za-dla	*zavazadla*
handbag	ka-bel-ku	*kabelku*
money	pe-nyee-ze	*peníze*
papers	do-kla-di	*doklady*
travellers	tses-tov-nye	*cestovní*
cheques	she-ki	*šeky*
passport	pas	*pas*
wallet	pe-nye-zhen-ku	*peněženku*

My possessions are insured.
maam po-yish-tye-nyee   *Mám pojištění.*

I'm sorry/I apologise.
ye mi lee-to/li-tu-yi/   *Je mi líto/Lituji/*
pro-miny-te   *Promiňte.*

I didn't realise I was
doing anything wrong.
ne-oo-vye-do-mil ysem si zhe   *Neuvědomil jsem si, že*
ysem u-dye-lal nye-tso   *jsem udělal něco*
shpat-neh-ho   *špatného.*

EMERGENCIES

I didn't do it.
    ja ysem to ne-u-dye-lal/-a
    Ja jsem to neudělal/a. (m/f)

We're innocent.
    ysme ne-vin-nyi
    Jsme nevinni.

We're foreigners.
    ysme tsi-zin-tsi
    Jsme cizinci.

I wish to contact my
embassy/consulate.
    khtyel bikh mlu-vit zmeem
    vel-vi-sla-nets-tveem/
    kon-zu-laa-tem
    Chtěl bych mluvit s mým
    velvyslanectvím/
    konzulátem.

Can I call someone?
    mo-hu nye-ko-mu za-vo-lat?
    Mohu někomu zavolat?

Can I have a lawyer
who speaks English?
    mo-hu do-stat an-glits-ki
    mlu-vee-tsee-ho praa-vnyee-ka?
    Mohu dostat anglicky
    mluvícího právníka?

Is there a fine we can
pay to clear this?
    daa se to vi-rzhe-shit
    za-la-tse-neem po-ku-ti?
    Dá se to vyřešit
    zaplacením pokuty?

I (don't) understand.
    (ne-)ro-zu-meem
    (Ne)rozumím.

I know my rights.
    znaam-svaa praa-va
    Znám svá práva.

YOU MAY HEAR ...

och yde?	What happened?
o tso se yed-naa?	What's wrong?
u-kazh-te mi (las-ka-vye) *proo-kaz to-to-zhno-styi?*	Can I have your ID, please?
vi-plny-te las-ka-vye ten-to *form-u-laarzh*	Please fill out this form.

EMERGENCIES

arrested	za-yi-shtyen	*zajištěn*
cell	tse-la	*cela*
consulate	kon-su-lat	*konzulát*
embassy	vel-vi-sla-ne-tstvee	*velvyslanectví*
fine (payment)	po-ku-ta	*pokuta*
guilty	vi-nen	*vinen*
lawyer	praa-vneek/ad-vo-kaat	*právník/advokát*
not guilty	ne-vi-nen	*nevinen*
police officer	po-li-tsayt	*policajt*
police station	po-li-tsey-nyee	*policejní*
	sta-nyi-tse	*stanice*
prison	vye-ze-nyee	*vězení*
trial	sohd	*soud*

SIGNS

NEMOCNICE	HOSPITAL
POHOTOVOST	EMERGENCY
POHOTOVOSTNÍ	EMERGENCY SERVICE
SLUŽBA	
POLICIE	POLICE
PRVNÍ POMOC/	FIRST AID
STANICE PRVNÍ	
POMOCI	

What am I accused of?	zche-ho ysem ob-zha-lo-vaan?	*Z čeho jsem obžalován?*
You will be charged with ...	yste ob-zha-lo-vaan za/z ...	*Jste obžalován za/z ...*
He/She will be charged with ...	bu-de ob-zha-lo-vaan/-a za ...	*Bude obžalován/a za ... (m/f)*
anti-government activity	pro-tyi-vlaa-dnee chin-no-styi	*protivládní činnosti*
assault	na-pa-de-nyee	*napadení*
disturbing the peace	po-ru-sho-vaa-nyee kli-du	*porušování klidu*
possession (of illegal substances)	vla-stnyi-tstvee (ne-le-gaal-nyeekh laa-tek)	*vlastnictví (nelegálních látek)*
illegal entry	ne-le-gaal-nyee vstup	*nelegální vstup*
murder	vra-zhdu	*vraždu*
no visa	przhe-kro-che-nyee hra-nyi-tse bez vee-za	*překročení hranice bez víza*
overstaying your visa	ne-le-gaal-nyee pro-dloh-zhe-nyee po-bi-tu	*nelegální prodloužení pobytu*
rape	znaa-sil-nye-nyee	*znásilnění*
robbery/theft	loh-pezh	*loupež*
shoplifting	kraa-dezh v ob-kho-dye	*krádež v obchodě*
traffic violation	do-prav-nyee przhe-stu-pek	*dopravní přestupek*
working with no permit	praa-tsi bez po-vo-le-nyee	*práci bez povolení*

EMERGENCIES

HEALTH

Call a doctor!
za-vo-ley-te leh-ka-rzhe!
Call an ambulance!
za-vo-ley-te sa-ni-tku!
I'm ill.
**ysem ne-mots-en/
ne-mots-naa**
My friend is ill.
mooy przhee-tel ye ne-mots-en
I have medical insurance.
**maam zdra-vot-nyee
po-yisht-ye-nyee**

PRVNÍ POMOC

Zavolejte lékaře!

Zavolejte sanitku!

*Jsem nemocen/
nemocná.* (m/f)

Můj přítel je nemocen.

*Mám zdravotní
pojištění.*

ENGLISH–CZECH DICTIONARY

A

| able (to be); can | mo-tsi | moci |

Can you show me on the map?
mu-zhesh mi to
u-kaa-zat na ma-pye?
Můžeš mi to ukázat na mapě?

aboard	na pa-lu-bye	na palubě
abortion	pot-rat	potrat
above	nad	nad
abroad	v tsi-zi-nye	v cizině
to accept	przhi-yat	přijat
accident	nye-ho-da	nehoda
accommodation	u-bit-o-vaa -nyee	ubytování
across	przhez	přes
activist	ak-ti-vis-ta	aktivista
adaptor	a-dap-tor	adaptor
addiction	nar-ko-ma-ni-e • toks-i-ko-ma-ni-e	narkomanie • toxikomanie
address	a-dre-sa	adresa
to admire	ob-dyi-vo-vat	obdivovat
admission	vstup • vstup-neh	vstup • vstupné
to admit	vpus-tyit • przhi-ymoht	vpustit • přijmout
adult	dos-pye-lee	dospělý
advantage	vee-ho-da	výhoda
advice	ra-da	rada
aeroplane	leh-ta-dlo	létadlo
to be afraid of	baat se	bát se
after (in the) afternoon	po od-po-led-ne	po odpoledne
this afternoon	dnes od-po-led-ne	dnes odpoledne
again	zno-vu • o-pyet • za-se	znovu • opět • zase
against	pro-tyi	proti
age	vyek	věk
aggressive	a-gres-iv-nyee	agresivní

(a while) ago	przhed • yizh daav-no	před • již dávno
to agree	soh-hla-siht	souhlasit
agriculture	zem-ye-dyel-stvee	zemědělství
ahead	vprzhed • przhed naa-mi	vpřed • před námi
aid (help)	po-mots	pomoc
AIDS	a-ids	AIDS
air	vzdukh	vzduch
air-conditioned	kli-ma-ti-za-tse	klimatizace
air mail	le-tyets-ki	letecky
airport	le-tyish-tye	letiště
airport tax	le-tyisht-nyee po-pla-tek	letištní poplatek
alarm clock	bu-dyeek	budík
all	vshi-knyi	všichni
an allergy	a-ler-gi-ye	alergie
to allow	do-vo-lit • po-vo-lit	dovolit • povolit

It's allowed.
ye po-vo-le-no
Je povoleno.

It's not allowed.
ne-nyee po-vo le-no
Není povoleno.

almost	sko-ro • tem-yerzh	skoro • temĕř
alone	saam • o-sam-ye-lee	sám • osamělý
already	yizh • uzh	již • už
also	ta-keh • tehzh • rov-nyezh	také • též • rovněž
altitude	veesh-ka	výška
always	vzhdi	vždy
amateur	a-ma-tehr	amatér
ambassador	vel-vi-sla-nets	velvyslanec
among	me-zi	mezi
anarchist	an-ar-khis-ta	anarchista
ancient	sta-ro-daav-nee	starodávný
and	a	a
angry	roz-hnye-va-nee	rozhněvaný

animals	zvee-rzha-ta	zvířata
annual	roch-nyee	roční
answer	od-po-vye-dy	odpověď
answering	od-po-vee-dat	odpovídat
ant	mra-ve-nets	mravenec
antibiotics	an-ti-bi-o-ti-ka	antibiotika
anti-nuclear	an-ti-nuk-le-aar-nyee	anti-nukleární
antiques	sta-ro-zhit-nos-tyi	starožitnosti
antiseptic	an-ti-sep-tits-kee • dez-in-fek-chnyee pro-strzhed-ek	antisep-tický • dezinfekční prostředek
any	ya-kee-ko-li • kte-ree-ko-li	jakýkoli • kterýkoli
appointment	ter-meen	termín
archaeological	ar-khe-o-log-its-kee	archeo-logický
architect	ar-khi-tekt	architekt
architecture	ar-khi-tek-tu-ra	architektura
to argue	de-but-o-vat • przheet se • haa-dat se	debatovat • přít se • hádat se
arm	pa-zhe • raa-mye	paže • rámě
to arrive	przhi-yeet • przhi-yet • przhi-leht-noht	přijít • přijet • přilétnout
arrivals	przhee-kho-di	příchody
art	u-mye-nyee	umění
art gallery	ga-le-ri-ye	galerie
artist	u-mye-lets	umělec
artwork	u-mye-lets-keh dyee-lo	umělecké dílo
ashtray	po-pel-nyeek	popelník
to ask (for something)	po-pro-sit • po-zhaa-dat	poprosit • požádat
to ask (a question)	ptaat se	ptát se
aspirin	a-spi-rin • a-tsil-pi-rin	aspirin • acylpiryn

asthmatic	ast-ma-tik	astmatik
atmosphere	at-mos-feh-ra	atmosféra
aunt	te-ta	teta
automatic teller (ATM)	bank-o-mat	bankomat
autumn	pod-zim	podzim
avenue	a-ley • tses-ta • trzhee-da	alej • cesta • třída
awful	hroz-nee • strash-nee	hrozný • strašný

B

baby	dye-tyat-ko • dyets-ko • ko-ye-nets	děťátko • děcko • kojenec
baby food	ko-ye-nets-kaa vee-zhi-va	kojenecká výživa
baby powder	dye-tskee pu-dr	dětský pudr
baby-sitter	pa-nyee u dyee-tye-te	paní u dítěte
back (body)	zaa-da • hrzh-bet	záda • hřbet
at the back (behind)	vza-du	vzadu
backpack	ba-toh	batoh
bad	shpat-nee	špatný
bag	pi-tel • tash-ka	pytel • taška
baggage	za-va-za-dlo • ba-to-zhi-na	zavazadlo • batožina
baggage claim	vee-dey ba-to-zhin	výdej batožin
bakery	pe-kaar-na	pekárna
balcony	bal-kawn	balkón
ball	ku-lich-ka • meech • ples	kulička • míč • ples
ballet	ba-let	balet
band (music)	sku-pi-na	skupina
bandage	ban-daazh • ob-vaz	bandáž • obvaz

bank	bank-a • spohrzh-ih-tel-nah	banka/ spořitelna
banknotes	bank-ov-ki	bankovky
baptism	krzhest	křest
a bar/ café	bar/ ka-vaar-na	bar/ kavárna
basket	kosh • kosh-eek	koš • košík
bath	laa-ze-ny • koh-pel • va-na	lázeň • koupel • vana
bathing suit	plav-ki	plavky
bathroom	koh-pel-na	koupelna
battery	ba-te-ri-ye	baterie
to be	beet	být
beach	plaazh	pláž
beautiful	kraa-snee	krásný
because	pro-to-zhe	protože
bed	post-el • loozh-ko	postel • lůžko
bedroom	lozh-nyits-e	ložnice
before	przhed	před
beggar	zheb-raak	žebrák
begin	za-cheet	začít
behind	vza-du • po-za-du • da-le-ko	vzadu • pozadu • daleko
below	pod	pod
beside	ved-le	vedle
best	ney-lep-shee	nejlepší
a bet	saaz-ka	sázka
better	lep-shee	lepší
between	me-zi	mezi
the Bible	bib-le	bible
bicycle	ko-lo	kolo
big	vel-kee	velký
bike	ko-lo	kolo
bill (account)	oo-chet • fak-tu-ra	účet • faktura
binoculars	da-le-ko-hled	dalekohled
biodegrad-able	skhop-ne roz-kla-du	schopný rozkladu
biography	zhi-vo-to-pis • bi-o-gra-fi-e	životopis • biografie
bird	ptaak	pták

birth certificate	rod-nee list	rodný list
birthday	na-ro-ze-nyi-ni	narozeniny
birthday cake	na-ro-ze-nyi-no-vee dort	narozeni nový dort
bite (dog)	kohs-nu-tyee • u-kohst-noh-tyee	kousnutí • ukoustnutí
bite (insect)	shteep-nu-tyee • peekh-nu-tyee	štípnutí • píchnutí
black	cher-nee	černý
B&W (film)	cher-no-bee-lee film	černo-bílý film
blanket	de-ka • przhi-kreev-na	deka • přikrývka
to bleed	krvaa-tset	krvácet
to bless	po-zhe-nat	požehnat

Bless you! (when sneezing)
na-zdra-vee!
Nazdraví!

blind	sle-pee	slepý
blood	kref	krev
blood group	kref-nyee sku-pi-na	krevní skupina
blood pressure	krev-nyee tlak	krevní tlak
blood test	krev-nyee zkoh-shka	krevní zkouška
blue	mod-ree	modrý
to board (ship etc)	nas-toh-pit	nastoupit
boarding pass	pa-lub-nyee kar-ta	palubní karta
boat	chlun • lo-dy	člun • loď
body	tye-lo	tělo

Bon appétit!
dob-roh khu-ty!
dobrou chuť!

Bon voyage!
shtya-stnoh tses-tu!
šťastnou cestu!

bone	kost	kost

book	knyi-ha	*kniha*
to book (make a booking)	ob-yed-nat	*objednat*
bookshop	knyi-hku-pet-stvee	*knihku-pectví*
boots	bo-ti	*boty*
border	kray • oh-kray • po-hra-nyich-nyee oo-ze-mee • hra-nyi-chit	*kraj • okraj • pohra-niční • území • hraničit*
bored	z-nu-dye-nee	*znuděný*
boring	nud-nee	*nudný*
to borrow	pooy-chit	*půjčit*
both	o-ba	*oba*
bottle	laa-hev	*láhev*
bottle opener	ot-vee-rach na laa-hve	*otvírač na láhve*
(at the) bottom	na dnye	*na dně*
box	kra-bi-tse	*krabice*
boxing	boks	*box*
boy	hokh • khla-pets	*hoch • chlapec*
boyfriend	prhee-tel	*přítel*
branch	vye-tev • od-vye-tvee • o-bor	*větev • odvětví • obor*
brave	od-vaazh-nee • sta-tech-nee	*odvážný • statečný*
bread	khlehb	*chléb*
to break	zlo-mit • roz-beet • laa-mat	*zlomit • rozbít • lámat*
broken	roz-bi-tee • zka-zhe-nee	*rozbitý • zkažený*
breakfast	snyee-da-nye	*snídaně*
to breathe	dee-khat	*dýchat*
a bribe	oo-pla-tek • pod-pla-tse-nyee	*úplatek • podplacení*
to bribe	pod-plaa-tset	*podplácet*
bridge	most	*most*
brilliant	skvye-lee	*skvělý*

to bring	przhi-nehst	*přinést*
brother	bra-tr	*bratr*
brown	hnye-dee	*hnědý*
a bruise	po-mozh-dye-nyi-na	*pohmožděnina*
bucket	vye-dro • kbe-leek	*vědro • kbelík*
Buddhist	bud-his-ta	*budhista*
bug	brohk • shvaab	*brouk • šváb*
to build	sta-vyet	*stavět*
building	stav-ba • bu-do-va	*stavba • budova*
bus (city/intercity)	ow-to-bus	*autobus*
bus station	ow-to-bus-o-veh naa-dra-zhee	*autobusové nádraží*
bus stop	ow-to-bus-o-vaa za-staav-ka	*autobusová zastávka*
business	ob-khod • pod-nyik • fir-ma	*obchod • podnik • firma*
business person	ob-khod-nyeek • pod-nyi-ka-tel	*obchodník • podnikatel*
busy	za-ne-praaz-dnye-nyee	*zaneprázdněný*
but	a-le • av-shak	*ale • avšak*
butterfly	mo-teel	*motýl*
buttons	knof-lee-ki	*knoflíky*
to buy	koh-pit	*koupit*

I'd like to buy ...
ktyel/-a bikh koh-pit ...
Chtěl/a bych koupit ... (m/f)

Where can I buy a ticket?
gde si mo-hu koh-pit yeez-den-ku?
Kde si mohu koupit jízdenku?

C

calendar	ka-len-daarzh	*kalendář*
camera	ka-me-ra • fo-to-a-pa-raat	*kamera • fotoaparát*
camera shop	ob-khod ska-me-ra-mi • fo-to-ki-no	*obchod s kamerami • foto-kino*

to camp	kem-po-vat	*kempovat*

> Can we camp here?
> moo-zhem ta-di kem-po-vat?
> *Můžem tady kempovat?*

campsite	kem-pink	*kempink*
can (to be able)	mo-hu • ysem skho-pen	*mohu • jsem schopen*

> We can do it.
> moo-zhe-me to u-dye-lat
> *Můžeme to udělat.*

> I can't do it.
> ne-u-meem to u-dye-lat
> *Neumím to udělat.*

can (tin)	kon-zer-va • ple-khov-ka	*konzerva • plechovka*
can opener	ot-vee-rach na ple-khov-ki	*otvírač na plechovky*
to cancel	zru-shit	*zrušit*
candle	svee-chka	*svíčka*
car	ow-to • vooz	*auto • vůz*
cards	kar-ti	*karty*

> Careful!
> po-zor!
> *Pozor!*

caring	sta-rost-li-vee	*starostlivý*
to carry	no-sit	*nosit*
carton	kra-bi-tse • kar-tawn	*krabice • kartón*
cartoons	kre-sle-neh film-i • ka-ri-ka-too-ri	*kreslené filmy • karikatúry*
cash register	po-klad-na	*pokladna*
cashier	po-klad-nyeek	*pokladník*
cassette	ka-ze-ta	*kazeta*
castle	hrad	*hrad*
cat	koch-ka	*kočka*
cathedral	ka-te-draa-la	*katedrála*
Catholic	ka-to-lits-kee	*katolický*
caves	yes-ki-nye	*jeskyně*
CD	tseh-deh • kom-pakt	*cédé • kompakt*

celebrate	sla-vit	*slavit*
centimetre	tsen-ti-me-tr	*centimetr*
ceramic	ke-ram-its-kee	*keramický*
certificate	vis-vyed-che-nee	*vysvědčení*
chair	zhid-le • krzhe-slo	*židle • křeslo*
champagne	sham-pany-skeh	*šampaňské*
chance	naa-ho-da	*náhoda*
to change	zmye-nyit	*změnit*
change (coins)	drob-neh (min-tse)	*drobné (mince)*
changing rooms	shat-ni	*šatny*
charming	o-koz-lu-yee-tsi	*okouzlující*
to chat up	u-mlu-vit-si	*umluvit si*
cheap	lev-nee	*levný*

> cheap hotel
> lev-nee ho-tel
> *levný hotel*

a cheat	pod-vod-nyeek	*podvodník*
to check	kon-tro-la • kon-tro-lo-vat • przhe-kon-tro-lo-vaa-nee	*kontrola • kontrolovat • překontrolování*
check-in (desk)	za-psat se • za-reg-is-tro-vat se • przhi-hlaa-sit se	*zapsat se • zaregistrovat se • přihlásit se*
checkpoint	kon-trol-nyee sta-no-vish-tye	*kontrolní stanoviště*

> Cheers! Good health!
> na-zdra-vee!
> *Nazdraví!*

cheese	sir	*syr*
chemist	leh-kaar-na • leh-kaar-nyeek	*lékárna • lékárník*
chess	sha-khy	*šachy*
chess board	sha-khov-nyits-e	*šachovnice*
chest	hru-dy • pr-sa	*hruď • prsa*

English	Pronunciation	Czech
chewing gum	zhvee-kach-ka	žvýkačka
chicken	ku-rzhe	kuře
child	dyee-tye	dítě
child-minding	o-pa-tye-ra dyee-tye-te	opatěra dítěte
children	dye-tyi	děti
chocolate	cho-ko-laa-da	čokoláda
to choose	vi-braat si	vybrát si
Christian	krzhe-styan	křesťan
christian name	ymeh-no	jméno
Christmas Day	prv-nyee svaa-tek vaa-noch-nyee	První svátek vánoční
Christmas Eve	shtye-dree ve-cher	Štědrý večer
church	kos-tel	kostel
cigarette papers	tsi-ga-ret-o-vee pa-peer	cigaretový papír
cigarettes	tsi-ga-re-ti	cigarety
cinema	ki-no	kino
circus	tsir-kus	cirkus
citizenship	ob-chan-stvee	občanství
city	mye-sto	město
city centre	strzhed mye-sta • tsen-trum	střed města • centrum
class	trzhee-da	třída
class system	trzheed-nyee sis-tem	třídní systém
clean	chis-tee	čistý

clean hotel
chis-tee ho-tel
čistý hotel

cleaning	u-pra-to-vaa-nyee	upratování
client	kli-ent • zaa-kaz-nyeek	klient • zákazník
cliff	oo-tyes • sraaz	útes • sráz
to climb	stoh-pat • lehst • vi-lehst	stoupat • lézt • vylézt
cloakroom	shat-na	šatna
clock	ho-dyi-ni	hodiny
to close	za-vee-rat	zavírat

closed	zav-rzhe-no	zavřeno
clothing	sha-ti	šaty
clothing store	od-ye-vi	oděvy
cloud	o-blak • mrak • mrach-no	oblak • mrak • mračno
cloudy	za-mra-che-no • za-ta-zhe-no	zamračeno • zataženo
clown	sha-shek	šašek
coast	po-brzhe-zhee	pobřeží
coat	ka-baat • sa-ko • plaa-shty	kabát • sako • plášť
cocaine	ko-ka-in	kokain
coins	min-tse	mince
cold (adj)	stu-de-nee	studený

It's cold.
ye khlad-no/zi-ma
Je chladno/zima.

a cold	nakh-la-ze-nyee • ree-ma	nachlazení • rýma

I have a cold.
ysem nakh-la-ze-nee/-aa • maam ree-mu
Jsem nachlazený/á.
Mám rýmu. (m/f)

cold water	stu-de-naa vo-da	studená voda
colleague	ko-le-ga	kolega
college	shko-la • fa-kul-ta	škola • fakulta
colour	bar-va	barva
comb	hrzhe-ben	hřeben
to come/ arrive	przhi-yeet • do-sta-vit se • przhi-ploht • przhi-le-tyet	přijít • dostavit se • připlout • přiletět
comedy	ko-me-di-ye	komedie
comfortable	po-ho-dl-nee	pohodlný
communion	przhi-yee-maa-nyee svaa-to-styi ol-taar-nyee	přijímání svátosti oltární

communist	ko-mun-ist-a	komunista
company	spo-lech-nost	společnost
compass	kom-pas	kompas
computer games	po-chee-ta-cho-veh hri	počítačové hry
a concert	kon-tsert	koncert
confession (religious)	zpo-vye-dy	zpověď
to confirm (a booking)	pot-vr-dyit	potvrdit

Congratulations!
bla-ho-przhe-yi! • gra-tu-lu-yi!
Blahopřeji! • Gratuluji!

conservative	kon-zer-va-tiv-nyee	konzervativní
constipation	zaats-pa	zácpa

to be constipated
meet zaats-pu
mít zácpu

construction work	sta-veb-nyee praa-tse	stavební práce
consulate	kon-zu-laat	konzulát
contact lenses	kon-takt-nyee choch-ki	kontaktní čočky

contraception
an-ti-kon-tsep-tse
antikoncepce

contraceptives	an-ti-kon-tsep-chnyee pro-strzhed-ki	antikon-cepční prostředky
contract	kon-trakt	kontrakt
convent	klaa-shter	klášter
to cook	va-rzhit	vařit
cool (colloquial)	v po-ho-dye	v pohodě
corner	ro-h	roh
corrupt	zko-rum-po-va-nee	zkorumpo-vaný
to cost	staat	stát

How much does it cost to go to …?
ko-lik sto-yee tses-ta do …?
Kolik stojí cesta do …?

cotton	ba-vl-na	bavlna
country	zem-ye	země
country-side	ven-kov	venkov
a cough	ka-shel	kašel
to count	po-chee-tat	počítat
coupon	ku-pawn	kupón
court (legal)	sohd	soud
(tennis)	kurt	kurt
cow	kraa-va	kráva
crafts	u-mye-lets-keh rzhe-me-sla	umělecké řemesla
crazy	blaaz-nyi-vee • shee-le-nyee	bláznivý • šílený
credit card	kre-dit-nyee kar-ta	kreditní karta

Can I pay by credit card?
mo-hu pla-tyit kre-dit-nyee kar-toh?
Mohu platit kreditní kartou?

cricket	kri-ket	kriket
cross (religious)	krzheezh	kříž
(angry)	mr-zu-tee	mrzutý
a cuddle	o-bye-tyee	objetí
cup	shaa-lek	šálek
cupboard	kre-de-nets • skrzheeny	kredenec • skříň
current affairs	ak-tu-a-li-ti	aktuality
customs	tsel-ni-tse	celnice
to cut	strzhi-hat	stříhat
to cycle	yez-dyit na ko-le	jezdit na kole
cycling	tsik-list-i-ka	cyklistika
cyclist	tsik-lis-ta	cyklista
cystitis	tsis-ti-ti-da • zaa-nyet mo-cho-veh-ho	cystitida • zánět močového

D

dad	taa-ta	táta
daily	den-nyee	denní
dairy products	mleh-chneh vee-rob-ki	mléčné výrobky
to dance	tan-tso-vat	tancovat
dancing	tan-tso-vaa-nyee	tancování
dangerous	ne-bez-pech-nee	nebez-pečný
dark	tma-vee	tmavý
date (appoint-ment)	ran-de	rande
(time)	da-tum	datum
to date (some-one)	kho-dyit (s nye-keem)	chodit (s někým)
date of birth	da-tum na-ro-ze-nyee	datum narození
daughter	tse-ra	dcera
dawn	svi-taa-nyee	svítání
day	den	den

day after tomorrow
po-zit-rzhee
pozítří

day before yesterday
przhe-dev-chee-rem
předevčírem

dead	mr-tvee	mrtvý
deaf	hlu-khee	hluchý
dear	dra-hee	drahý
death	smrt	smrt
to decide	roz-hod-noht	rozhodnout
deck (of cards)	ba-lee-chek ka-ret	balíček karet
(of ship)	pa-lu-ba lo-dye	paluba lodě
deep	hlu-bo-ko	hluboko
deer	ye-len	jelen
deforest-ation	od-les-nyo-vaa-nyee	odlesňo-vání
degree	stu-pe-ny • u-ni-ver-zit-nyee	stupeň • univerzit-ní
	dip-lom	diplom

delay	od-lo-zhit • od-su-noht	odložit • odsunout
deli-catessen	la-hood-ki	lahůdky
delirious	de-li-rant-nyee • blohz-nyee-tsee	delirantní • blouzníci
democracy	de-mo-kra-tse	demokrace
demon-stration	de-mon-stra-tse	demonst-race
dentist	zu-barzh	zubař
to deny	za-przheet	zapřít
deodorant	de-zo-do-rant	dezodorant
to depart (leave)	o-de-yeet	odejít
departm-ent stores	ob-khod-nyee doom	obchodní dům
departure	od-khod	odchod
desert	poh-shty	poušť
design	di-zain	design
destination	mee-sto ur-che-nyee • tseel tses-ti	místo určení • cíl cesty
to destroy	zny-i-chit	zničit
detail	de-tail	detail
diabetic	di-a-be-tik	diabetik
dial tone	vi-taa-che-tsee tawn	vytáčecí tón
diaper	plehn-kah	plénka
diarrhoea	proo-yem	průjem
diary	den-nyeek	denník
dice/die	kost-ka	kostka
dictionary	slov-nyeek	slovník
to die	zem-rzheet • um-rzheet	zemřít • umřít
different	od-lish-nee	odlišný
difficult	tyezh-kee	těžký
dining car	yee-del-nyee vooz	jídelní vůz
dinner	ve-che-rzhe	večeře
direct	przhe-mo	přímo
director	di-rek-tor • rzhe-dyi-tel	direktor • ředitel
dirty	shpi-na-vee	špinavý
disad-vantage	ne-vee-ho-da • va-da	nevýhoda • vada

ENGLISH–CZECH DICTIONARY

discount	sle-va	sleva
to discover	ob-ye-vit	objevit
discrimination	disk-rim-in-a-tse	diskriminace
disease	o-ne-mots-nye-nyee	onemocnění
distributor	dis-tri-bu-tor	distributor
diving	po-taa-pye-nyee	potápění
dizzy	zaa-vra-ty	závrať
to do	dye-lat	dělat

> What are you doing?
> tso dye-laash?
> *Co děláš?*

> I didn't do it.
> *Já jsem to neudělal.*
> yaa ysem to ne-u-dye-lal

doctor	dok-tor • leh-karzh	doktor • lékař
a documentary	do-ku-men-taar-nyee film	dokumentární film
dog	pes	pes
dole	pod-po-ra v ne-za-mye-sta-nos-tyi	podpora v nezaměstanosti
dolls	pa-nen-ki	panenky
door	dve-rzhe	dveře
dope (drugs)	dro-gi	drogy
double	dvo-yi-tee	dvojitý
double bed	dvoh-loozh-ko	dvoulůžko
double room	dvoh-loozh-ko-vee po-koy	dvoulůžkový pokoj
a dozen	tu-tset	tucet
drama	draa-ma	dráma
dramatic	dra-ma-tits-kee	dramatický
to dream	snyee-vat	snívat
a dress	sha-ti	šaty
to dress	ob-leh-kat	oblékat
a drink	drink	drink

to drink	peet	pít
to drive	yez-dyit • rzhee-dyit • vehzt	jezdit • řídit • vézt
driver's licence	rzhi-dyich-skee proo-kaz	řidičský průkaz
drug	dro-ga	droga
drug addiction	nar-ko-ma-ni-ye	narkomanie
drug dealer	di-la	dyla
drugs	dro-gi	drogy
drums	bub-ni	bubny
to be drunk	o-peet se	opít se
to dry (clothes)	su-shit	sušit
	praa-dlo	prádlo
dummy (baby's)	dud-leek	dudlík

E

each	kazh-dee	každý
ear	u-kho	ucho
early	chas-nee • ra-nee	časný • raný
to earn	vi-dye-lat	vydělat
earrings	naa-ush-nyi-tse	náušnice
ears	u-shi	uši
Earth	ze-mye	Země
earth (soil)	poo-da	půda
earthquake	ze-mye-trzhe-se-nye	zemětřesení
east	vee-khod	východ
Easter	ve-li-ko-no-tse	Velikonoce
easy	leh-ko	lehko
to eat	yeest	jíst
economy	e-ko-no-mi-e • hos-pod-aarzh-stvee	ekonomie • hospodářství
editor	e-di-tor	editor
education	vzdye-laa-nyee	vzdělání
elections	vol-bi	volby
electorate	vo-leb-nyee o-kr-sek	volební okrsek

electricity	e-lek-trzhi-na	elektřina
elevator	vee-ta-h	výtah
embarassed	v roz-pa-tseekh	v rozpacích
embarassment	roz-pa-ki	rozpaky
embassy	vel-vi-sla-nets-tvee	velvyslanectví
emergency	naa-hla przhee-ho-da • po-ho-to-vost	náhla příhoda • pohotovost
employee	za-myest-na-nets	zaměstnanec
employer	za-mest-naa-va-tel	zaměstnávatel
empty	praazd-ni	prázdny
end	ko-nets	konec
to end	kon-chit • u-kon-chit	končit • ukončit
endangered species	o-hro-ze-neh dru-hi	ohrozené druhy
engagement	zaa-va-zek • za-snoh-be-nyee	závazek • zasnoubení
engine	mo-tor	motor
engineer	in-zhe-neer	inženýr
engineering	stroy-ee-ren-stvee	strojírenství
English	an-glits-kee • an-glich-tyi-na	anglický • angličtina
to enjoy (oneself)	vi-khut-naa-vat • u-zhee-vat	vychutnávat • užívat
enough	dost • do-sta-tek	dost • dostatek

Enough!
dost! • przhe-sta-ny!
Dost! • Přestaň!

to enter	vstoh-pit • ve-yeet • vkro-chit	vstoupit • vejít • vkročit
entertaining	zaa-bav-nyee	zábavní

envelope	o-baal-ka	obálka
environment	pro-strzhe-dyee	prostředí
epileptic	e-pi-lep-tits-kee	epileptický
equality	rov-nost	rovnost
equipment	vee-stroy • veez-broy • za-rzhee-ze-nyee	výstroj • výzbroj • zařízení
European	ev-rop-skee	evropský
euthanasia	e-u-ta-na-si-ye	euthanasie
evening	ve-cher	večer
every day	kazh-dee den	každý den
example	przhe-klad	příklad

For example ...
na-przhee-klad ...
Například ...

excellent	vee-bor-nee	výborný
exchange	vee-mye-na • smye-na • smye-naar-na	výměna • směna • směnárna
to exchange	vi-mye-nyit	vyměnit
exchange rate	kurz	kurz
excluded	vi-loh-chit	vyloučit

Excuse me.
pro-mi-nye-te
promiňte

to exhibit	vi-sta-vo-vat	vystavovat
exhibition	vee-sta-va	výstava
exit	vee-khod	východ
expensive	dra-hee • naa-klad-nee	drahý • nákladný
express	eks-pres-nyee	expresní
express mail	eks-pres-nyee zaa-sil-ka	expresní zásilka
eye	o-ko	oko

F

face	o-bli-chey	obličej
factory	to-vaar-na	továrna
factory worker	dyel-nyeek	dělník
fall (autumn)	pod-zim	podzim
family	ro-dyi-na	rodina
famous	sla-vnee	slavný
fan (hand-held)	vye-yeerzh	vějíř
	su-shich na vla-si	sušič na vlasy
(ma-chine)		
fans (of a team)	fa-nohsh-tsi	fanoušci
far	da-le-ko	daleko
farm	sta-tek • far-ma	statek • farma
farmer	far-maarzh	farmář
fast	ri-khlee	rychlý
fat	tlus-tee	tlustý
father	o-tets	otec
father-in-law	tkhaan	tchán
fault (someone's)	khi-ba • vi-na	chyba • vina
faulty	khib-nee • vad-nee • shpat-nee	chybný • vadný • špatný
fear	strakh	strach
to feel	tsee-tyit	cítit
feelings	tsi-ti	city
fence	plot • o-hra-da	plot • ohrada
festival	svaa-tek	svátek
fever	ho-rech-ka	horečka
few	maa-lo	málo
fiancé	snoh-be-nets	snoubenec
fiancée	snoh-ben-ka	snoubenka
fiction	be-le-tri-e • ro-maan	beletrie • román
field	po-le	pole
fight	boy • zaa-pas • bit-ka	boj • zápas • bitka

to fight	boy-o-vat • zaa-pa-sit	bojovat • zápasit
to fill	na-pl-nyit	naplnit
film (cinema)	film	film
(camera)	film	film
film speed	tsit-li-vost	citlivost
filtered	fil-tro-va-neh	filtrované
to find	na-yeet	najít
a fine	po-ku-ta	pokuta
finger	prst	prst
fir	yed-le	jedle
fire	o-heny	oheň
firewood	pa-li-vo-veh drzhe-vo	palivové dřevo
first	prv-nyee	první
first-aid kit	le-kaar-nyich-ka	lékárnička
	prv-nyee po-mo-tsi	první pomoci
fish (alive)	ri-ba	ryba
fish (as food)	ri-bi-na	rybina
fish shop	ri-ba	ryba
flag	zaa-sta-va	zástava
flat (adj)	ro-vi-na	rovina
flea	ble-kha	blecha
flashlight	ba-ter-ka	baterka
flight	let	let
floor (of room)	pod-la-ha	podlaha
(storey)	po-skho-dyee	poschodí
flour	moh-ka	mouka
flower	kvye-tyi-na	květina
a fly	moh-kha	moucha
to fly	leh-tat	létat
foggy	za-ml-zhe-no	zamlženo
to follow	naa-sle-do-vat	následovat
food	yeed-lo	jídlo
foot	no-ha	noha
football (soccer)	ko-pa-naa • fot-bal	kopaná • fotbal
footpath	stez-ka • khod-nyeek	stezka • chodník
foreign	za-hran-yich-nyee • tsi-zee	zahranič-ní • cizí

F

D I C T I O N A R Y

forest	les	*les*
forever	na-vye-ki •	*navěky* •
	po-rzhaad •	*pořád* •
	staa-le	*stále*
to forget	za-po-me-noht	*zapome-nout*

I forget.
za-po-mee-nam • ne-pa-ma-tu-yu si
Zapomínam • Nepamatuju si.

Forget about it! • Don't worry!
ne-dye-ley si sta-ros-tyi!
Nedělej si starosti!

to forgive	ot-pus-tyit •	*odpustit* •
	pro-mi-noht	*prominout*
fortnight	chtr-naatst	*čtrnáct*
	dnoo •	*dnů* •
	dva tee-dni	*dva týdny*
fortune teller	vyesht-ki-nye	*věštkyně*
foyer	przhed-seeny	*předsíň*
free (un-bound)	vol-nee	*volný*
(gratis)	zdar-ma	*zdarma*
to freeze	za-mrz-noht	*zamrznout*
Friday	paa-tek	*pátek*
friend	przhee-tel	*přítel*
frozen foods	mra-zhe-neh yee-dla	*mražené jídla*
full	pl-nee	*plný*
fun	zaa-ba-va	*zábava*

for fun
pro zaa-ba-vu • pro le-gra-tsi
pro zábavu • pro legraci

to have fun
ba-vit se
bavit se

to make fun of
dye-lat si le-gra-tsi
dělat si legraci

funeral	po-hrzheb	*pohřeb*
future	bu-dohts-nost	*budoucnost*

G

game (games/ sport)	hra	*hra*
game show	kveez	*kvíz*
garage	ga-raazh	*garáž*
garbage	ot-pat-ki • sme-tyee	*odpadky* • *smetí*
gardening	za-hrad-nyich-e-nye	*zahradničení*
gardens	za-hra-di	*zahrady*
gas	pli-no-vaa	*plynová*
cartridge	bom-bich-ka	*bombička*
gate	braa-na	*brána*
gay	gai • tep-lee	*gay • teplý*
general	o-bets-nee	*obecný*

Get lost!
z-miz!
zmiz!

gift	dar • daa-rek	*dar • dárek*
gig	kon-tsert	*koncert*
girl	dyev-che • hol-ka	*děvče • holka*
girlfriend	przhe-tel-ki-nye	*přítelkyně*
to give	daat	*dát*

Could you give me ...?
moo-zhe-te mi daat ...?
Můžete mi dát ...?

glass	skle-nyich-ku	*skleničku*
to go	yeet	*jít*

Let's go.
poydy-me!
Pojďme!

We'd like to go to ...
khtye-li bi-khom yeet do ...
Chtěli bychom jít do ...

Go straight ahead.
ydye-te rov-nye!
Jděte rovně!

222

to go out with ...
kho-dyit s ...
chodit s ...

goal	tseel	*cíl*
goal keeper	bran-karzh	*brankař*
goat	ko-za	*koza*
God	boo-h	*Bůh*
of gold	ze zla-ta	*ze zlata*

Good afternoon.
dob-ree den
Dobrý den.

Goodbye.
na-shle-da-noh
Na shledanou.

Good evening • night.
dob-ree ve-cher • dob-roh nots
Dobrý večer • Dobrou noc.

good hotel
dob-ree ho-tel
dobrý hotel

Good luck!
mno-ho shtye-styee!
Mnoho štěstí!

Good morning.
dob-re raa-no
Dobré ráno.

government	vlaa-da	*vláda*
gram	gram	*gram*
grandchild	vnuk • vnuch-ka	*vnuk • vnučka*
grandfather	dye-de-chek	*dědeček*
grandmother	ba-bich-ka	*babička*
grapes	hroz-na	*hrozna*
graphic art	gra-fi-ka	*grafika*
grass	traa-va	*tráva*

grave	hrob	*hrob*
great	vel-kee	*velký*

Great!
ve-bor-nye! • pri-ma! • fayn!
výborně! • prima! • fajn!

green	ze-le-nee	*zelený*
greengrocer	ob-khod-nyeek se ze-le-nyi-noh a o-vo-tseem	*obchodník se zeleninou a ovocím*
grey	she-dyi-vee	*šedivý*
to guess	haa-dat	*hádat*
guide (person)	proo-vot-tse • voot-tse • ve-doh-tsee	*průvodce • vůdce • vedoucí*
(audio)	przhee-ruch-ka	*příručka*
guidebook	proo-vot-tse	*průvodce*
guidedog	sle-pets-kee pes	*slepecký pes*
guided trek	tu-ris-tits-kaa stez-ka s proo-vod-tsem	*turistická stezka s průvodcem*
guitar	ki-ta-ra	*kytara*
gym	po-si-lov-na	*posilovna*
gymnastics	gim-nas-ti-ka	*gymnastika*

H

hair	vla-si	*vlasy*
hairbrush	kar-taach na vla-si	*kartáč na vlasy*
half	pool	*půl*
half a litre	pool lit-ra	*půl litra*
hallucinate meet	ha-lu-tsi-na-tse	*halucinace*
ham	shun-ka	*šunka*
hammer	kla-dyi-vo	*kladivo*
hammock	see-ty na hoh-paa-nyee	*síť na houpání*
hand	ru-ka	*ruka*
handbag	ka-bel-ka	*kabelka*
handicrafts	u-mye-lets-keh rzhe-mes-la	*umělecké řemesla*
handmade	ruch-nye vi-ro-be-no	*ručně vyrobeno*

handsome	hes-kee	hezký
happy	shtya-stnee	šťastný

Happy Birthday!
vshe-khno ney-lep-shee
kna-ro-ze-nyi-naam!
Všechno nejlepší k narozeninám!

harbour	przhee-stav	přístav
hard	tyezh-kee •	těžký •
	tvr-dee	tvrdý
harness	post-roy	postroj
harrass-ment	su-zho-vaa-nyee • shik-a-no-vaa-nyee	sužování • šikanování
hash	ha-shish • ma-ri-hu-a-na	hašiš • marihuana
to have	meet	mít

Do you have ...?
maa-te ...?
Máte ...?

I have ...
maam ...
Mám ...

hayfever	sen-naa ree-ma	senná rýma
he	on	on
head	hla-va • hlav-nyee	hlava • hlavní
headache	bo-le-nyee hla-vi	bolení hlavy
health	zdra-vee	zdraví
to hear	sli-shet	slyšet
hearing aid	slu-kha-dlo	sluchadlo
heart	srt-tse	srdce
heat	hor-ko	horko
heater	o-hrzhee-vach	ohřívač
heavy	tyezh-kee	těžký

Hello.
a-hoy
Ahoj.

Hello! (answering telephone)
ha-lo!
Halo!

helmet	hel-ma	helma
to help	po-mo-tsi	pomoci

Help!
po-mots!
Pomoc!

herbs	bi-li-ni	byliny
here	ta-di	tady
heroin	he-ro-in	heroin
high	vi-so-kee	vysoký
high school	strzhed-nyee shko-la	střední škola
to hike	tram-po-vat	trampovat
hiking	tu-ris-ti-ka	turistika
hiking routes	tu-ris-tits-keh stez-ki	turistické stezky
hill	ko-pets	kopec
Hindu	hind	Hind
to hire	pooy-chit	půjčit
to hitchhike	stop-o-vat	stopovat
HIV	HIV	HIV
positive	po-zi-tiv-nyee	pozitivní
holiday	svaa-tek	svátek
holidays	do-vo-le-naa	dovolená
Holy Week	sva-tee tee-den	svatý týden
homeless	bez-do-mo-vets	bezdomovec
homosexual	gay/tep-lee	gay/teplý
honey	met	med
honeymoon	sva-teb-nyee tses-ta	svatební cesta
horrible	hroz-nee	hrozný
horse	koony	kůň
horse riding	yez-dyit na ko-nyi	jezdit na koni
hospital	ne-mots-nyi-tse	nemocnice
hot	horzh-kee	hořký

It's hot.
ye hor-ko
Je horko.

I'm hot.
ye mi hor-ko
Je mi horko.

ENGLISH–CZECH DICTIONARY

hot water	tep-laa vo-da	*teplá voda*
house	doom	*dům*
how	yak	*jak*

How do I get to ...?
yak se dos-ta-nu do ...?
Jak se dostanu do ...?

How do you say ...?
yak se rzhee-ka ...?
Jak se říká ...?

hug	ob-ye-tyee	*objetí*
a hundred	sto	*sto*
to be hungry	meet hlad	*mít hlad*
husband	man-zhel • khoty	*manžel • choť*

I

I	yaa	*já*
ice	led	*led*
icecream	zmrz-li-na	*zmrzlina*
identification card	i-den-ti-fi-kach-naa kar-ta	*identifikačná karta*
idiot	i-di-ot	*idiot*
if	gdi	*kdy*
ill	ne-mo-tsen	*nemocen*
important	doo-le-zhi-tee	*důležitý*

It's important.
ye to doo-le-zhi-teh
Je to důležité.

It's not important.
ne-nyi to doo-le-zhi-teh
Není to důležité.

in a hurry	spye-khaam	*spěchám*
in front of	przhed	*před*
included	vchet-nye	*včetně*
income tax	da-ny z przhee-ymu	*daň z příjmu*
incomprehensible	ne-po-khop-it-el-neh	*nepochopitelné*
indicator	blih-kr	*blinkr*

indigestion	bo-le-nyee brzhi-kha	*bolení břicha*
industry	proo-misl	*průmysl*
inequality	ne-rov-nost	*nerovnost*
to inject	peekh-noht in-yek-tsi	*píchnout injekci*
injection	in-yek-tse	*injekce*
injury	zra-nye-nyee	*zranění*
inside	vndyit-rzhek	*vnitřek*
instructor	in-struk-tor	*instruktor*
insurance	po-yish-tye-nyee	*pojištění*
intense	in-ten-siv-nyee	*intensivní*
interesting	za-yee-ma-vee	*zajímavý*
intermission	przhe-staaf-ka	*přestávka*
international	me-zi-naa-rod-nyee	*mezinárodní*
interview	in-ter-vyoo	*interview*
island	os-trov	*ostrov*
itch	svr-bye-nyee	*svrbění*
itinerary	tses-tov-nyee plaan	*cestovní plán*

J

jail	vye-znyi-tse	*věznice*
jar	naa-do-ba	*nádoba*
jealous	zhaar-li-vee	*žárlivý*
jeans	dzheen-si	*džíny*
jeep	dzheep	*džíp*
jewellery	shper-ki	*šperky*
Jewish	zhi-dov-skee	*židovský*
job	za-myest-naa-nyee	*zaměstnání*
joke	vtyip	*vtip*
to joke	vtyip-ko-vat	*vtipkovat*
journalist	no-vin-aarzh	*novinář*
journey	tses-ta	*cesta*
judge	sohd-tse	*soudce*
juice	dzhus • shtyaa-va	*džus • šťáva*
to jump	sko-chit	*skočit*
jumper	sve-tr	*svetr*
justice	spra-ve-dl-nost	*spravedlnost*

K

key	kleech	*klíč*
keyboard	klaa-ves-nyi-tse	*klávesnice*
kick	ko-pat	*kopat*
to kill	za-beet	*zabít*
kilogram	ki-lo-gram	*kilogram*
kilometre	ki-lo-me-tr	*kilometr*
kind	druh •	*druh •*
	od-roo-da •	*odrůda •*
	la-ska-vee	*laskavý*
kinder-garten	shkol-ka	*školka*
king	kraal	*král*
kiss	po-li-bek •	*polibek •*
	hu-bich-ka	*hubička*
to kiss	lee-bat	*líbat*
kitchen	ku-khi-nye	*kuchyně*
kitten	ko-tye	*kotě*
knapsack	ba-to-h	*batoh*
knee	ko-le-no	*koleno*
knife	noozh	*nůž*
to know (some-one)	znaat	*znát*
(some-thing)	vye-dyet	*vědět*

I don't know.
ne-vim
Nevím.

L

lace	krai-ka	*krajka*
lake	ye-ze-ro	*jezero*
land	ze-mye	*země*
languages	ja-zi-ki	*jazyky*
large	vel-kee	*velký*
last	pos-led-nyee	*poslední*

last night
vche-ra ve-cher
včera večer

last week		
przhe-desh-lee tee den		
předešlý týden		
last year		
lo-nyi		
loni		
late	poz-dye	*pozdě*
laugh	smaat se •	*smát se •*
	smeekh	*smích*
launder-ette	prad-len-ka	*pradlenka*
law	zaa-kon	*zákon*
lawyer	praav-nyeek	*právník*
laxatives	pro-yee-mad-lo	*projímadlo*
lazy	lee-nee •	*líný •*
	le-nyi-vee	*lenivý*
leaded (petrol/gas)	o-lov-na-tee	*olovnatý*
leader	voot-se	*vůdce*
to learn	u-chit se	*učit se*
leather	koo-zhe	*kůže*
leather goods	ko-zhe-neh vee-rob-ki	*kožené výrobky*
ledge	rzheem-sa • lish-ta	*římsa • lišta*
to be left (behind/over)	zbi-lee • zbi-tek	*zbylý • zbytek*
left (not right)	vle-vo	*vlevo*
left luggage	oos-kho-va za-va-za-del	*úschova zavazadel*
left-wing	le-veh • krzhee-dlo • le-vi-tso-vee	*levé • křídlo • levicový*
leg (body)	no-ha	*noha*
(in race)	e-ta-pa • oo-sek	*etapa • úsek*
legislation	le-gi-sla-tse	*legislace*
lens	choch-ka	*čočka*
Lent	poost	*půst*
lesbian	les-bits-kee	*lesbický*
less	meh-nye • men-shee	*méně • menší*

ENGLISH–CZECH DICTIONARY

letter	do-pis	*dopis*
liar	lhaa-rzh	*lhář*
library	knyi-hov-na	*knihovna*
lice	vshi	*vši*
to lie	lhaat	*lhát*
life	zhi-vot	*život*
lift (elevator)	vee-tah	*výtah*
light (n)	svye-tlo	*světlo*
light (adj)	le-hkee	*lehký*
light (lamp)	lam-pa	*lampa*
light (clear)	yas-nee	*jasný*
light bulb	zhaa-rov-ka	*žárovka*
light meter	eks-po-zi-me-tr	*expozimetr*
lighter	za-pa-lo-vach	*zapalovač*
to like	meet raad	*mít rád*
line	shnoo-ra •	*šňůra •*
	chaa-ra	*čára*
lips	r-ti	*rty*
lipstick	rzh-tyen-ka	*rtěnka*
to listen	po-sloh-khat	*poslouchat*
little (small)	ma-lee	*malý*
(amount)	maa-lo	*málo*
a little bit	tro-khu	*trochu*
to live (life)	zheet	*žít*
(somewhere)	bid-let	*bydlet*

aty zhi-ye!
ať žije!

local	lo-kaal-nyee •	*lokální •*
	do-maa-tsee	*domácí*
local/city bus	myest-skee ow-to-bus	*městský autobus*
location	mee-sto	*místo*
lock	zaa-mek	*zámek*
to lock	zamk-noht	*zamknout*
long	dloh-hee	*dlouhý*
long distance	daal-ko-vee	*dálkový*
to look	po-dyee-vat se	*podívat se*
to look after	sta-rat se	*starat se*

to look for	hle-dat	*hledat*
loose change	drob-neh	*drobné*
to lose	ztra-tyit	*ztratit*
loss	straa-ta	*ztráta*
a lot	mots •	*moc •*
	mno-ho	*mnoho*
loud	hla-si-tye	*hlasitě*
to love	mi-lo-vat	*milovat*
lover	mi-le-nets •	*milenec •*
	mi-len-ka	*milenka (m/ f)*
low	neez-kee	*nízký*

low/high blood pressure
nyeez-kee/vi-so-kww krev-nee tlak
nízký/vysoký krevní tlak

loyal	vyer-nee	*věrný*
luck	shtye-styee	*štěstí*
lucky	shtya-stnee	*šťastný*
luggage	ba-to-zhi-na	*batožina*

luggage lockers
ow-to-ma-tits-kaa oos-khov-na
automatická úschovna

lump	boh-le	*boule*
lunch	o-byed	*oběd*
lunchtime	po-led-ne	*poledne*
luxury	lu-ksus	*luxus*

M

machine	stroy	*stroj*
mad	shee-le-nee	*šílený*
made (of)	vi-ro-be-no z	*vyrobeno z*
magazine	cha-so-pis	*časopis*
mail	posh-ta	*pošta*
mailbox	posh-tov-nyee skhraan-ka	*poštovní schránka*
majority	vyet-shi-na	*většina*
to make	u-dye-lat	*udělat*
make-up	meyk ap	*make up*
man	muzh	*muž*
manager	man-a-zher	*manažer*
manual worker	dyel-nyeek	*dělník*
many	mno-zee	*mnozí*

M

D
I
C
T
I
O
N
A
R
Y

227

map	ma-pa	*mapa*

Can you show me on the map?
moo-zhe-te mi to u-kaa-zat
na ma-pye?
Můžete mi to ukázat na mapě?

marital status	stav	*stav*
market	trzh-nyi-tse	*tržnice*
marriage	man-zhel-stvee	*manželství*
marvellous	skvye-lee	*skvělý*
mass (Catholic)	mshe	*mše*
massage	ma-saazh	*masáž*
match	vi-rov-nat • zaa-pas	*vyrovnat • zápas*
matches	sir-ki	*sirky*

It doesn't matter.
ne-va-dyee
Nevadí.

What's the matter?
tso se dye-ye?
Co se děje?

mattress	ma-tra-tse	*matrace*
maybe	mozh-naa	*možná*
mayor	sta-ros-ta	*starosta*
medicine	lehk • leh-karzh-stvee	*lék • lékařství*
to meet	pot-kat	*potkat*
menstruation	men-stru-a-tse	*menstruace*
menu	yee-del-nyee lees-tek	*jídelní lístek*
message	zpraa-va	*zpráva*
metre	me-tr	*metr*
midnight	pool-nots	*půlnoc*
migraine	mi-greh-na	*migréna*
military service	vo-yen-skaa sluzh-ba	*vojenská služba*
milk	mleh-ko	*mléko*
millimetre	mi-li-me-tr	*milimetr*
million	mi-li-on	*milion*
mind	mi-sl • mish-le-nyee	*mysl • myšlení*
mineral water	mi-ne-raal-ka	*minerálka*
a minute	mi-nu-ta	*minuta*

Just a minute.
mo-ment!
Moment!

in (five) minutes
za (pyet) mi-nut
za (pět) minut

mirror	zr-tsad-lo	*zrcadlo*
miscarriage	po-trat	*potrat*
to miss (feel absence)	pos-traa-dat	*postrádat*
mistake	khi-ba	*chyba*
to mix	mee-khat	*míchat*
mobile phone	mo-bil	*mobil*
moisturising cream	hi-dra-tach-nyee krehm	*hydratační krém*
monastery	klaa-shter	*klášter*
money	pe-nyee-ze	*peníze*
monk	mnyikh	*mnich*
month	mye-seets	*měsíc*
this month	ten-to myeh-seets	*tento měsíc*
monument	pom-nyeek • so-kha	*pomník • socha*
moon	mye-seets	*měsíc*
more	veets	*víc*
morning (6am – 1pm)	do-po-led-ne	*dopoledne*
mosque	me-shi-ta	*mešita*
mother	mat-ka	*matka*
mother-in-law	tkhee-nye	*tchýně*
motorboat	mo-to-ro-vee chlun	*motorový člun*
motorcycle	mo-to-tsi-kl	*motocykl*
motorway (tollway)	daal-nyi-tse	*dálnice*
mountain	ho-ra	*hora*

228

mountain bike	hor-skeh ko-lo	horské kolo
mountain range	po-hor-zhee	pohoří
mountaineering	ho-ro-lez-ets-tvee	horolezectví
mouse	mish	myš
mouth	oo-sta	ústa
movie	film	film
mud	blaa-to	bláto
Mum	maa-ma	máma
muscle	sval	sval
museum	mu-ze-um	muzeum
music	hud-ba	hudba
musician	hu-deb-nyek	hudebník
mute	nye-mee	němý

N

name	ymeh-no	jméno
nappy	plen-ka	plenka
nappy rash	dyet-skeh vi-raazh-ki	dětské vyrážky
national park	naa-rod-nyee park	národní park
nationality	naa-rod-nost	národnost
nature	przhee-ro-da	příroda
nausea	shpat-nye ot zha-luh-ku	špatně od žaludku
near	blee-zko	blízko
necessary	po-trzheb-nee	potřebný
necklace	naa-hr-del-nyeek	náhrdelník
to need	po-trzhe-bo-vat	potřebovat
needle (sewing)	ye-hla	jehla
needle (syringe)	strzhee-kach-ka	stříkačka
neither	zhaa-dnee	žádný
net	seety	síť
never	nyig-di	nikdy
new	no-vee	nový
news	spraa-vi	zprávy
news-agency	PNS	PNS

newspapers	no-vi-ni	noviny
New Year's Day	no-vee rok	Nový rok
New Year's Eve	sil-ves-tr	Silvestr
New Zealand	no-vee zeh-land	Nový Zéland
next	dal-shee • przhee-shtyee	další • příští
next to	ved-le	vedle
next week	przhee-shtyee tee-den	příští týden
next year	przhee-shtyee rok	příští rok
nice	pyek-nee	pěkný
night	nots	noc
no	ne	ne
noise	hluk	hluk
noisy	hluch-nyee	hluční
none	zhaa-dnee	žádný
noon	po-led-ne	poledne
north	se-ver	sever
nose	nos	nos
notebook	zaa-pis-nyeek	zápisník
nothing	nyits	nic
not yet	yesh-tye ne	ještě ne
novel (book)	ro-maan	román
now	tedy	teď
nuclear energy	a-to-mo-vaa e-ner-gi-ye	atomová energie
nun	yep-tyish-ka	jeptiška
nurse	zdra-vot-nyee ses-tra	zdravotní sestra

O

obvious	yas-nee	jasný
office	oo-rzhad	úřad
office work	praa-tse v kan-tse-laa-rzhi	práce v kanceláři
often	chas-to	často
oil (cooking)	o-ley	olej

English	Pronunciation	Czech
oil (crude)	ro-pa	ropa
OK	OK/do-brzhe	Ok/dobře
old	sta-ree	starý
old city	sta-reh mye-sto	staré město
olive oil	o-li-vo-vee o-ley	olivový olej
olives	o-li-vi	olivy
Olympic Games	o-lim-piy-skeh hri	olympijské hry
on	na	na
once • one time	yed-noh • ye-den-kraat	jednou • jedenkrát
one-way (ticket)	yed-no-smyer-nee	jedno-směrný
only	ye-nom	jenom
open	o-te-vrzhe-nee	otevřený
to open	o-te-vrzheet	otevřít
opening	ot-vor • o-te-vee-raa-nyee	otvor • otevírání
opera	o-pe-ra	opera
opera house	bu-do-va o-pe-ri • o-pe-ra	budova opery • opera
operation	o-pe-ra-tse	operace
opinion	naa-zor	názor
opposite	o-pach-nee	opačný
or	ne-bo	nebo
oral	oos-tnyee	ústní
orange (colour)	o-ran-zho-vaa	oranžová
orchestra	or-khes-tr	orchestr
order	po-rzhaa-dek • roz-kaz • ob-yed-naav-ka	pořádek • rozkaz • objednávka
to order	ob-yed-nat	objednat
ordinary	nor-maal-nyee	normální
organise	or-ga-ni-zo-vat	organizovat
other	yi-nee•dru-hee	jiný • druhý
outside	ven	ven
overdose	prze-daav-ko-vaa-nyee	předávkování
owner	ma-yi-tel	majitel
oxygen	ki-sleek	kyslík

English	Pronunciation	Czech
pacifier (dummy)	dud-leek	dudlík
package	ba-lee-chek	balíček
padlock	zaa-mek	zámek
page	stra-na	strana
a pain	bo-lest	bolest
painful	bo-les-tyi-veh	bolestivé
painkillers	praa-shki pro-tyi bo-les-tyi	prášky proti bolesti
to paint	ma-lo-vat • na-tyee-rat	malovat • natírat
painter	ma-leerzh	malíř
painting (the art)	ma-lo-vat	malovat
painting	o-braz	obraz
paintings	o-bra-zy	obrazy
pair (a couple)	paar	pár
palace	pa-laats	palác
pan	pan-vi-tse	panvice
paper	pa-peer	papír
parcel	ba-lee-chek	balíček
parents	ro-dyi-che	rodiče
a park	park	park
to park	par-ko-vat	parkovat
parliament	par-la-ment	parlament
part	chaast	část
party	fes-ti-val	festival
party (politics)	stra-na	strana
pass	yeet • slo-zhit skoh-shku • proo-smik	jít • složit skoušku • průsmyk
passenger	pa-sa-zhehr	pasažér
passport	pas	pas
passport number	chee-slo pa-su	číslo pasu
past	mi-nu-lee • mi-nu-lost	minulý • minulost
path	stez-ka • khod-nyeek	stezka • chodník

patient (adj)	tr-pye-li-vee	trpělivý
to pay	pla-tyit	platit
payment	plat-ba	platba
peace	meer	mír
peak	vr-khol	vrchol
pedestrian	pye-shee	pěší
pen (ballpoint)	pe-ro	pero
pencil	tuzh-ka	tužka
penknife	ka-pes-nyee noozh	kapesní nůž
pensioner	pen-zis-ta	penzista
people	li-dyi	lidi
pepper	pe-przh	pepř
percent	pro-tsen-to	procento
performance	pro-ve-de-nyee	provedení
permanent	per-ma-nen-tnyee	permanentní
permission	po-vo-le-nyee • soh-hlas	povolení • souhlas
permit	po-vo-le-nyee • le-gi-ti-ma-tse	povolení • legitimace
person	o-so-ba	osoba
personality	o-sob-nost	osobnost
petrol	ben-zeen	benzín
pharmacy	leh-kaar-na	lékárna
phone book	te-le-fon-nyee sez-nam	telefonní seznam
phone box	te-le-fon-nyee bud-ka	telefonní budka
phonecard	te-le-fon-nyee kar-ta	telefonní karta
photo	fot-ka	fotka

Can (May) I take a photo?
mo-hu tye vi-fo-tyit?
Mohu tě vyfotit?

photographer	fo-to-graf	fotograf
photography	fo-to-gra-fi-ye	fotografie
piece	kus	kus
pig	pra-se	prase

pill	ta-blet-ka	tabletka
the Pill	an-ti-kon-tsep-chnyee tab-let-ka	antikoncepční tabletka
pillow	pol-shtaarzh	polštář
pillowcase	pov-lak na pol-shtaarzh	povlak na polštář
pine	bo-ro-vi-tse	borovice
pink	roo-zho-vee	růžový
pipe	deem-ka	dýmka
place	mee-sto	místo
place of birth	na-ro-ze-nye	narození
plain	o-bi-chey-nee	obyčejný
plane	le-tad-lo	letadlo
planet	pla-ne-ta	planeta
plant	rost-li-na	rostlina
plate	ta-leerzh	talíř
plateau	ro-vi-na	rovina
platform	naa-stu-pish-tye	nástupiště
play (theatre)	hra	hra
to play (a game, music)	hraat	hrát
playing cards	kar-ti	karty
plug (electrical)	zaa-suv-ka	zásuvka
pocket	kap-sa	kapsa
poetry	po-e-zi-ye	poezie
to point	u-ka-zo-vat	ukazovat
poker	po-ker	poker
police	po-li-tsi-ye	policie
politics	po-li-ti-ka	politika
pollution	zne-chish-tye-nyee	znečištění
pool (swimming)	ba-zehn	bazén
poor	khu-dee	chudý
popular	po-pu-laar-nyee	populární
port	przhe-stav • port-skeh	přístav • portské
possible	mozh-nee	možný

It's (not) possible.
to ne-nyi mozh-neh
To neni možné.

postcard	po-hled-nyi-tse	pohlednice
post code	posh-tov-nyee smye-ro-va-tsee chee-slo	poštovní směrovací číslo
postage	posh-tov-neh	poštovné
poster	pla-kaat	plakát
post office	posh-ta	pošta
poverty	khu-do-ba	chudoba
power	mots	moc
prayer	mod-lit-ba	modlitba
to prefer	daat przhed-nost	dát přednost
pregnant	tye-hot-naa	těhotná
prehistoric art	pra-vye-keh u-mye-nyee	pravěké umění
to prepare	przhi-pra-vit	připravit
present (gift)	daa-rek	dárek
president	pre-zi-dent	prezident
pressure	tlak	tlak
pretty	hez-kee	hezký
prevent	za-braa-nyit	zabránit
price	tse-na	cena
pride	hr-dost	hrdost
priest	knyez	kněz
prime minister	mi-ni-ster-skee przhed-se-da • przhed-se-da vlaa-di	ministerský předseda • předseda vlády
a print (artwork)	tyisk • re-pro-duk-tse	tisk • reprodukce
prison	vye-ze-nyee	vězení
private	pri-vaat-nyee • soh-kro-mee	privátní • soukromý
privatisation	pri-va-ti-za-tse	privatizace
profession	pro-fe-se	profese
profit	pro-fit	profit
program	pro-gram	program
promise	slib	slib
proposal	naa-vrh	návrh

to protect	khraa-nyit	chránit
protected species	khraa-nye-neh dru-hi	chráněné druhy
protest	pro-test	protest
to protest	pro-tes-to-vat	protestovat
public toilet	ve-rzhey-neh zaa-kho-di	veřejné záchody
to pull	taah-noht	táhnout
pump	pum-pa	pumpa
puncture	de-fekt	defekt
to punish	po-tres-tat	potrestat
puppy	shtye-nye	štěně
pure	chis-tee	čistý
purple	pur-pur-o-vee	purpurový
to push	tla-chit	tlačit
to put	daat • vlo-zhit	dát • vložit

Q

qualifications	kva-li-fi-ka-tse	kvalifikace
quality	kva-li-ta	kvalita
quarantine	ka-ran-teh-na	karanténa
quarrel	spor • haad-ka	spor • hádka
quarter	ch-tvr-tyi-na	čtvrtina
queen	kraa-lov-na	královna
question	o-taaz-ka	otázka
to question	ptaat se	ptát se
question (topic)	vyets	věc
queue	fron-ta	fronta
quick	rikh-lee	rychlý
quiet (adj)	tyi-khee	tichý

R

rabbit	kraa-lick	králík
race (breed)	ra-sa	rasa
race (sport)	zaa-vod	závod
racism	ra-sis-mus	rasismus
racquet	ra-ke-ta	raketa
radiator	ra-di-aa-tor	radiátor
railroad	zhe-lez-nyi-tse	železnice
railway station	naa-dra-zhee	nádraží

rain	deh-shty	déšť

It's raining.
pr-shee
Prší.

rape	znaa-sil-nye-nyee	znásilnění
rare	vzaats-nee	vzácný
a rash	vi-raazh-ki	vyrážky
rat	pot-kan • kri-sa	potkan • krysa
razor	brzhi-tva • ho-lee-tsee stro-yek	břitva • holící strojek
razor blades	zhi-let-ki	žiletky
to read	cheest	číst
ready	ho-to-vee • przhi-pra-ve-nee	hotový • připravený
reason	doo-vod	důvod
receipt	stvr-zen-ka	stvrzenka
to receive	dos-tat	dostat
recent	ne-daav-nee	nedávný
recently	ne-daav-no	nedávno
to recognise	poz-nat	poznat
to recommend	do-po-ru-chit	doporučit
red	cher-ve-nee • ru-dee	červený • rudý
reflection (mirror)	od-raz • zr-tsad-le-nyee	odraz • zrcadlení
reflection (thinking)	u-va-zho-vaa-nyee • oo-va-ha	uvažování • úvaha
refrigerator	led-nyich-ka	lednička
refugee	u-prkh-leek	uprchlík
refund	re-fun-da-tse • naa-hra-da	refundace • náhrada
to refund	vraa-tyit pe-nyee-ze	vrátit peníze
to refuse	od-meet-noht	odmítnout
regional	ob-last-nyee	oblastní
registered mail	do-po-ru-che-naa zaa-sil-ka	doporučená zásilka

to regret	li-to-vat	litovat
relationship	vsta-h	vztah
to relax	re-laks-o-vat	relaxovat
religion	naa-boh-zhen-stvee	náboženství
religious	naa-bozh-nee	nábožený
to remember	pa-ma-to-vat si	pamatovat si
remote	vzdaa-le-nee	vzdálený
remote control	daal-ko-veh o-vlaa-da-nyee	dálkové ovládání
rent	naa-yem-neh	nájemné
to rent	pro-nay-moht	pronajmout
to repair	o-pra-vit	opravit
to repeat	o-pa-ko-vat	opakovat
republic	re-pub-li-ka	republika
reservation	re-zer-va-tse	rezervace
to reserve	re-zer-vo-vat	rezervovat
respect	re-spekt	respekt
rest (relaxation)	ot-po-chi-nek	odpočinek
rest (what's left)	sbi-tek • os-ta-tek	zbytek • ostatek
to rest	ot-po-chee-vat	odpočívat
restaurant	res-tow-ra-tse	restaurace
retired	vdoo-kho-du	v důchodu
to return	vraa-tyit se	vrátit se
return (ticket)	zpaa-tech-nyee yeez-den-ka	zpáteční jízdenka
review	re-vi-ze	revize
rhythm	rit-mus	rytmus
rich (wealthy)	bo-ha-tee	bohatý
to ride (a horse)	yez-dyit na ko-nyi	jezdit na koni
right (correct)	spraa-vnee	správný
right (not left)	vpra-vo	vpravo
to be right	meet prav-du	mít pravdu

You're right.
maash prav-du
Máš pravdu.

civil rights	ob-chan-skeh praa-va	občanské práva
right now	praa-vye tety	právě teď
right-wing	pra-vi-tso-vee	pravicový
ring (on finger)	pr-sten	prsten
ring (of phone)	zvo-nyit	zvonit

I'll give you a ring.
za-vo-laam tyi • brnk-nu tyi
Zavolám ti. • *Brnknu ti.*

ring (sound)	zvo-nye-nyee	zvonění
risk	risk	risk
river	rzhe-ka	řeka
road (main)	tses-ta • sil-nyi-tse	cesta • silnice
road map	ow-to-ma-pa	automapa
to rob	o-kraast • u-kraa-st	okrást • ukrást
rock	skaa-la	skála
rock climbing	ho-ro-le-zets-tvee	horole-zectví
rock (wall of)	oo-tyes • skaa-la	útěs • skála
romance	ro-man-tse	romance
room	meest-nost	místnost
room number	chee-slo po-ko-ye	číslo pokoje
rope	pro-vaz	provaz
round	ku-la-tee	kulatý
(at the) round-about	kru-ho-vee ob-yezd	kruhový objezd
rubbish	od-pad-ki	odpadky
rug	ko-ber-chek • hoh-nye	koberček • houně
ruins	ru-i-ni	ruiny
to run	bye-zhet	běžet

S

sad	smut-nee	smutný
safe (adj)	bes-pech-nee	bezpečný
saint	sva-tee	svatý

salary	plat	plat
(on) sale	vee-pro-dey	výprodej
sales	ob-khod-nyee	obchodní
department	od dye-le-nyee	oddělení
salt	sool	sůl
sand	pee-sek	písek
sanitary napkins	men-shtru-a-chnyee vlozh-ki	menštru-ační vložky
Saturday	so-bo-ta	sobota
to save	u-shet-rzhit • za-khraa-nyit	ušetřit • zachránit
to say	rzhee-tsi	říci
to scale • climb	vi-stoh-pit • vish-plhat se	vystoupit • vyšplhat se
school	shko-la	škola
science	vye-da	věda
scientist	vye-dets	vědec
scissors	noozh-ki	nůžky
screen	stye-na • o-bra-zof-ka	stěna • obrazovka
script	ma-nu-skript	manuskript
sculpture	so-kha	socha
sea	mo-rzhe	moře
seasick	trpee-tsee morzh-skoh ne-mo-tsee	trpící mořskou nemocí
seaside	pob-rzhe-zhee	pobřeží
seat	se-da-dlo • mee-sto	sedadlo • místo
seatbelt	bez-pech-nost-nee paas	bezpeč-nostní pás
second (n)	vte-rzhi-na	vteřina
second	dru-hee	druhý
secretary	sek-re-taarzh-ka	sekretářka
to see	vi-dyet	vidět

We'll see!
uy-vi-dyee-me!
Uvidíme!

I see. (understand)
ro-zu-meem
Rozumím.

ENGLISH–CZECH DICTIONARY

See you tomorrow.
na-shle-da-noh zee-tra
Na shledanou zítra.

self-service	sa-mo-op-slu-ha	samoob-sluha
to sell	pro-daa-vat	prodávat
to send	pos-lat	poslat
sentence (words)	vye-ta	věta
sentence (prison)	roz-su-dek	rozsudek
to separate	se-pa-ro-vat	separovat
serious	vaazh-nee	vážný
service (ance)	sluzh-ba •	služba • servis
service (religious)	bo-ho-sluzh-ba	bohoslužba
to sew	sheet	šít
sex	seks	sex
shade • shadow	styeen	stín
shampoo	sham-pon	šampon
shape	tvar	tvar
to shave	ho-lit se	holit se
she	o-na	ona
sheep	of-tse	ovce
sheet (bed)	pro-stye-rad-lo • pla-khta	prostě-radlo • plachta
sheet (of paper)	list	list
ship	lody	loď
shirt	ko-shi-le	košile
shoes	bo-ti	boty
shop	ob-khod	obchod

to go shopping
na-ku-po-vat
nakupovat

short (length)	kraat-ki	krátky
short (height)	ma-lee	malý
shortage	ne-dos-ta-tek	nedostatek
shorts	short-ki	šortky

shoulders	ra-mye-na	ramena
to shout	za-vo-lat • krzhi-chet	zavolat • křičet
a show	shoh	show
to show	u-kaa-zat	ukázat

Can you show me on the map?
moo-zhe-te mi to
u-kaa-zat na ma-pye?
Můžete mi to ukázat na mapě?

shower	spr-kha	sprcha
to shut	zahv-rzheet	zavřít
shy	pla-khee • stid-li-vee	plachý • stydlivý
sick	ne-mots-nee	nemocný
a sickness	ne-mots	nemoc
side	stra-na	strana
a sign	znak • zna-mye-nee	znak • zna-mění
to sign	po-dep-sat	podepsat
signature	pod-pis	podpis
silk	hed-vaab	hedváb
of silver	strzhee-br-nee	stříbrný
similar	po-dob-nee	podobný
simple	yed-no-du-khee	jednodu-chý
sin	hrzheekh	hřích
since (May)	od (kvyet-na)	od (května)
to sing	zpee-vat	zpívat
singer	zpye-vaak	zpěvák
single (person)	saam • svo-bod-nee	sám • svo-bodný
single (unique)	ye-den	jeden
single (unique)	ye-di-nee	jediný
single room	yed-no-loozh-ko-vee po-koy	jednolůž-kový pokoj
sister	ses-tra	sestra
to sit	se-dyet	sedět
size (of anything)	ve-li-kost	velikost
size (clothes)	ve-li-kost • chee-slo	velikost • číslo
size (shoes)	ve-li-kost • chee-slo	velikost • číslo

skiing	li-zho-vaa-nee	lyžování
to ski	li-zho-vat	lyžovat
skin	koo-zhe	kůže
sky	ob-lo-ha • ne-be	obloha • nebe
to sleep	spaat	spát
sleeping bag	spa-tsaak	spacák
sleeping car	spa-tsee vooz	spací vůz
sleeping pills	praa-shki	prášky
sleepy	o-spa-lee	ospalý
slide (film)	di-ya-po-zi-tiv	diapozitiv
slow • slowly	po-ma-li	pomaly
small	ma-lee	malý
a smell	pakh • smrad	pach•smrad
to smell	paakh-noht • smr-dyet	páchnout • smrdět
to smile	smaat se	smát se
to smoke	koh-rzhit	kouřit
soap	meed-lo	mýdlo
soccer	fot-bal • ko-pa-naa	fotbal • kopaná
social welfare	so-tsi-aal-nee peh-che	sociální péče
somebody • someone	nye-kdo	někdo
something	nye-tso	něco
sometimes	nye-kdi	někdy
son	sin	syn
song	pee-se-nye	píseň
soon	br-zi	brzy

I'm sorry.
ye mi lee-to
Je mi líto.

sound	z-vuk	zvuk
south	yih	jih
souvenir	su-ve-neer	suvenír
souvenir shop	ob-khod se su-ve-nee-ri	obchod se suveníry
to speak	mlu-vit	mluvit
special	spe-tsi-al-nee	speciální

speed	rikh-lost	rychlost
speed limit	o-me-ze-nee rikh-lo-sti	omezení rychlosti
spicy (hot)	pi-kant-nee	pikantní
sport	sport	sport
sportsperson	spor-to-vets	sportovec
a sprain	vee-ron	výron
spring (season)	ya-ro	jaro
spring (coil)	pru-zhi-na • stru-na	pružina • struna
square (shape)	ch-tve-rets	čtverec
square (in town)	naa-mye-stee	náměstí
stadium	sta-di-on	stadion
stage	paw-di-um • ye-vish-tye	pódium • jeviště
stairway	skho-dish-tye	schodiště
stamps	znaam-ki	známky
standard (usual)	stan-dard	standard
standard of living	zhi-vot-nee oo-ro-ve-nye • stil	životní úroveň • styl
stars	hvye-zdi	hvězdy
to start	za-cheet	začít
station	za-staav-ka	zastávka
stationers	pa-peer-nits-tvee	papírnictví
statue	so-kha	socha
to stay (remain)	zoo-stat	zůstat
to stay (somewhere)	zoo-stat	zůstat
to steal	kraast	krást
steep	str-mee	strmý
step	u-dye-lat krok • skhod	udělat krok • schod
stomach	zha-lu-dek	žaludek
stomachache	bo-le-nee brzhi-kha	bolení břicha
stone	kaa-men	kámen
stop	staat • za-staav-ka	stát • zastávka

ENGLISH–CZECH DICTIONARY

to stop	za-sta-vit	zastavit

> Stop!
> stooy!
> *Stůj!*

stork	chaap	čáp
storm	bohr-zhe	bouře
story	po-haad-ka	pohádka
stove	kam-na •	kamna •
	spo-raak	sporák
straight	rov-nee	rovný
strange	tsi-zee •	cizí •
	ne-znaa-mee	neznámý
stranger	tsi-zi-nets	cizinec
stream	prohd •	proud•
	po-tok	potok
street	u-li-tse	ulice
strength	see-la	síla
a strike	staav-ka	stávka
on strike	staav-ko-vat	stávkovat
string	shpa-gaat	špagát
stroll •	pro-khaaz-ka	procházka
walk		
strong	sil-nee	silný
stubborn	tvr-do-hla-vee	tvrdohlavý
student	stu-dent	student
studio	stu-di-o	studio
stupid	hloh-pee •	hloupý •
	pi-to-mee	pitomý
style	stil	styl
subtitles	pod-ti-tul-ki	podtitulky
suburb	seed-lish-tye	sídliště
suburbs of	przhed-mye-stee	předměstí
subway station	met-ro	metro
success	oo-spyekh	úspěch
to suffer	tr-pyet	trpět
sugar	tsu-kr	cukr
suitcase	ku-fr	kufr
summer	leh-to	léto
sun	slun-tse	slunce
sunblock	o-pa-lo-va-tsee krehm	opalovací krém

sunburn	spaa-le-nee	spálený
	slun-tsem	sluncem
sunglasses	slu-nech-nee	sluneční
	bree-le	brýle
sunny	slu-nech-nee	slunečný
sunrise	vee-khod	východ
	slun-tse	slunce
sunset	zaa-pad	západ
	slun-tse	slunce

> Sure.
> yis-tye.
> *Jistě.*

surface mail	o-bi-chey-naa posh-ta	obyčej-ná pošta
surname	przhee-me-nee	příjmení
a surprise	przhe-kva-pe-nee	překva-pení
to survive	przhe-zheet	přežít
sweater	sve-tr	svetr
sweet	slad-kee	sladký
to swim	pla-vat	plavat
swimming	pla-vaa-nee	plavání
swimming pool	ba-zehn	bazén
swimsuit	plav-ki	plavky
sword	mech	meč
sympathetic	sim-pa-tits-kee	sympatický
synagogue	si-na-gaw-ga	synagóga
synthetic	sin-te-tits-kee	syntetický
syringe	strzhee-kach-ka	stří-kačka

T

table	stool	stůl
table tennis	stol-nee te-nis	stolní tenis
tail	o-hon • o-tsas	ohon • ocas
to take (away)	vzeet se-boh	vzít sebou
to take (food/ the train)	vzeet	vzít
to take photographs	ot-fo-tit	odfotit

to talk	mlu-vit • po-vee-dat si	mluvit • povídat si
tall	vi-so-kee	vysoký
tampons	tam-paw-ni	tampóny
tasty	khut-nee	chutný
tax	da-nye	daň
taxi stand	sta-no-vish-tye taks-ee-koo	stanoviště taxíků
teacher	u-chi-tel	učitel
team	teem	tím
tear (crying)	plaach	pláč
technique	tekh-ni-ka	technika
teeth	zu-bi	zuby
telegram	te-le-gram	telegram
telephone	te-le-fon	telefon
to telephone	te-le-fo-no-vat	telefonovat
television	te-le-vi-ze	televize
to tell	vi-praa-vyet	vyprávět
temperature (fever)	ho-rech-ka	horečka
temperature (weather)	te-plo-ta	teplota
temple	khraam	chrám
tennis	te-nis	tenis
tennis court	te-ni-so-vee kurt	tenisový kurt
tent	stan	stan
terrible	hro-zne	hrozný
test	test	test
to thank	dye-ko-vat	děkovat

Thank you.
dye-ku-yi
Děkuji.

theatre	di-va-dlo	divadlo
thick	sil-nee • tlu-stee	silný • tlustý
thief	zlo-dyey	zloděj
thin	sla-bee • ten-kee	slabý • tenký
to think	mis-let	myslet
third	trzhe-tee	třetí
thirsty	zhee-zni-vee	žíznivý
thought	mish-len-ka	myšlenka

throat	krk • hrd-lo	krk • hrdlo
ticket	vstoo-pen-ka • lee-stek	vstupenka • lístek
ticket collector	proo-vod-chee	průvodčí
ticket office	po-klad-na	pokladna
time	chas	čas
timetable	yeez-dnee rzhaad•roz-vr-h ho-din	jízdní řád • rozvrh hodin
tin (can)	ple-khof-ka	plechovka
tin opener	ot-vee-rach na ple-khof-ki	otvírač na plechovky
tip (gratuity)	spro-pit-neh	spropitné
tired	u-na-ve-nee	unavený
toad	ro-pu-kha	ropucha
toast	tohst	toast
tobacco	ta-baak	tabák
today	dnes	dnes
together	spo-lu	spolu
toilet paper	to-a-let-nee pa-peer	toaletní papír
toilets	to-a-le-ti • zaa-kho-di	toalety • záchody
tomorrow	zee-tra	zítra

tomorrow afternoon/evening
zee-tra fpo-led-ne/ve-cher
zítra v poledne/večer

tomorrow morning
zee-tra raa-no
zítra ráno

tonight	dnes ve-cher	dnes večer
too (as well)	tehzh • ta-ki	též • taky
too expensive	przhe-lish dra-hee	příliš drahý
too much • many	przhe-lish mots	příliš moc
tooth (front)	zub (przhed-nee)	zub (přední)
tooth (back)	zub (zad-nee • sto-lich-ka)	zub (zadní • stolička)

toothache	bo-le-nee zu-boo	bolení zubů
toothbrush	zub-nee kar-taa-chek	zubní kartáček
toothpaste	zub-nee pa-sta	zubní pasta
torch (flashlight)	ba-ter-ka	baterka
to touch	dot-knoht se	dotknout se
tourist	tu-ris-ta	turista

tourist information office
in-for-much-nee tsen-trum
informační centrum

towel	ruch-neek	ručník
tower	vyezh	věž
track (path)	stez-ka	stezka
trade union	ot-bo-ri	odbory
traffic	do-pra-va • pro-voz	doprava • provoz
traffic lights	se-ma-for	semafor
trail • route	tra-tye	trať
train	vlak	vlak
train station	naa-dra-zhee	nádraží
tram	tram-vai	tramvaj
to translate	przhe-lo-zhit	přeložit
to travel	tses-to-vat	cestovat
travel agency	tses-to-vnee a-gen-tu-ra	cestovní agentura
travel sickness	ne-mots stses-to-vaa-nee	nemoc z cestování
travellers cheques	tses-to-vnee she-ki	cestovní šeky
tree	strom	strom
trendy (person)	mawd-nee chlo-vyehk	módní člověk
trip	tses-ta • vee-let	cesta • výlet
trousers	kal-ho-ti	kalhoty
truck	naa-kla-dyaak	náklaďák

It's true.
ye to prav-da
Je to pravda.

trust	vee-ra • doo-vye-ra	víra • důvěra
to trust	vye-rzhit • spo-le-h-noht se	věřit • spolehnout se
truth	prav-da	pravda
to try	zku-sit	zkusit
to try (to attempt)	po-kus	pokus
T-shirt	trich-ko	tričko
tune	me-lo-di-ye	melodie

Turn left.
za-boch vle-vo
Zaboč vlevo.

Turn right.
za-boch fpra-vo
Zaboč vpravo.

TV set	te-le-vi-ze • te-le-viz-nee a-pa-raat	televize • televizní aparát
twice	dva-kraat	dvakrát
twin beds	dvo-yi-taa pos-tel	dvojitá postel
twins	dvoy-cha-ta	dvojčata
to type	kle-pat • psaat na stro-yi	klepat • psát na stroji
typical	ti-pits-kee	typický
tyres	pne-u-ma-ti-ki	pneumatiky

U

umbrella	desht-neek	deštník
to understand	ro-zu-myet • khaa-pat	rozumět • chápat
unemployed	ne-za-myest-na-nee	nezaměstnaný
unemployment	ne-za-myest-na-nost	nezaměstnanost
unions	ot-bo-ri	odbory
universe	ves-meer	vesmír
university	u-ni-ver-zi-ta	univerzita

unleaded	bez o-lo-va	*bez olova*
unsafe	ne-bez-pech-nee	*nebez-pečný*
until (June)	do (cher-vna)	*do (června)*
unusual	ne-zvi-klee • z-vlaasht-nee	*nezvyklý • zvláštní*
up	vzhoo-ru	*vzhůru*
urgent	ur-gent-nee	*urgentní*
useful	u-zhi-tech-nee	*užitečný*

V

vacant	vol-nee	*volný*
vacation	praazd-ni-ni • do-vo-le-naa	*prázdniny • dovolená*
vaccination	och-ko-vaa-nee	*očkování*
valley	oo-do-lee	*údolí*
valuable	tsen-nee • hod-not-nee	*cenný • hodnotný*
value (price)	tse-na	*cena*
van	do-daav-ka	*dodávka*
vegetable	ze-le-ni-na	*zelenina*
vegetarian	ve-ge-ta-ri-aan	*vegetarián*

I'm vegetarian.
ysem ve-ge-ta-ri-aan
Jsem vegetarián.

vegetation	ve-ge-ta-tse	*vegetace*
vein	zhee-la	*žíla*
venereal disease	po-hlav-nee ne-mots	*pohlavní nemoc*
venue	mee-sto	*místo*
very	mots	*moc*
video tape	vi-de-o paa-ska	*video páska*
view	po-dee-vaa-ni	*podívání*
village	ves-ni-tse	*vesnice*
virus	vi-rus	*virus*
visa	vee-zum	*vízum*
to visit	nav-shtee-vit	*navštívit*
vitamins	vi-ta-mee-ni	*vitamíny*
voice	hlas	*hlas*
to vote	vo-lit	*volit*

W

Wait!	poch-key!	*Počkej!*
waiter	cheesh-neek	*číšník*
waiting room	che-kaar-na	*čekárna*
to walk	kho-dit • przhe-khaa-zet se	*chodit • přecházet se*
wall (inside)	stye-na	*stěna*
wall (outside)	ze-dye	*zeď*
to want	khteet	*chtít*
war	vaal-ka	*válka*
wardrobe	shat-neek	*šatník*
warm	te-plee	*teplý*
to warn	va-ro-vat	*varovat*
to wash (something)	meet • praat	*mýt • prát*
to wash (oneself)	u-meet se	*umýt se*
washing machine	pra-chka	*pračka*
watch	ho-din-ki	*hodinky*
to watch	sle-do-vat	*sledovat*
water	vo-da	*voda*

mineral water
mi-ne-raal-ka
minerálka

waterfall	vo-do-paad	*vodopád*
wave	vl-na	*vlna*
way	tses-ta	*cesta*

Please tell me the way to ...
proh-seem u-kazh • -te mi tses-tu do ...
Prosím ukaž • te mi cestu do ... (inf/pol)

Which way?
kte-reem smye-rem?
Kterým směrem?

Way Out	vee-khod	*východ*
we	mi	*my*
weak	sla-bee	*slabý*

ENGLISH–CZECH DICTIONARY

wealthy	bo-ha-tee	*bohatý*
weather	po-cha-see	*počasí*
wedding	svat-ba	*svatba*
	daa-rek	*dárek*
week	tee-den	*týden*
this week	ten-to tee-den	*tento týden*
to weigh	vaa-zhit	*vážit*
weight	vaa-ha	*váha*
welcome	vee-tey/-te	*vitej/te (inf/pol)*
welfare	so-tsi-aal-nee	*sociální*
	peh-che/	*péče/*
	bla-ho	*blaho*
west	zaa-pad	*západ*
wet	mok-ree	*mokrý*
what	tso	*co*

What is he saying?
tso rzhee-ka?
Co říká?

wheel	ko-le-so	*koleso*
wheelchair	in-va-lid-nee	*invalidní*
	vo-zeek	*vozík*
when	gdi	*kdy*

When does it leave?
gdi/v ko-lik ho-din od-khaa-zee?
Kdy/v kolik hodin odchází?

where	gde	*kde*

Where is the bank?
gde ye ban-ka?
Kde je banka?

white	bee-lee	*bílý*
who	gdo	*kdo*

Who is it?
gdo ye to?
Kdo je to?

why	proch	*proč*

Why is the museum closed?
proch ye mu-ze-um za-tvo-rzhe-no?
Proč je muzeum zatvořeno?

wide	shi-ro-kee	*široký*

wife	man-zhel-ka •	*manželka •*
	kho-tye	*choť*
wild		
animal	di-veh zvee-rzhe	*divé zvíře*
to win	vi-hraat	*vyhrát*
wind	vee-tr	*vítr*
window	ok-no	*okno*

to (go) window-shopping
po-dee-vat se na vee-kla-di
podívat se na výklady

windscreen	chel-nee sklo	*čelní sklo*
wine	vee-no	*víno*
wings	krzhee-dla	*křídla*
winter	zi-ma	*zima*
wire	draat	*drát*
wise	mohd-ree	*moudrý*
to wish	przhaat	*přát*
with	s • se	*s • se*
without	bez	*bez*
woman	zhe-na	*žena*
wonderful	naad-her-nee	*nádherný*
wood	les • drzhe-vo	*les • dřevo*
wool	vl-na	*vlna*
word	slo-vo	*slovo*
work	praa-tse	*práce*
to work	pra-tso-vat	*pracovat*
workshop	deel-na	*dílna*
world	svyet	*svět*
worried	u-sta-ra-nee	*ustaraný*
worth	meet hod-no-tu	*mít hodnotu*
wound	raa-na	*rána*
to write	p-saat	*psát*
writer	spi-so-va-tel	*spisovatel*
wrong	ne-spraav-nee	*nesprávný*

I'm wrong. (my fault)
mo-ye khi-ba
Moje chyba.

I'm wrong. (not right)
ne-maam prav-du
Nemám pravdu.

Y

year	rok	*rok*
this year	ten-to rok	*tento rok*
yellow	zhlu-tee	*žlutý*
yesterday	vche-ra	*včera*

yesterday afternoon/evening
fche-ra ot-po-led-ne/ve-cher
včera odpoledne/večer

yesterday morning
fche-ra raa-no • do-po-led-ne
včera ráno • dopoledne

yet	yizh	*již*
you (pol)	vi	*vy*
young	mla-dee	*mladý*
youth (collective)	mlaa-dezh	*mládež*
youth hostel •	no-tsle-haar-na pro mlaa-dezh	*noclehárna pro mládež*

Z

zebra	ze-bra	*zebra*
zoo	zo-o • zo-o-lo-gits-kaa za-hra-da	*zoo • zoologická zahrada*

CZECH–ENGLISH DICTIONARY

A

a	a	and
acylpirin	a-tsil-pi-rin	aspirin
adaptor	a-dap-tor	adaptor
adresa	a-dre-sa	address
agresivní	a-gres-iv-nyee	aggressive

Ahoj.	
a-hoy	
Hello • Hi.	

AIDS	a-ids	AIDS
aktivista	ak-ti-vis-ta	activist
aktuality	ak-tu-a-li-ti	current affairs
ale	a-le	but
alej	a-ley	avenue
alergie	a-ler-gi-ye	allergy
amatér	a-ma-tehr	amateur
anarchista	a-nar-khis-ta	anarchist
anglický	an-glits-kee	English
antikoncepce	an-ti-kon-tsep-tse	contraception
antikoncepční prostředky	an-ti-kon-tsep-chnee pro-strzhed-ki	contraceptives
antikoncepční tabletka	an-ti-kon-tsep-chnee tab-let-ka	the Pill
antinukleární	an-ti-nuk-le-aar-nyee	anti-nuclear
antiseptický	an-ti-sep-tits-kee	antiseptic
archeologický	ar-khe-o-log-its-kee	archaeological
architektura	ar-khi-tek-tu-ra	architecture
astmatik	ast-ma-tik	asthmatic
atmosféra	at-mos-feh-ra	atmosphere
atomová energie	a-to-mo-vaa e-ner-gi-ye	nuclear energy
atomové zkoušky	a-to-mo-veh skoh-sh-ki	nuclear testing
auto	ow-to	car
autobus	ow-to-bus	bus (city)
autobusová zastávka	ow-to-bus-o-vaa za-staaf-ka	bus stop
autobusové nádraží	ow-to-bus-o-veh naa-dra-zhee	bus station
autokar	ow-to-kar	bus (intercity)
automapa	ow-to-ma-pa	road map
automat na lístky	ow-to-mat na lees-tki	ticket machine
automatická úschovna	ow-to-ma-tits-kaa oos-khov-na	luggage lockers
auto mechanik	ow-to-me-kha-nik	mechanic
avšak	af-shak	but

B

babička	ba-bich-ka	grandmother
balíček	ba-lee-chek	package • parcel
balíček (karet)	ba-lee-chek (ka-ret)	deck (of cards)
balíček (cigaret)	ba-lee-chek (tsi-ga-ret)	packet (of cigarettes)
balík	ba-leek	packet (general)
balkón	bal-kawn	balcony
bandáž	ban-daazh	bandage
bankomat	bank-o-mat	automatic teller (ATM)
bankovky	bank-ov-ki	banknotes
barva	bar-va	colour
bát se	baat se	to be afraid of
baterie	ba-te-ri-ye	battery
baterka	ba-ter-ka	torch (flashlight)
batoh	ba-to-h	backpack
batožina	ba-to-zhi-na	luggage • baggage
bavit se	ba-vit se	to have fun

bavlna	bah-vl-na	cotton
bazén	ba-zehn	swimming pool
během hodiny	bye-hem ho-dyi-ni	within an hour
beletrie	be-le-tri-ye	fiction
benzín	ben-zeen	petrol
bez	bez	without
bez filtra	bez fil-tra	without filter
bez olova	bez o-lo-va	unleaded
bezdomovec	bez-do-mo-vets	homeless
běžet	byezh-et	to run
bezpečnost	bes-pech-nost	safe (n)
bezpečnostní pás	bez-pech-nost-nyee paas	seatbelt
bezpečný	bes-pech-nee	safe (adj)
bezpečný sex	bes-pech-nee seks	safe sex
bible	bib-le	the Bible
bílý	bee-lee	white
bitka	bit-ka	fight

Blahopřeji!
bla-ho-przhe-yi!
Congratulations!

bláto	blaa-to	mud
bláznivý	blaaz-nyi-vee	crazy
blbec	bl-bets	creep (slang)
blecha	ble-kha	flea
blinkr	blinkr	indicator
blízko	blee-zko	near
blouznící	blohz-nyee-tsee	delirious
bohatý	bo-ha-tee	wealthy
bohoslužba	bo-ho-sluzh-ba	service (religious)
boj	boy	a fight
bojovat	boy-o-vat	to fight

bolení břicha	bo-le-nyee brzhi-kha	indigestion • stomachache
bolení hlavy	bo-le-nyee hla-vi	headache
bolení zubů	bo-le-nyee zu-boo	toothache
bolest	bo-lest	a pain
bolestivé	bo-les-tyi-veh	painful
borovice	bo-ro-vi-tse	pine
boty	bo-ti	boots • shoes
boule	boh-le	lump
bouře	bohr-zhe	storm
box	boks	boxing
brána	braa-na	gate
brankař	bran-karzh	goalkeeper
bratr	bra-tr	brother
brouk	brohk	bug
brzy	br-zi	soon
břitva	brzhi-tva	razor
bubny	bub-ni	drums
budík	bu-dyeek	alarm clock
budoucnost	bu-dohts-nost	future
budova	bu-do-va	building
budova opery	bu-do-va o-pe-ri	opera house
Bůh	boo-h	God
bydlet	bid-let	to live (somewhere)
bydlet spolu	bid-let spo-lu	to share a dorm
byliny	bi-li-ni	herbs
být	beet	to be
být	beet	appointment

CZECH–ENGLISH DICTIONARY

C

cédé	tseh-deh	CD
celnice	tsel-nyi-tse	customs
celý	tse-lee	whole
cena	tse-na	price • value
cenný	tsen-nee	valuable
centrum	tsen-trum	city centre
cesta	tses-ta	journey • way • avenue • road (main) • trek • trip
cestopisy	tses-to-pi-si	travel books
cestovat	tses-to-vat	to travel
cestovní agentura	tses-tov-nyee a-gen-tu-ra	travel agency
cestovní horečka	tses-tov-nyee ho-rech-ka	travel sickness
cestovní plán	tses-tov-nyee plaan	itinerary
cestovní šeky	tses-tov-nyee she-ki	travellers cheques
cifry	tsi-fri	figures
cigaretový papír	tsi-ga-ret-o-vee pa-peer	cigarette papers
cigarety	tsi-ga-re-ti	cigarettes
cíl	tseel	goal • destination
cítit	tsee-tyit	to feel
citlivost	tsit-li-vost	film speed
city	tsi-ti	feelings
cizí	tsi-zee	strange • foreign
cizinec	tsi-zi-nets	stranger
co	tso	what
cukr	tsu-kr	sugar
cvičení	tsvi-che-nyee	workout
cyklista	tsik-lis-ta	cyclist
cyklistika	tsik-list-i-ka	cycling
cystitida	tsis-ti-ti-da	cystitis

Č

čáp	chaap	stork
čára	chaa-ra	line
čas	chas	time
časný	chas-nee	early
časopis	cha-so-pis	magazine
část	chaast	part
často	chas-to	often
čekárna	che-kaar-na	waiting room
čelní sklo	chel-nyee sklo	windscreen
černo-bílý film	cher-no-bee-lee film	B&W (film)
černý	cher-nee	black
červený	cher-ve-nee	red
červy	cher-vi	worms
číslice	chee-sli-tse	figures
číslo	chee-slo	size
číslo pasu	chee-slo pa-su	passport number
číslo pokoje	chee-slo po-ko-ye	room number
číšník	cheesh-nyeek	waiter
číst	cheest	to read
čistý	chis-tee	clean • pure
člen	chlen	member
člun	chlun	boat
čočka	choch-ka	lens
čokoláda	cho-ko-laa-da	chocolate
čtrnáct dnů	chtr-naatst dnoo	fortnight
čtverec	ch-tve-rets	square (shape)
čtvrtina	ch-tvr-tyi-na	quarter

D

daleko	da-le-ko	far
dalekohled	da-le-ko-hled	binoculars
dálkové ovládání	daal-ko-veh o-vlaa-da-nyee	remote control
dálkový	daal-ko-vee	long distance

dálnice	daal-nyits-e	motorway (tollway)
další	dal-shee	next
daň	dany	tax
daň z příjmu	da-nye z przhee-ymu	income tax
dar	dar	gift
dárek	daa-rek	present (gift)
dát	daat	to give • to put
dát přednost	daat przhed-nost	to prefer
datum	da-tum	date (time)
datum narození	da-tum na-ro-ze-nyee	date of birth
dcera	tse-ra	daughter
děcko	dyets-ko	baby
dědeček	dye-de-chek	grandfather
defekt	de-fekt	puncture
deka	de-ka	blanket
děkovat	dye-ko-vat	to thank

Děkuji.
dye-ku-yi
Thank you.

dělat	dye-lat	to do
dělat si legraci	dye-lat le-gra-tsi	to make fun of
delirantní	de-li-rant-nyee	delirious
dělit se s	dye-lit se s	to share (with)
dělník	dyel-nyeek	factory/ manual worker
demokrace	de-mo-kra-tse	democracy
demonstrace	de-mon-stra-tse	demonstration
den	den	day
denní	den-nyee	daily
deník	dyen-nyeek	diary
dentální nit	den-taal-nyee nyit	dental floss

desátý	de-saa-tee	tenth
déšť	deh-shty	rain
deštník	desht-nyeek	umbrella
detail	de-tail	detail
dezinfekční prostředek	dez-in-fek-chnyee pro-strzhed-ek	anti-septic
děťátko	dye-tyaat-ko	baby
děti	dye-tyi	children
dětské vyrážky	dyet-skeh vi-raazh-ki	nappy rash
dětský pudr	dye-tskee pu-dr	baby powder
dezodorant	de-zo-do-rant	deodorant
diapozitiv	di-ya-po-zi-tiv	slide (film)
dílna	dyeel-na	workshop
diskriminace	disk-rim-in-a-tse	discrimination
diskriminace žen	dis-kri-mi-na-tse zhen	sexism
dítě	dyee-tyeh	child
divadlo	dyi-va-dlo	theatre
divé zvíře	dyi-veh z-vee-rzhe	wild animal
dizajn	di-zain	design
dlouhý	dloh-hee	long
dlužit	dlu-zhit	to owe
dnes	dnes	today
dnes	dnes	this
dnes odpoledne	dnes od-po-led-ne	afternoon
dnes večer	dnes ve-cher	tonight
do (června)	do (cher-vna)	until (June)
dobře	dob-rzhe	well • OK

Dobrou chuť!
dob-roh khuty!
Bon appétit!

Dobrý večer • Dobrou noc.
dob-ree ve-cher • dob-roh nots
Good evening • night.

dodávka	do-daav-ka	van
doktor	dok-tor	doctor
dokumen-	do-ku-men-	a documen-
tární film	taar-nyee film	tary
domácí	do-maa-tsee	local
domácí	dom-aa-tsee	house-
úkol	oo-kol	work
dopis	do-pis	letter
dopoledne	do-po-led-ne	morning (6am - 1pm)
doporuče-	do-po-ru-che-	registered
ná zásilka	naa zaa-sil-ka	mail
doporučit	do-po-ru-chit	to recommend
doprava	do-pra-va	traffic
dospělý	dos-pye-lee	adult
dost	dost	enough
dostat	do-stat	to receive
dostatek	do-sta-tek	enough
dostavit se	do-sta-vit se	to come • to arrive
dotknout se	dot-knoht se	to touch
dovolená	do-vo-le-naa	holidays • vacation
dovolit	do-vo-lit	to allow
drahý	dra-hee	dear • expensive
dráma	draa-ma	drama
dramatický	dra-ma-tits-kee	dramatic
drát	draat	wire
drink	drink	a drink
drobné (mince)	drob-neh (min-tse)	change (coins)
droga	dro-ga	drug
drogy	dro-gi	drugs
druh (adj)	druh	kind
druhý	dru-hee	second • other
dřevo	drzhe-vo	wood
dudlík	dud-leek	pacifier • (baby's) dummy
důležitý	doo-le-zhi-tee	important
dům	doom	house
důvěra	doo-vye-ra	trust
důvod	doo-vod	reason
dva týdny	dva tee-dni	fortnight
dvakrát	dva-kraat	twice
dveře	dve-rzhe	door
dvojčata	dvoy-cha-ta	twins
dvojitá postel	dvo-yi-taa pos-tel	twin beds
dvojitý	dvo-yi-tee	double
dvoulůžko	dvoh-loozh-ko	double bed
dvoulůž kový pokoj	dvoh-loozh- ko-vee po-koy	double room
dýchat	dee-khat	to breathe
dyla	di-la	drug dealer
dýmka	deem-ka	pipe
džínsy	dzheen-si	jeans
džíp	dzheep	jeep
džus	dzhus	juice

E

ekonomie	e-ko-no-mi-e	economy
elektřina	e-lek-trzhi-na	electricity
emigrace	e-mi-gra-tse	immigration
epileptický	e-pi-lep-tits-kee	epileptic
etapa	e-ta-pa	leg (in race)
evropský	ev-rop-skee	European
expozimetr	eks-po-zi-me-tr	light meter
expresní	eks-pres-nyee	express
expresní zásilka	eks-pres-nyee zaa-sil-ka	express mail

F

| Fajn! | Fain! | Great! |
| faktura | fak-tu-ra | bill (account) |

fakulta	fa-kul-ta	college
fanoušci	fa-nohsh-tsi	fans (of a team)
farma	far-ma	farm
farmář	far-maarzh	farmer
festival	fes-ti-val	party
film	film	a film (camera) • movie
filtrované	fil-tro-va-neh	filtered
firma	fir-ma	business
fotbal	fot-bal	football • soccer
fotka	fot-ka	photo
foto-kino	fo-to-ki-no	camera shop
fotoaparát	fo-to-a-pa-raat	camera
fotograf	fo-to-graf	photographer
fotografie	fo-to-gra-fi-ye	photography
fronta	fron-ta	queue

galerie	ga-le-ri-ye	art gallery
garáž	ga-raazh	garage
gay	gay	gay
grafika	gra-fi-ka	graphic art

Gratuluji!
gra-tu-lu-yi!
Congratulations!

gymnastika	gim-nas-ti-ka	gymnastics

hádat	haa-dat	to guess
hádat se	haa-dat se	to argue
hádka	haad-ka	quarrel
hašiš	ha-shish	hash
hedváb	hed-vaab	silk

helma	hel-ma	helmet
hezký	hes-kee	handsome • pretty
HIV	HIV	HIV
pozitivní	po-zi-tiv-nyee	positive
hlas	hlas	voice
hlásatel/ka (m/f)	hlaa-sa-tel/-ka	presenter (TV etc)
hlasitě	hla-si-tye	loud
hlasování	hla-so-vaa-nyee	polls
hlava	hla-va	head
hlavní	hlav-nyee	head
hlavní	hlav-nyee	main
hlavní cesta	hlav-nyee tses-ta	main road
hlavní náměstí	hlav-nyee naa-mye-stee	main square
hledat	hle-dat	to look for
hloupý	hloh-pee	stupid
hluboko	hlu-bo-ko	deep
hluchý	hlu-khee	deaf
hluční	hluch-nyee	noisy
hluk	hluk	noise
hnědý	hnye-dee	brown
hoch	hokh	boy
hodinky	ho-dyin-ki	watch
hodiny	ho-dyi-ni	clock
hodnotný	hod-not-nee	valuable
holit se	ho-lit se	to shave
holící strojek	ho-lee-tsee stro-yek	razor
holka	hol-ka	girl
homeopatie	ho-me-o-pa-ti-ye	homeopathy
homosexuál	ho-mo-seks-u-aal	homosexual
hora	ho-ra	mountain
horečka	ho-rech-ka	fever • temperature (fever)
horko	hor-ko	heat
hořký	horzh-kee	hot

horolezectví	ho-ro-lez-ets-tvee	mountaineering • rock climbing
horská chata	hor-skaa kha-ta	mountain hut
horské kolo	hor-skeh ko-lo	mountain bike
hospodářství	hos-pod-aarzh-stvee	economy
hotový	ho-to-vee	ready
houně	hoh-nye	rug
hra	hra	game (sport/ games) • play (the atre)
hráč (sports)	hraach	player
hrací automat	hra-tsee ow-to-mat	pinball
hrad	hrad	castle
hraničit	hra-nyi-chit	border
hrát	hraat	to play (a game/ music)
hrát karty	hraat kar-ti	to play cards
hrdlo	hrd-lo	throat
hrdost	hr-dost	pride
hřbet	hrzh-bet	back (body)
hřeben	hrzhe-ben	comb
hřích	hrzheekh	sin
hrnčířství	hrn-cheerzh-stvee	pottery
hrob	hrob	grave
hrozna	hroz-na	grapes
hrozný	hroz-nee	horrible • terrible • awful
hruď	hrudy	chest
hubička	hu-bich-ka	kiss
hudba	hud-ba	music
hudebník	hu-deb-nyeek	musician
hvězdy	hvye-zdi	stars
hydratační krém	hi-dra-tach-nee krem	moisturiser

CH

chápat	khaa-pat	to understand
chlapec	khla-pets	boy
chléb	khlehb	bread
chodit	kho-dyit	to walk
chodník	khod-nyeek	footpath • path
chrám	khraam	temple
chráněné druhy	khraa-nye-neh dru-hi	protected species
chráněný les	khraa-nye-nee les	protected forest
chránit	khraa-nyit	to protect
chtít	khtyeet	to want
chudoba	khu-do-ba	poverty
chudý	khu-dee	poor
chutný	khut-nee	tasty
chyba	khi-ba	mistake • fault
chybný	khib-nee	faulty

I

identifikačná karta	i-den-ti-fi-kach-naa kar-ta	identification card
informační centrum	in-for-mach-nee tsen-trum	tourist information office
injekce	in-yek-tse	injection
intensivní	in-ten-siv-nyee	intense
invalida	in-va-lida	disabled
invalidní vozík	in-vah-lid-nyee vo-zeek	wheelchair
inženýr	in-zhe-neer	engineer

J

já	yaa	I
jak	yak	how
jakýkoli	ya-kee-ko-li	any
jaro	ya-ro	spring (season)
jasný	yas-nee	light (clear)
jasný	yas-nee	obvious

Je mi líto.
ye mi lee-to
I'm sorry.

jazyky	ja-zi-ki	languages
jeden	ye-den	single
jediný	ye-di-nye	(unique)
jedenkrát	ye-den-kraat	one time
jedle	yed-le	fir
jedno-duchý	yed-no-du-khee	simple
jedno-lůžkový pokoj	yed-no-loozh-ko-vee po-koy	single room
jedno-směrná (jízdenka)	yed-no-smyer-naa (yeez-den-ka)	one-way (ticket)
jednou	yed-noh	once
jehla	ye-hla	needle (sewing)
jelen	ye-len	deer
jenom	ye-nom	only
jeptiška	yep-tyish-ka	nun
jeskyně	yes-ki-nye	caves
ještě ne	yesh-tye ne	not yet
jezdit na kole	yez-dyit na ko-le	to cycle
jezdit na koni	yez-dyit na ko-nyi	horse riding • to ride (a horse)
jezdit	yez-dyit	to drive
jezero	ye-ze-ro	lake
jídelní lístek	yee-del-nyee lees-tek	menu

jídelní vůz	yee-del-nyee vooz	dining car
jídlo	yeed-lo	food
jih	yih	south
jiný	yi-nee	other
jíst	yeest	to eat

Jistě.
yis-tye
Sure.

jít	yeet	to go • pass
již	yizh	yet • already
jízdní řád	yeez-dnyee rzhaad	timetable
jízvy	yeez-vi	scarves
již dávno	yizh daav-no	(a while) ago
jméno	ymeh-no	(christian) name
jsem schopen	ysem skho-pen	can (to be able)

K

K	k	towards
kabát	ka-baat	(over)coat
kabelka	ka-bel-ka	handbag
kalendář	ka-len-daarzh	calendar
kalhoty	kal-ho-ti	trousers
kámen	kaa-men	stone
kamera	ka-me-ra	camera
kamna	kam-na	stove
kapesní nůž	ka-pes-nyee noozh	penknife
kapsa	kap-sa	pocket
karanténa	ka-ran-teh-na	quarantine
karikatúry	ka-ri-ka-too-ri	cartoons
kartáč na vlasy	kar-taach na vla-si	hairbrush
kartón	kar-tawn	carton
karty	kar-ti	cards • playing cards
kašel	ka-shel	a cough

CZECH–ENGLISH DICTIONARY

katedrála	ka-te-draa-la	cathedral
katolický	ka-to-lits-kee	Catholic
kavárna	ka-vaar-na	a bar/café
každý	kazh-dee	each
každý den	kazh-dee den	every day
kazeta	ka-ze-ta	cassette
kde	gde	where
kdo	gdo	who
kdy	gdi	if • when
ke	ke	towards
kempink	kem-pink	campsite
kempovat	kem-po-vat	to camp
keramický	ke-ram-its-kee	ceramic
keramika	ke-ra-mi-ka	pot (ceramic)
kino	ki-no	cinema
kladivo	kla-dyi-vo	hammer
klášter	klaa-shter	convent • monastery
klávesnice	klaa-ves-nyi-tse	keyboard
klepat	kle-pat	to type
klíč	kleech	key
klient	kli-ent	client
klimatizace	kli-ma-ti-za-tse	air-conditioned
kluk	kluk	boy
kněz	knyez	priest
kniha	knyi-ha	book
knihkupectví	knyi-ku-pet-stvee	bookshop
knihovna	knyi-hov-na	library
knoflíky	knof-lee-ki	buttons
koberček	ko-ber-chek	rug
kočka	koch-ka	cat
kojenec	ko-ye-nets	baby
kojenecká výživa	ko-ye-nets-kaa vee-zhi-va	baby food
kokain	ko-ka-in	cocaine
koláč	ko-laach	pie
kolega	ko-le-ga	colleague
koleno	ko-le-no	knee
koleso	ko-le-so	wheel
kolo	ko-lo	bicycle • bike

komedie	ko-me-di-ye	comedy
kompas	kom-pas	compass
kompakt	kom-pakt	CD
komunista	ko-mun-ist-a	communist
končit	kon-chit	to end
konec	ko-nets	end
kontaktní čočky	kon-takt-nyee choch-ki	contact lenses
kontrakt	kon-trakt	contract
kontrola	kon-tro-la	to check
kontrolní stanoviště	kon-trol-nyee sta-no-vish-tye	checkpoint
konzerva	kon-zer-va	can (tin)
konzervativní	kon-zer-va-tiv-nyee	conservative
konzulát	kon-zu-laat	consulate
kopaná	ko-pa-naa	football (soccer)
kopat	ko-pat	kick
kopec	ko-pets	hill
koš	kosh	basket
košík	kosh-eek	basket
košile	ko-shi-le	shirt
kost	kost	bone
kostel	kos-tel	church
kostka	kost-ka	dice • die
kostka mýdla	kost-ka meed-la	bar of soap
kotě	ko-tye	kitten
koupel	koh-pel	bath
koupelna	koh-pel-na	bathroom
koupit	koh-pit	to buy
kouřit	kohr-zhit	to smoke
kousnutí	kohs-nu-tyee	bite (dog)
kouzelník	koh-zel-nyeek	magician
kov	kov	metal
koza	ko-za	goat
kožené výrobky	ko-zhe-neh vee-rob-ki	leather-goods
krabice	kra-bi-tse	box • carton
kraj	kray	border
krajka	kray-ka	lace
král	kraal	king

králík	kraa-lick	rabbit
královna	kraa-lov-na	queen
krásný	kraa-snee	beautiful
krást	kraast	to steal
krátke filmy	kraat-ke fil-mi	short films
krátke povídky	kraat-ke po-veet-ki	short stories
krátky	kraat-ki	short (length)
kráva	kraa-va	cow
kredenec	kre-de-nets	cupboard
kreditní karta	kre-dit-nyee kar-ta	credit card
kreslené filmy	kre-sleh-neh film-i	cartoons
krev	kref	blood
krevní skupina	krev-nyee sku-pi-na	blood group
krevní tlak	krev-nyee tlak	blood pressure
krevní zkouška	kref-nee zkoh-shka	blood test
kriket	kri-ket	cricket
krk	krk	throat
kruhový objezd	kru-ho-vee ob-yezd	(at the) round-about
krumpáč	krum-paach	pick • pickaxe
krvácet	krvaa-tset	to bleed
krysa	kri-sa	rat
křeslo	krzhe-slo	chair
křest	krzhest	baptism
křičet	krzhi-chet	to shout
křídla	krzhee-dla	wings
kříž	krzheezh	cross (religious)
kterýkoli	kte-ree-ko-li	any
kuchyně	ku-khi-nye	kitchen
kufr	ku-fr	suitcase
kulatý	ku-la-tee	round
kulečník	ku-lech-nyeek	pool (game)
kulička	ku-lich-ka	ball
kůň	koony	horse
kupón	ku-pawn	coupon
kuře	ku-rzhe	chicken
kurt	kurt	court (tennis)
kurz	kurz	exchange rate
kus	kus	piece
kůže	koo-zhe	leather • skin
kvalifikace	kva-li-fi-ka-tse	qualifications
kvalita	kva-li-ta	quality
květina	kvye-tyi-na	flower
kvíz	kveez	a game show
kyslík	ki-sleek	oxygen
kytara	ki-ta-ra	guitar

L

láhev	laa-hev	bottle
láhev na vodu	laa-hev na vo-du	water bottle
lahůdky	la-hood-ki	delicatessen
lámat	laa-mat	to break
lampa	lam-pa	light (sun/lamp)
laskavý	la-ska-vee	kind
lázeň	laa-zeny	bath
led	led	ice
lednička	led-nyich-ka	refrigerator
legalizace	le-ga-li-za-tse	legalisation
legislace	le-gi-sla-tse	legislation
legitimace	le-gi-ti-ma-tse	permit
lehko	leh-ko	easy
lehký	le-hkee	light (adj)
lék	lehk	medicine
lékárna	leh-kaar-na	pharmacy • chemist

lekárnička	le-kaar-nyich-ka	first-aid kit
první pomoci	prv-nyee po-mo-tsi	
lékař	leh-karzh	doctor
lékařství	leh-karzh-stvee	medicine
lenivý	le-nyi-vee	lazy
lepší	lep-shee	better
les	les	forest • wood
lesbický	les-bits-kee	lesbian
let	let	flight
letadlo	le-tad-lo	aeroplane
létat	leh-tat	to fly
letěcky	le-tyets-ki	air mail
letiště	le-tyish-tye	airport
letištní poplatek	le-tyisht-nyee po-pla-tek	airport tax
léto	leh-to	summer
levé křídlo	le-veh krzhee-dlo	left-wing
levicový	le-vi-tso-vee	left-wing
levný	lev-nee	cheap
lézt	lehst	to climb
lhář	lhaarzh	liar
lhát	lhaat	to lie
líbat	lee-bat	to kiss
lidi	li-dyi	people
lidská práva	lid-skaa praa-va	human rights
líný	lee-nee	lazy
list	list	sheet (of paper)
lístek	lee-stek	ticket
lišta	lish-ta	ledge
litovat	li-to-vat	to regret
loď	lody	ship
lokální	lo-kaal-nyee	local
loni	lo-nyi	last year
ložnice	lozh-nyits-e	bedroom
lukra- tivnost	lu-kra- tiv-nost	profit- ability
luxus	lu-ksus	luxury
lúzer	loo-zer	loser
lůžko	loozh-ko	bed

lyžování	li-zho-vaa-nyee	skiing
lyžovat	li-zho-vat	to ski

M

majitel	ma-yi-tel	owner
malíř	ma-leerzh	painter
málo	maa-lo	few • a little (amount)
malovat obraz	ma-lo-vat o-braz	painting (the art)
malovat	ma-lo-vat	to paint
malý	ma-lee	little (small) • short (height)
máma	maa-ma	Mum
manažer	ma-na-zher	manager
manifes- tace	ma-ni-fes- ta-tse	rally
manuskript	ma-nu-skript	script
manžel	man-zhel	husband
manželka	man-zhel-ka	wife
manželství	man-zhel-stvee	marriage
mapa	ma-pa	map
marihuana	ma-ri-hu-a-na	marijuana • pot (dope)
matka	mat-ka	mother
matrace	ma-tra-tse	mattress
meč	mech	sword
med	med	honey
medaile	me-daile	medal
meditace	me-di-ta-tse	meditation
melodie	me-lo-di-ye	tune
méně	meh-nye	less
menstru- ace	men-stru- a-tse	menstru- ation
menstru- ační bolesti	men-stru- ach-nyee bo-les-tyi	period pain
menší	men-shee	less
menštru- ační vložky	men-shtru- ach-nyee vlozh-ki	sanitary napkins

mentolové (cigarety)	men-to-lo-veh (tsi-ga-re-ti)	menthol (cigarettes)
měsíc	mye-seets	month • moon
mešita	me-shi-ta	mosque
město	mye-sto	city
městský autobus	myest-skee ow-to-bus	local/city bus
meteor	me-te-or	meteor
metro	met-ro	subway station
mezi	me-zi	among • between
mezinárodní	me-zi-naa-rod-nyee	international
míchat	mee-khat	to mix
migréna	mi-greh-na	migraine
milenec (m)	mi-le-nets	lover (m)
milenka (f)	mi-len-ka	lover (f)
milovat	mi-lo-vat	to love
mince	min-tse	coins
minerálka	mi-ne-raal-ka	mineral water
ministerský předseda	mi-ni-ster-skee przhed-se-da	prime minister
minulý měsíc	mi-nu-lee mye-seets	last month
minulý	mi-nu-lee	past
minulost	mi-nu-lost	past
minuta	mi-nu-ta	a minute
mír	meer	peace
místnost	meest-nost	room
místo	mee-sto	location • place • venue • seat
místo narození	mee-sto na-ro-ze-nyee	place of birth
místo určení	mee-sto ur-che-nyee	destination
mít	meet	to have
mít halucinace	meet ha-lu-tsi-na-tse	to hallucinate
mít hlad	meet hlad	to be hungry
mít hodnotu	meet hod-no-tu	worth
mít pravdu	meet prav-du	to be right
mít rád	meet raad	to like
mít zácpu	meet zaats-pu	to be constipated
mládež	mlaa-dezh	youth (collective)
mladý	mla-dee	young
mléčné výrobky	mleh-chneh vee-rob-ki	dairy products
mléko	mleh-ko	milk
mluvit	mlu-vit	to speak • to talk
mnich	mnyikh	monk
mnoho	mno-ho	a lot

Mnoho štěstí!
mno-ho shtye-styee!
Good luck!

mnozí	mno-zee	many
množství	mnozh-stvee	volume
mobil	mo-bil	mobile phone
moc	mots	power • a lot
moct	mo-tst	able (to be) • can
modem	mo-dem	modem
modlitba	mod-lit-ba	prayer
modlitební knížka	mod-li-teb-nyee knyeezh-ka	prayer book
módní člověk	mawd-nyee chlo-vyek	trendy (person)
modrý	mod-ree	blue
mohu	mo-hu	can (to be able)
mokrý	mok-ree	wet

Moment!
mo-ment!
Just a minute.

CZECH–ENGLISH DICTIONARY

morče	mor-che	guinea pig
moře	mo-rzhe	sea
most	most	bridge
motocykl	mo-to-tsi-kl	motorcycle
motor	mo-tor	engine
motorový člun	mo-to-ro-vee chlun	motorboat
motýl	mo-teel	butterfly
moucha	moh-kha	a fly
moudrý	mohd-ree	wise
mouka	moh-ka	flour
možná	mozh-naa	maybe
možný	mozh-nee	possible
mračno	mrach-no	cloud
mrak	mrak	cloud
mravenec	mra-ve-nets	ant
mražené jídla	mra-zhe-neh yee-dla	frozen foods
mrtvý	mr-tvee	dead
mrzutý	mr-zu-tee	cross (angry)
mše	mshe	mass (Catholic)
mušle	mush-le	shell
muž	muzh	man
my	mi	we
mýdlo	meed-lo	soap
mysl	mi-sl	mind
myslet	mis-let	to think
myš	mish	mouse
myšlení	mish-le-nyee	mind
myšlenka	mish-len-ka	thought
mýt	meet	to wash (something)

N

na	na	on
na dně	na dnye	(at the) bottom
na palubě	na pa-lu-bye	aboard
na volné noze	na vol-neh no-ze	self-employed
náboženství	naa-bozhen-stvee	religion
nábožný	naa-bozh-nee	religious
načas	na-chas	on time
nachlazení	nakh-la-ze-nyee	a cold
nad	nad	above
nádherný	naad-her-nee	wonderful
nádoba	naa-do-ba	jar
nádraží	naa-dra-zhee	railway station
nadrogovaný	na-drogo-va-nee	stoned (drugged)
náhlá	naa-hla	emergency
příhoda	przhe-ho-da	
náhoda	naa-ho-da	chance
náhrada	naa-hra-da	refund
nahrávka	na-hraav-ka	recording
náhrdelník	naa-hr-del-nyeek	necklace
nájemné	naa-yem-neh	rent
najít	na-yeet	to find
náklaďák	naa-kla-dyaak	truck
nákladný	naa-klad-nee	expensive
nakupovat	na-ku-po-vat	to go shopping
náměstí	naa-mye-styee	square (town)
naplnit	na-pl-nyit	to fill
například ...	na-przhih-klahd	for example ...
narkoman	nar-ko-man	heroin addict
narkomanie	nar-koma-ni-ye	drug addiction
národní park	naa-rod-nyee park	national park
národnost	naa-rod-nost	nationality
narozeninový dort	na-ro-zenyi-no-vee dort	birthday cake
narozeniny	na-ro-ze-nyi-ni	birthday

Na shledanou zítra.
na-shle-da-noh zee-tra
See you tomorrow.

Na shledanou.
na-shle-da-noh
Goodbye. • See you later.

následovat	naa-sle-do-vat	to follow
nastoupit	nas-toh-pit	to board (ship/etc)
nástupiště	naa-stu-pish-tye	platform
natírat	na-tyee-rat	to paint
náušnice	naa-ush-nyi-tse	earrings
navěky	na-vye-ki	forever
návrh	naa-vrh	proposal
navštívit	nav-shtyee-vit	to visit

Nazdraví!
na-zdra-vee!
Bless you! (when sneezing) •
Good health! • Cheers!

názor	naa-zor	opinion
ne	ne	no
nebe	ne-be	sky
nebez-	ne-bez-	dangerous
pečný	pech-nee	• unsafe
nebo	ne-bo	or
něco	nye-tso	something
nedávno	ne-daav-no	recently
nedávný	ne-daav-nee	recent

Nedělej si starosti!
ne-dye-ley si sta-ros-tyi!
Forget about it! • Don't worry!

nedostatek	ne-dos-ta-tek	shortage
něhoda	nye-ho-da	accident
nejlepší	ney-lep-shee	best
někdo	nye-gdo	somebody • someone
někdy	nye-gdi	sometimes
několik	nye-ko-lik	several
některý	nye-kte-ree	some
nemoc	ne-mots	a sickness
nemocnice	ne-mots-nyi-tse	hospital

nemocný	ne-mots-nee	sick • ill
němý	nye-mee	mute

Není povoleno.
ne-nyee po-vo le-no
It's not allowed.

Není to důležité.
ne-nee to doo-le-zhi-teh
It's not important.

nepocho-	ne-po-kho-	incompre-
pitelné	pi-tel-neh	hensible
nepřímý	ne-przhee-mee	non-direct
nerovnost	ne-rov-nost	inequality
nesprávný	ne-spraav-nee	wrong

Nevadí.
ne-va-dyee
(It doesn't) matter.

Nevím.
ne-veem
I don't know.

nevýhoda	ne-vee-ho-da	disad-vantage
nezaměst-	ne-za-myest-	unem-
nanost	na-nost	ployment
nezaměst-	ne-za-myest-	unem-
naný	na-nee	ployed
neznámý	ne-znaa-mee	strange
nezpů-	nez-poo-	disabled
sobilý	so-bi-lee	
nezvyklý	ne-zvi-klee	unusual
nic	nyits	nothing
nikdy	nyik-di	never
nízký	neez-kee	low
nízký/	neez-kee/	low/high
vysoký	vi-so-kee	
krevní tlak	krev-nyee tlak	blood pressure
noc	nots	night
nocle-	no-tsle-	youth
hárna pro	haar-na pro	hostel
mládež	mlaa-dezh	
noha	no-ha	leg • foot

CZECH–ENGLISH DICTIONARY

normální	nor-maal-nyee	ordinary
nos	nos	nose
nosit	no-siht	to carry • to wear
novinář	no-vin-aarzh	journalist
noviny	no-vih-ni	newspaper(s)
nový	no-vee	new
Nový rok	no-vee rok	New Year's Day
nudný	nud-nee	boring
nůž	noozh	knife
nůžky	noozh-ki	scissors

O

oba	o-ba	both
obálka	o-baal-ka	envelope
občanské práva	ob-chan-skeh praa-va	civil rights
občanství	ob-chan-stvee	citizenship
obchod	ob-khod	shop • business
obchod s kamerami	ob-khod ska-me-ra-mi	camera shop
obchod se suvenýry	ob-khod se su-ve-nee-ri	souvenir shop
obchodní dům	ob-khod-nyee doom	department stores
obchodní oddělení	ob-khod-nyee od dye-le-nyee	sales department
obchod se zeleninou a ovocím	ob-khod se ze-le-nyi-noh a o-vo-tseem	greengrocer
obchodník	ob-khod-nyeek	business person
obdivovat	ob-dyi-vo-vat	to admire
obecný	oh-bets-nee	general
oběd	o-byed	lunch
objednat	ob-yed-nat	to book (make a booking) • to order

objednávka	ob-yed-naav-ka	order
objem	ob-yem	volume
objetí	o-bye-tee	a cuddle • a hug
objevit	ob-ye-vit	to discover
oblak	o-blak	cloud
oblastní	ob-last-nyee	regional
oblékat	ob-leh-kat	to dress
obličej	o-bli-chey	face
obloha	o-lo-ha	sky
obrazovka	o-bra-zof-ka	screen • monitor
obrazy	o-bra-zy	paintings
obuv	o-buf	shoe shop
obvaz	ob-vaz	bandage
obyčejná pošta	o-bi-chey-naa posh-ta	surface mail
obyčejný	o-bi-chey-nee	plain
ocas	o-tsas	tail
oceán	o-tse-aan	ocean
očkování	och-ko-vaa-nyee	vaccination
od (května)	od (kvyet-na)	since (May)
obor	o-bor	branch
odbor pro nezaměstnané	od-bor pro ne-za-myest-na-neh	job centre
odborník	od-bor-nyeek	specialist
odbory	ot-bo-ri	trade union(s)
odchod	od-khod	departure
odejít	o-de-yeet	to depart (leave)
oděvy	od-ye-vi	clothing store
odfotit	ot-fo-tyit	to take photographs
odlesňování	od-les-nyo-vaa-nyee	deforestation
odlišný	od-lish-nee	different
odložit	od-lo-zhit	delay

odmítnout	od-meet-noht	to refuse
odpadky	od-pad-ki	rubbish • garbage
odpočinek	ot-po-chi-nek	rest (relaxation)
odpočívat	ot-po-chee-vat	to rest
odpoledne	od-po-led-ne	(in the) afternoon
odpověď	od-po-vyedy	answer
odpovídat	od-po-vee-dat	answering
odpustit	ot-pus-tyit	to forgive
odraz	od-raz	reflection (mirror)
okrást	o-kraa-st	rip-off
odrůda	od-roo-da	kind
odsunout	od-su-noht	delay
odvážný	od-vaazh-nee	brave
odvětví	od-vye-tvee	branch
ofsajd	of-sayd	offside
oheň	o-heny	fire
ohrada	o-hra-da	fence
ohřívač	o-hrzhee-vach	heater
ohrozené druhy	o-hro-ze-neh dru-hi	endangered species
okno	ok-no	window
oko	o-ko	eye
okouzlující	o-kohz-lu-yee-tsi	charming
okradnout	o-krad-noht	rip-off
okraj	o-kray	border
okrást	o-kraast	to rob
olej	o-ley	oil (cooking)
olivový olej	o-li-vo-vee o-ley	olive oil
olivy	o-li-vi	olives
olovnatý	o-lov-na-tee	leaded (petrol/gas)
olympijské hry	o-lim-pi-yskeh hri	Olympic Games
omezení rychlosti	o-me-ze-nyee rikh-lo-styi	speed limit
on	on	he
ona	o-na	she
onemocnění	o-ne-mots-nye-nyee	disease
oni	o-nyi	they
opačný	o-pach-nee	opposite
opakovat	o-pa-ko-vat	to repeat
opalovací krém	o-pa-lo-va-tsee krehm	sunblock
opatěra dítěte	o-pa-tye-ra dyee-tye-te	child-minding
operace	o-pe-ra-tse	operation
operatér	o-pe-ra-tehr	operator
opět	o-pyet	again
opít se	o-peet se	to be drunk
opravit	o-pra-vit	to repair
oranžová	o-ran-zho-vaa	orange (colour)
organizovat	or-ga-ni-zo-vat	organise
orgasmus	or-gas-mus	orgasm
originální	o-ri-gi-naal-nyee	original
osamělý	o-sam-ye-lee	alone
osoba	o-so-ba	person
osobnost	o-sob-nost	personality
ospalý	o-spa-lee	sleepy
ostrov	os-trov	island
otázka	o-taaz-ka	question
otec	o-tets	father
otevírání	o-te-vee-raa-nyee	opening
otevřený	o-te-vrzhe-nee	open
otevřít	o-te-vrzheet	to open
otvírač na láhve	ot-vee-rach na laa-hve	bottle opener
otvírač na konzervy	ot-vee-rach na kon-zer-vi	can opener
otvírač na plechovky	ot-vee-rach na ple-khof-ki	tin opener
otvor	ot-vor	opening
ovce	of-tse	sheep
ověření	o-vye-rzhe-nyee	to check

CZECH–ENGLISH DICTIONARY

ozonová vrstva	o-zo-no-vaa vr-stva	ozone layer
oženit se (m)	o-zhe-nyit se	to marry (m)

P

pach	pakh	a smell
páchnout	paakh-noht	to smell
palác	pa-laats	palace
palivové dřevo	pa-li-vo-veh drzhe-vo	firewood
paluba (lodě)	pa-lu-ba (lo-dye)	deck (of ship)
palubní karta	pa-lub-nyee kar-ta	boarding pass
pamatovat si	pa-ma-to-vat si	to remember
panenky	pa-nen-ki	dolls
paní u dítěte	pa-nyee u dyee-tye-te	baby-sitter
panvice	pan-vi-tse	pan
papír	pa-peer	paper
papírnictví	pa-peer-nits-tvee	stationers
papírový kapesník	pa-pee-ro-vee ka-pes-nyeek	tissues
pár	paar	pair (a couple)
pára	paa-ra	steam
park	park	a park
parkovat	park-o-vat	to park
parlament	par-la-ment	parliament
pas	pas	passport
pasažér	pa-sa-zhehr	passenger
pasivní	pa-siv-nyee	passive
pátek	paa-tek	Friday
paže	pa-zhe	arm
pekárna	pe-kaar-na	bakery
pěkný	pyek-nee	nice
penis	pe-nis	penis
peníze	pe-nyee-ze	money
penzista	pen-zis-ta	pensioner

pepř	pe-przh	pepper
permanentní	per-ma-nen-tnyee	permanent
pero (kuličkové)	pe-ro (ku-lich-ko-veh)	pen (ball point)
pes	pes	dog
pěší	pye-shee	pedestrian
petice	pe-ti-tse	petition
pevný	pev-nee	solid
píchnout injekci	peekh-noht in-yek-tsi	to inject
pikantní (pálivý)	pi-kant-nyee (paa-li-vee)	spicy (hot)
písek	pee-sek	sand
píseň	pee-seny	song
pít	peet	to drink
pitomý	pi-to-mee	stupid
plachý	pla-khee	shy
plachta	pla-khta	sheet (bed)
plakát	pla-kaat	poster
planeta	pla-ne-ta	planet
plášť	plaa-shty	coat • cloak
plat	plat	salary
platba	plat-ba	payment
platit	pla-tyit	to pay
plavání	pla-vaa-nyee	swimming
plavat	pla-vat	to swim
plavky	plav-ki	bathing suit • swimsuit
pláž	plaazh	beach
konzerva	kon-zer-va	tin (can)
plechovka	ple-khov-ka	can (tin)
plénka	plehn-ka	nappy • diaper
plný	pl-nee	full
plot	plot	fence
plynová bombička	pli-no-vaa bom-bich-ka	gas cartridge
pneumatiky	pne-u-ma-ti-ki	tyres
PNS	PNS	news-agency

po	po	after
pobožnost	po-bozh-nohst	worship
pobřeží	po-brzhe-zhee	coast
počasí	po-cha-see	weather
počíta-čové hry	po-chee-ta-cho-veh hri	computer games
počítat	po-chee-tat	to count
pod	pod	below
podepsat	po-dep-sat	to sign
pódium • jeviště	paw-di-um • ye-vish-tye	stage
podívat se	po-dyee-vat se	to look
podívat se na výklady		
po-dyee-vat se na vee-kla-di		
to (go) window-shopping		
podlaha	pod-la-ha	floor
podnik	pod-nyik	business
podnikatel	pod-nyi-ka-tel	business person
podobný	po-dob-nee	similar
podpis	pod-pis	signature
podplácet	pod-plaa-tset	to bribe
podpora v nezaměstanosti	pod-po-ra v ne-za-mye-sta-nos-tyi	dole
podtitulky	pod-ti-tul-ki	subtitles
podvodník	pod-vod-nyeek	a cheat
podzim	pod-zim	autumn • fall
poezie	po-e-zi-ye	poetry
pohádka	po-haad-ka	story
pohlavní nemoc	po-hlav-nyee ne-mots	venereal disease
pohlednice	po-hled-ni-tse	postcard
pohmož-děnina	po-mozh-dye-nyi-na	a bruise
pohodlný	po-ho-dl-nee	comfortable
pohoří	po-ho-rzhee	mountain range
pohotovost	po-ho-to-vost	emergency

pohraniční území	po-hra-nich-nyee oo-ze-mee	border
pohřeb	po-hrzheb	funeral
pojištění	po-yish-tye-nyee	insurance
pokladna	po-klad-na	cash register • ticket office
pokladník	po-klad-nyeek	cashier
pokus	po-kus	to try (to attempt)
pokuta	po-ku-ta	a fine
pole	po-le	field
poledne	po-led-ne	lunchtime • noon
polibek	po-li-bek	kiss
police	po-li-tse	shelves
policie	po-li-tsi-ye	police
politici	po-li-ti-tsi	politicians
politický projev	po-li-tits-kee pro-yev	political speech
politika	po-li-ti-ka	politics
polštář	pol-shtaarzh	pillow
pomaly	po-ma-li	slow • slowly
pomník	pom-nyeek	shrine • monument
pomoc	po-mots	aid (help)

Pomoc!
po-mots!
Help!

pomoct	po-mo-tst	to help
popelník	po-pel-nyeek	ashtray
popis prácovní náplně	po-pis praa-tsov-nye naa-pl-nye	job description
poprosit	po-pro-sit	to ask (for something)
populární	po-pu-laar-nyee	popular
portské	port-skeh	port
portrétista	por-treh-tis-ta	portrait sketcher
pořád	po-rzhaad	forever

pořádek	po-rzhaa-dek	order
poschodí	po-skho-dyee	floor (storey)
posílat	po-see-lat	to ship
posilovna	po-si-lov-na	gym
poslat	pos-lat	to send
poslední	pos-led-nyee	last
poslouchat	po-sloh-khat	to listen
pošta	posh-ta	mail• post office
postel	post-el	bed
postižený paraplegií	po-styi-zhe-nee pa-ra-pleg-i-ee	paraplegic
poštovné	posh-tov-neh	postage
poštovní schránka	posh-tov-nyee skhraan-ka	mailbox
poštovní směrovací číslo	posh-tov-nee smye-ro-va-tsee chee-slo	post code
postrádat	pos-traa-dat	to miss (feel absence)
postroj	post-roy	harness
posudek	po-su-dek	reference
potápění	po-taa-pye-nyee	diving
potit se	po-tyit se	to perspire
potkan	pot-kan	rat
potkat	pot-kat	to meet
potok	po-tok	stream
potrat	pot-rat	abortion • miscarriage
potřebný	po-trzheb-nee	necessary
potřebovat	po-trzhe-bo-vat	to need
potrestat	po-tres-tat	to punish
potvrdit	pot-vr-dyit	to confirm (a booking)
poušť	poh-shty	desert
povídat si	po-vee-dat si	to talk
povlak na polštář	pov-lak na pol-shtaarzh	pillowcase
povolení	po-vo-le-nee	permit (n)• permision

povolit	po-vo-lit	to allow
pozadu	po-zah-du	behind
pozdě	poz-dye	late
pozítří	po-zit-rzhee	day after tomorrow
poznat	poz-nat	to recognise

Pozor!
po-zor!
Careful!

požádat	po-zhaa-dat	to ask (for something)
požehnat	po-zheh-nat	to bless
práce	praa-tse	work
práce v kanceláři	praa-tse v kan-tsel-aarzhi	office work
pračka	pra-chka	washing machine
pracovat	pra-tso-vat	to work
pracovní inzerát	pra-tsov-nyee in-ze-raat	job advertisement
pracovní povolení	pra-tsov-nyee po-vo-le-nyee	work permit
pradlenka	prad-len-ka	launderette
prase	pra-se	pig
prášky proti bolesti	praa-shki pro-tyi bo-les-tyi	painkillers
prát	praat	to wash (something)
pravda	prav-da	truth
právě teď	pra-vye te-dye	right now
pravěké umění	pra-vye-keh u-mye-nyee	pre-historic art
pravicový	pra-vi-tso-vee	right-wing
právník	praav-nyeek	lawyer
prázdniny	praazd-nyi-ni	vacation

prázdny	praazd-ni	empty
přát	przhaat	to wish
přečin	przhe-chin	offence
před	przhed	before • in front of
před námi	przhed naa-mi	ahead
před	przhed	(a while) ago
předávkování	przhe-daav-ko-vaa-nyee	overdose
předešlý týden	przhe-desh-lee tee-den	last week
předevčírem	przhe-dev-chee-rem	day before yesterday
předmenstruační napětí	przhed-men-stru-ach-nyee na-pye-tyee	pre-menstrual tension
předměstí	przhed-mye-styee	suburbs of
předseda vlády	przhed-se-da vlaa-di	prime minister
předsíň	przhed-seeny	foyer
představení	przhed-sta-ve-nyee	performance art
přecházet se	przhe-khaa-zet se	to walk
překvapení	przhe-kva-pe-nyee	a surprise
přeložit	przhe-lo-zhit	to translate
přes	przhez	across
přestat	przhes-tat	to quit
přestávka	przhe-staaf-ka	intermission
přez	przhez	over
prezentace	pre-zen-ta-tse	presentation
prezident	pre-zi-dent	president
přežít	przhe-zheet	to survive
přezývka	przhe-zeev-ka	nickname
příchody	przhee-kho-di	arrivals
přihlásit se	przhi-hlaa-sit se	check-in (desk)

přijat	przhi-yat	to accept
přijet	przhi-yet	to come • arrive
přijímání svátosti oltární	przhi-yee-maa-nyee svaa-to-styi ol-taar-nyee	communion
přijít	przhi-yeet	to come • to arrive
příjmení	przhee-me-nyee	surname
přijmout	przhi-ymoht	to admit
příklad	przhee-klad	example
přikrývka	przhi-kreev-ka	blanket
přiletět	przhi-le-tyet	to come • to arrive
příliš drahý	przhe-lish dra-hee	too expensive
příliš moc	przhe-lish mots	too much • many
příliv a odliv	przhee-liv a od-liv	tide

> **Prima!**
> pri-ma!
> **Great!**

přímo	przhee-mo	direct
přinést	przhi-nehst	to bring
připlout	przhi-ploht	to come • to arrive
připravit	przhi-pra-vit	to prepare
připravený	przhi-pra-ve-nee	ready
příroda	przhee-ro-da	nature
příručka	przhee-ruch-ka	guide (audio)
přístav	przhee-stav	harbour
příští měsíc	przhee-shtyee mye-seets	next month
příští rok	przhee-shtyee rok	next year
příští týden	przhee-shtyee tee-den	next week
přítel	prhee-tel	friend • boyfriend

262

CZECH–ENGLISH DICTIONARY

přítelkyně	przeeh-tel-ki-nye	girlfriend
přítomnost	przhee-tom-nost	present (time)
privatizace	pri-va-ti-za-tse	privatisation
privátní nemocnice	pri-vaat-nyee ne-mots-ni-tse	private hospital
privátní	pri-vaat-nyee	private
prominout	pro-min-oht	to forgive
pro legraci	pro le-gra-tsi	for fun
pro zábavu	pro zaa-ba-vu	for fun
proč	proch	why
procento	pro-tsen-to	percent
procházka	pro-khaaz-ka	stroll • walk
prodávat	pro-daa-vat	to sell
produkovat	pro-du-ko-vat	to produce
profese	pro-fe-se	profession
profit	pro-fit	profit
program	pro-gram	program
projektor	pro-yek-tor	projector
projímadlo	pro-yee-mad-lo	laxatives

Promiňte.
pro-mi-ny-te
Excuse me.

pronajmout	pro-nai-moht	to rent
prostěradlo	pro-stye-rad-lo	sheet (bed)
prostor	pro-stor	space
prostředek komárům	pros-trzhe-dek ko-maa-room	mosquito coil
proti	pro-tyi	
prostředí	pro-strzhe-dyee	environment
protest	pro-test	protest
protestovat	pro-tes-to-vat	to protest
proti	pro-tyi	against
protože	pro-to-zhe	because
proud	prohd	stream
provaz	pro-vaz	rope
provedení	pro-ve-de-nee	performance

provoz	pro-voz	traffic

Prší.
prshee
It's raining.

prsa	pr-sa	chest
prst	prst	finger
prsten	pr-sten	ring (on finger)
průjem	proo-yem	diarrhoea
průmysl	proo-misl	industry
průsmyk	proos-mik	mountain path/pass
průvodce	proo-vot-tse	guidebook • guide (person)
průvodčí	proo-vod-chee	ticket collector
pružina	pru-zhi-na	spring (coil)
první	prv-nyee	first
První svátek vánoční	prv-nyee svaa-tek vaa-noch-nyee	Christmas Day
příští	przhee-shtyee	next
psát	psaat	to write
psát na stroji	psaat na stro-yi	to type
pták	ptaak	bird
ptát se	ptaat se	to ask (a question)
půda (soil)	poo-da	earth
půjčit	pooy-chit	to borrow • to hire
půl	pool	half
půl litra	pool lit-ra	half a litre
půlnoc	pool-nots	midnight
pumpa	pum-pa	pump
purpurový	pur-pur-o-vee	purple
půst	poost	Lent
pyl	pil	pollen
pytel	pi-tel	bag

R

rada	ra-da	advice
radiátor	ra-di-aa-tor	radiator
raketa	ra-ke-ta	racquet
rámě	raa-mye	arm
raměna	ra-mye-na	shoulders
rána	raa-na	wound
rande	ran-de	date (appointment)
raný	ra-nee	early
rasa	ra-sa	race (breed)
rasismus	ra-sis-mus	racism
realizovat	re-a-li-zo-vat	to realise
recirkulace	re-tsir-ku-la-tse	recycling
recirkulovatelný	re-tsir-ku-lo-va-tel-nee	recyclable
reference	re-fe-ren-tse	reference
refundace	re-fun-da-tse	refund
relaxovat	re-laks-o-vat	to relax
reprodukce	re-pro-duk-tse	a print (artwork)
republika	re-pub-li-ka	republic
restaurace	res-tow-ra-tse	restaurant
resumé	re-su-meh	resumé
revize	re-vi-ze	review
rezervace	re-zer-va-tse	reservation
rezervovat	re-zer-vo-vat	to reserve
rezignovat	re-zig-no-vat	resignation
rocková skupina	rok-o-vaa sku-pi-na	rock group
roční	roch-nyee	annual
rodiče	ro-dyi-che	parents
rodina	ro-dyi-na	family
rodný list	rod-nee list	birth certificate
roh	ro-h	corner
rohož	ro-hozh	mat
rok	rok	year
román	ro-maan	novel (book) • fiction
romance	ro-man-tse	romance
ropa	ro-pa	oil (crude)
ropucha	ro-pu-kha	toad
rostlina	rost-li-na	plant
rovina	ro-vi-na	flat (land etc) • plateau
rovněž	rov-nyezh	also
rovnost	rov-nost	equality
rovný	rov-nee	straight
rozbít	roz-beet	to break
rozbitý	roz-bi-tee	broken
rozhněvaný	roz-hnye-va-nee	angry
rozhodčí	roz-hod-chee	referee
rozhodnout	roz-hod-noht	to decide
rozkaz	roz-kaz	order
rozpaky	roz-pa-ki	embarrassment
rozsudek	roz-su-dek	sentence (prison)
rozumět	ro-zu-myet	to understand
rozumný	ro-zum-nee	sensible
rozvrh hodin	roz-vr-h ho-din	timetable
rty	r-ti	lips
ručně vyrobeno	ruch-nye vi-ro-be-no	handmade
ručník	ruch-nyeek	towel
rudý	ru-dee	red
ruiny	ru-i-ni	ruins
ruka	ru-ka	hand
růžový	roo-zho-vee	pink
ryba	ri-ba	fish (alive)
Ryba	ri-ba	fish shop
rybina	ri-bi-na	fish (as food)
rychlost	rikh-lost	speed
rychlý	ri-khlee	fast • quick
rýma	ree-ma	a cold
rytmus	rit-mus	rhythm
rýže	ree-zhe	rice

Ř

ředitel	rzhe-dyi-tel	director
řeka	rzhe-ka	river
říct	rzhee-tst	to say
řidičský průkaz	rzhi-dich-skee proo-kaz	driver's licence
řídit	rzhee-dyit	to drive
římsa	rzheem-sa	ledge
řtěnka	rzh-tyen-ka	lipstick

S

s	s	with
sako	sa-ko	coat
sadit	sa-dyit	to plant
sám	saam	alone • single (person)
samoob- sluha	sa-mo-op- slu-ha	self- service
sazba	saz-ba	rate of pay
sázka	saaz-ka	a bet
schodiště	skho-dyish-tye	stairway
schopný rozkladu	skhopn-ee roz-kla-du	biode- gradable
se	se	with
sedadlo	se-da-dlo	seat
sedět	se-dyet	to sit
sekretářka	sek-re-taarzh-ka	secretary
semafor	se-ma-for	traffic lights
senná rýma	sen-naa ree-ma	hayfever
separovat	se-pa-ro-vat	to separate
seriál	se-ri-yaal	soap opera
série	seh-ri-ye	series
servis	ser-vis	service (assist- ance)

sestra	ses-tra	sister
sever	se-ver	north
schod	skhod	step
sídliště	seed-lish-tye	suburb
síla	see-la	strength
silnice	sil-nyi-tse	road (main)
silný	sil-nee	strong • thick
Silvestr	sil-ves-tr	New Year's Eve
sirky	sir-ki	matches
síť	seety	net
síť na houpání	seety na hoh-paa-nyee	hammock
síť proti komárům	see-ty pro-tyi ko-maa-room	mosquito net
skála	skaa-la	rock • wall of rock
sklenička	skle-nyich-ka	glass
skočit	sko-chit	to jump
skoro	sko-ro	almost
skórovat	skaw-ro-vat	to score
skříň	skrzheeny	cupboard
skupina	sku-pi-na	band (music)
skvělý	skvye-lee	brilliant • marvellous
slabý	sla-bee	weak • thin
sladký	slad-kee	sweet
slavit	sla-vit	to celebrate
slavný	sla-vnee	famous
sledovat	sle-do-vat	to watch
slepecký pes	sle-pets-kee pes	guidedog
slepý	sle-pee	blind
sleva	sle-va	discount
slib	slib	promise
slovník	slov-nyeek	dictionary
slovo	slo-vo	word

složit skoušku	slo-zhit skoh-shku	pass
sluchadlo	slu-kha-dlo	hearing aid
slunce	slun-tse	sun
sluneční brýle	slu-nech-nee bree-le	sunglasses
slunečný	slu-nech-nyee	sunny
služba	sluzh-bah	service (assist-ance)
slyšet	sli-shet	to hear
slza (pláč)	slza (plaach)	tear (crying)
smát se	smaat se	to smile • to laugh
smetí	sme-tyee	garbage
směna	smye-na	exchange
smích	smeekh	laugh
smrad	smrad	a smell
smrdět	smr-dyet	to smell
smrt	smrt	death
smutný	smut-nee	sad
snídaně	snyee-da-nye	breakfast
snívat	snyee-vat	to dream
snou-benec (m)	snoh-be-nets	fiancé
snou-benka (f)	snoh-ben-ka	fiancée
sobecký	so-bets-kee	selfish
sobota	so-bo-ta	Saturday
socha	soh-kha	sculpture • statue • monu-ment
socialis-tický	so-tsi-a-lis-tits-kee	socialist
sociálně-demo-kratický	so-tsi-aal-nye-de-mo-kra-tits-kee	social-demo-cratic
sociální péče	so-tsi-aal-nyee peh-che	social welfare

sociální zabez pečení	so-tsi-aal-nyee za-bes-pe-che-nyee	social security
solidní	so-lid-nyee	solid
soud	sohd	court (legal)
soudce	sohd-tse	judge
souhlas	soh-hlas	permis-sion
souhlasit	soh-hla-sit	to agree
soukromý	soh-kro-mee	private
spacák	spa-tsaak	sleeping bag
spací prášky	spa-tsee praa-shki	sleeping pills
spací vůz	spa-tsee vooz	sleeping car
spálený sluncem	spaa-le-nee slun-tsem	sunburn
spát	spaat	to sleep
spěchám	spye-khaam	in a hurry
specialista	spe-tsi-a-lis-ta	specialist
speciální	spe-tsi-aal-nyee	special
spisovatel	spi-so-va-tel	writer
spole-čenské vědy	spo-le-chen-skeh vye-di	social sciences
spole-čenský	spo-le-chen-skee	outgoing
společnost	spo-lech-nost	company
spolehnout se	spo-le-h-noht se	to trust
spolu	spo-lu	together
spor	spor	quarrel
sporák	spo-raak	stove
sportovec	spor-to-vets	sports-person
spořitelna	sporzh-i-tel-na	bank
správce	spraav-tse	curator
spravedl-nost	spra-ve-dl-nost	justice
správný	spraa-vnee	right (correct)
sprcha	spr-kha	shower

CZECH–ENGLISH DICTIONARY

spropitné	spro-pit-neh	tip (gratuity)
sráz	sraaz	cliff
srdce	srt-tse	heart
stadion	sta-di-on	stadium
stálá výstava	staa-laa vee-sta-va	permanent collection
stále	staa-le	forever
stan	stan	tent
standard	stan-dard	standard (usual)
stanové kolíky	sta-no-veh ko-lee-ki	tent pegs
stanoviště taxíků	sta-no-vish-tye taks-ee-koo	taxi stand
starat se	sta-rat se	to look after
staré město	sta-reh mye-sto	old city
starodávný	sta-ro-daav-nee	ancient
starosta	sta-ros-ta	mayor
starostlivý	sta-rost-li-vee	caring
starožitnosti	sta-ro-zhit-nos-tyi	antiques
starý	sta-ree	old
stát	staat	to cost • stop • state
statečný	sta-tech-nee	brave
statek	sta-tek	farm
stav	stav	marital status
stavba	stav-ba	building
stavební práce	sta-veb-nyee praa-tse	construction work
stavět	sta-vyet	to build
stávka	staav-ka	a strike
stávkovat	staav-ko-vat	on strike
stejný	stey-nee	same
stěna	stye-na	wall (inside) • screen
stezka	stez-ka	track (path) • footpath
stín	styeen	shade • shadow
sto	sto	a hundred
stolní tenis	stol-nyee te-nis	table tennis
stopovat	stop-oh-vat	to hitch-hike
stopy	sto-pi	track (foot prints)
stoupat	stoh-pat	to climb
strach	strakh	fear
strana	stra-na	side • page • party (politics)
strašný	strash-nee	awful
střed města	strzhed mye-sta	city centre
střední škola	strzhed-nyee shko-la	high school
stříbrný	strzhee-br-nee	of silver
stříhat	strzhi-hat	to cut
stříkačka	strzhee-kach-ka	needle (syringe)
střílet	strzhee-let	to shoot
strmý	str-mee	steep
stroj	stroy	machine
strojírenství	stroy-ee-ren-stvee	engin-eering
strom	strom	tree
struna	stru-na	spring (coil)
studená voda	stu-de-naa vo-da	cold water
studený	stu-de-nee	cold (adj)
studna	stud-na	well

Stůj!
stooy!
Stop!

stůl	stool	table
stupeň	stu-pe-ny	degree
stvrzenka	stvr-zehn-kah	receipt

stydlivý	stid-li-vee	shy
styl	stil	style
sůl	sool	salt
surfovací prkno	sur-fo-va-tsee prk-no	surfboard
sušič na vlasy	su-shich na vla-si	fan (machine)
sušit prádlo	su-shit praa-dlo	to dry (clothes)
suvenýr	su-ve-neer	souvenir
sužování	su-zho-vaa-nyee	harrassment
svah	sva-h	uphill
sval	sval	muscle
svatba	svat-ba	wedding
svatební cesta	sva-teb-nyee tses-ta	honeymoon
svatební dárek	sva-teb-nyee daa-rek	wedding present
svatební dort	sva-teb-nyee dort	wedding cake
svátek	svaa-tek	festival • holiday
svatý	sva-tee	saint
svatý týden	sva-tee tee-den	Holy Week
svazek	sva-zek	volume
svět	svyet	world
světlo	svye-tlo	light (n)
světový pohár	svye-to-vee po-haar	World Cup
svetr	sve-tr	jumper (sweater)
svíčka	svee-chka	candle
svitání	svi-taa-nyee	dawn
svobodný	svo-bod-nee	single (person)
svrbění	svr-bye-nyee	itch
svrchník	svrkh-nyeek	overcoat
sympatický	sim-pa-tits-kee	sympathetic
syn	sin	son
synagóga	si-na-gaw-ga	synagogue
syntetický	sin-te-tits-kee	synthetic
syr	sir	cheese
syrový	si-ro-vee	raw
sytý	si-tee	rich (food)

Š

šachovnice	sha-khov-nyits-e	chess board
šachy	sha-khy	chess
šálek	shaa-lek	cup
šampaňské	sham-pany-skeh	champagne
šampon	sham-pon	shampoo
šašek	sha-shek	clown
šatna	shut-na	cloakroom
šatník	shat-nyeek	wardrobe
šatny	shat-ni	changing rooms
šaty	sha-ti	clothing • a dress
šedivý	she-dyi-vee	grey
šermování	sher-mo-vaa-nyee	fencing
šikanování	shik-a-no-vaa-nyee	harrassment
šílený	shee-le-nee	crazy • mad
široký	shi-ro-kee	wide
šít	sheet	to sew
škeble	shkeb-le	shell
škola	shkoh-la	school • college
školka	shkol-ka	kindergarten
šňůra	shnoo-ra	line
šortky	short-ki	shorts
špagát	shpa-gaat	string
špatně od žaludku	shpat-nye ot zha-lud-ku	nausea
špatný	shpat-nee	bad • faulty

268

CZECH–ENGLISH DICTIONARY

šperky	shper-ki	jewellery
špinavý	shpi-na-vee	dirty

> **Šťastnou cestu!**
> shtya-stnoh tses-tu!
> Bon voyage!

šťastný	shtya-stnee	happy • lucky
šťáva	shtyaa-va	juice
Štědrý	shtye-dree	Christmas
večer	ve-cher	Eve
štěně	shtye-nye	puppy
štěstí	shtye-styee	luck
štípnutí	shtyeep-nu-tyee	bite (insect)
šunka	shun-ka	ham
šváb	shvaab	bug

T

tabák	ta-baak	tobacco
tabletka	ta-blet-ka	pill
tabule	ta-bu-le	scoreboard
ukazující	u-ka-zu-yee-tsi	
skóre	skaw-re	
tady	ta-di	here
táhnout	taah-noht	to pull
také	ta-keh	also
taky	ta-ki	too (as well)
talíř	ta-leerzh	plate
tampóny	tam-paw-ni	tampons
tancování	tan-tso-vaa-nyee	dancing
tancovat	tan-tso-vat	to dance
taška	tash-ka	bag
táta	taa-ta	dad
technika	tekh-ni-ka	technique
teď	te-ty	now
těhotná	tye-hot-naa	pregnant
telefonní budka	te-le-fon-nyee bud-ka	phone box
telefonní karta	te-le-fon-nyee kar-ta	phone-card
telefonní seznam	te-le-fon-nyee sez-nam	phone book

telefonní ústředna	te-le-fon-nyee oo-strzhed-na	telephone office
telefonovat	te-le-fo-no-vat	to telephone
teleskop	te-le-skop	telescope
televize	te-le-vi-ze	television
televizní aparát	te-le-viz-nyee a-pa-raat	TV set
telka	tel-ka	TV
tělo	tye-lo	body
téměř	tem-yerzh	almost
tenis	te-nis	tennis
tenisový kurt	te-ni-so-vee kurt	tennis court
tenhle	ten-hle	this (one)
tenký	ten-kee	thin
tento měsíc	ten-to mye-seets	this month
tento rok	ten-to rok	this year
tento týden	ten-to tee-den	this week
tento	ten-to	this (one)
teplá voda	tep-laa vo-da	hot water
teplota	te-plo-ta	temperature (weather)
teplý	te-plee	warm • gay/homosexual
termín	ter-meen	appointment
těsný	tyes-nee	tight
teta	te-ta	aunt
též	teh-zh	too (as well) • also
těžký	tye-zh-kee	difficult • heavy • rich (food)
tchán	tkhaan	father-in-law
tchýně	t-khee-nye	mother-in-law
tichý	tyi-khee	quiet (adj)
tým	teem	team

tisk	tisk	a print (artwork)
tlačit	tla-chit	to push
tlak	tlak	pressure
tlustý	tlus-tee	fat • thick
tmavý	tma-vee	dark
toaletní	to-a-let-nyee	toilet
papír	pa-peer	paper
toast	tohst	toast
továrna	to-vaar-na	factory
toxiko-	toks-i-ko-	addiction
manie	ma-ni-e	
toxický	toks-its-kee	toxic
odpad	ot-pad	waste
trafika	tra-fi-ka	tobacco kiosk
trampovat	tram-po-vat	to hike
tramvaj	tram-vai	tram
tranzitní	tran-zit-nyee	transit
hala	ha-la	lounge
trať	traty	track (car-racing/sports) • trail • route
tráva	traa-va	grass
trénink	treh-nink	workout
trezor	tre-zor	safe (n)
tričko	trich-ko	T-shirt
trochu	tro-khu	a little bit
trpělivý	tr-pye-li-vee	patient (adj)
trpět	tr-pyet	to suffer
trpící	trpee-tsee	seasick
mořskou	morzh-skoh	
nemocí	ne-mo-tsee	
tržnice	trzh-nyi-tse	market
třetí	trzhe-tyee	third
třída	trzhee-da	class • avenue
třídní	trzheed-nyee	class
systém	sis-tehm	system
tucet	tu-tset	a dozen
tuhý	tu-hee	solid
túra	too-ra	tour
turista	tu-ris-ta	tourist
turistická	tu-ris-tits-kaa	guided
stezka s	stez-ka s	trek
průvod-	proo-vod-	
cem	tsem	
turistické	tu-ris-tits-keh	hiking
boty	bo-ti	boots
turistické	tu-ris-tits-keh	hiking
stezky	stez-ki	routes
turistika	tu-ris-ti-ka	hiking
tužka	tuzh-ka	pencil
tvar	tvar	shape
tvrdohlavý	tvr-do-hla-vee	stubborn
tvrdý	tvr-dee	hard
týden	tee-den	week
typický	ti-pits-kee	typical

U

ubytování	u-bit-o-vaa-nyee	accommodation
uctívání	uts-tyee-vaa-nyee	worship
učení	u-che-nyee	teaching
účet	oo-chet	bill (account)
ucho	u-kho	ear
učit se	u-chit se	to learn
učitel	u-chi-tel	teacher
udělat	u-dye-lat	to make
udělat krok	u-dye-lat krok	step
údolí	oo-do-lee	valley
ukázat	u-kaa-zat	to show
ukazovat	u-ka-zo-vat	to point
ukončit	u-kon-chit	to end
ukoustnutí	u-kohst-noh-tyee	bite (dog)
ulice	u-li-tse	street
umělá	u-mye-laa	plastic
hmota	hmo-ta	
umělec	u-mye-lets	artist
umělecké	u-myeh-lets-keh	artwork
dílo	dyee-lo	

umělecké	u-mye-lets-keh	crafts •
řemesla	rzhe-me-sla	handicrafts
umění	u-mye-nyee	art
umluvit si	um-lu-vit-si	to chat up
umřít	um-rzheet	to die
umýt se	u-meet se	to wash (oneself)
unavený	u-na-ve-nee	tired
univerzita	u-ni-ver-zi-ta	university
univerzitní diplom	u-ni-ver-zit-nyee dip-lom	degree
úplatek	oo-pla-tek	a bribe
upratování	u-pra-to-vaa-nyee	cleaning
uprchlík	u-prkh-leek	refugee
úřad	oo-rzhad	office
úředník	oo-rzhed-nyeek	office worker
urgentní	ur-gent-nyee	urgent
úschova zava zadel	oos-kho-va za-va-za-del	locker
úsek	oo-sek	trek • leg (in race)
ušetřit	u-shet-rzhit	to save
uši	u-shi	ears
uskutečnit	u-sku-tech-nyit	to realise
úspěch	oo-spyekh	success
ústa	oo-sta	mouth
ustaraný	u-sta-ra-nee	worried
ústní	oos-tnyee	oral
útěs	oo-tyes	(wall of) rock • cliff
úvaha	oo-va-ha	reflection (thinking)
uvažování	u-va-zho-vaa-nyee	reflection (thinking)
uvnitř	u-vnyi-trzh	within
už	uzh	already
užitečný	u-zhi-tech-nee	useful
užívat	u-zhee-vat	to enjoy (oneself)

V

v	v	within
v cizině	v tsi-zi-nye	abroad
v důchodu	vdoo-kho-du	retired
v pohodě	v po-ho-dye	cool (colloquial)
v pohybu	vpo-hi-bu	rolling
v rozpacích	v roz-pa-tseekh	embarassed
vada	va-da	disadvantage
vadný	vad-nee	faulty
váha	vaa-ha	weight
válka	vaal-ka	war
vana	va-na	bath
vařit	va-rzhit	to cook
varovat	va-ro-vat	to warn
vážit	vaa-zhit	to weigh
vážný	vaazh-nee	serious
včera	fche-ra	yesterday

včera odpoledne/večer
fche-ra ot-po-led-ne/ve-cher
yesterday afternoon/evening

včera ráno/dopoledne
fche-ra raa-no/do-po-led-ne
yesterday morning

včera večer	fche-ra ve-cher	last night
včetně	fchet-nye	included
věc	vyets	question (topic)
vdát se (f)	vdaat se	to marry (f)
večer	ve-cher	evening
večeře	ve-che-rzhe	dinner
věda	vye-da	science
vědec	vye-dets	scientist
vědět	vye-dyet	to know (something)
vedle	ved-le	beside • next to
vedoucí	ved-oh-tsee	guide (person)

vegetace	ve-ge-ta-tse	vegetation
vegetarián	ve-ge-ta-ri-aan	vegetarian
vějíř	vye-yeerzh	fan (hand-held)
vejít	ve-yeet	to enter
věk	vyek	age
Velikonoce	veh-li-ko-no-tse	Easter
velikost	ve-li-kost	size
velký	vel-kee	big • great • large
velvyslanec	vel-vi-sla-nets	ambassador
velvyslanectví	vel-vi-sla-nets-tvee	embassy
ven	ven	outside
venkov	ven-kov	countryside
veřejné záchody	ve-rzhey-neh zaa-kho-di	public toilet
věřit	vye-rzhit	to trust
věrný	vyer-nee	loyal
veslování	ve-slo-vaa-nyee	rowing
vesmír	ves-meer	universe
vesnice	ves-nyi-tse	village
věštkyně	vyesht-ki-nye	fortune teller
věta	vye-ta	sentence (words)
větev	vye-tev	branch
většina	vyet-shi-na	majority
věž	vyezh	tower
vězeň	vye-ze-ny	prisoner
vězení	vye-ze-nyee	prison
věznice	vye-znyi-tse	jail
vézt	vehzt	to drive
víc	veets	more
video páska	vi-de-o paa-ska	video tape
vidět	vi-dyet	to see
víkend	vee-kend	weekend

vina	vi-na	fault (someone's)
vinárna	vi-naar-na	winery
vinice	vi-nyi-tse	vineyard
vinná réva	vin-naa reh-va	vine
víno	vee-no	wine
víra	vee-ra	trust
vitamíny	vi-ta-mee-ni	vitamins
vítej/te (inf/pol)	vee-tey/-te	welcome (inf/pol)
vítěz	vee-tyez	winner
vítr	vee-tr	wind
vízum	vee-zum	visa
vkročit	vkro-chit	to enter
vláda	vlaa-da	government
vlak	vlak	train
vlasy	vla-si	hair
vlevo	vle-vo	left (not right)
vlna	vl-na	wave • wool
vložit	vlo-zhit	to put inside
vnitřek	vnyit-rzhek	inside
vnučka (f)	vnuch-ka	grandchild (f)
vnuk (m)	vnuk	grandchild (m)
voda	vo-da	water
vodopád	vo-do-paad	waterfall
vojenská služba	voy-en-skaa sluzh-ba	military service
volby	vol-bi	elections • polls
volební období	vo-leb-nyee ob-do-bee	term of office
volební okrsek	vo-leb-nyee o-kr-sek	electorate
volit	vo-lit	to vote
volný	vol-nee	free (not bound) • vacant
vpravo	vpra-vo	right (not left)

272

CZECH–ENGLISH DICTIONARY

vpřed	vprzhed	ahead
vpustit	vpus-tyit	to admit
vrátit	vraa-tyit	to refund
peníze	pe-nyee-ze	
vrátit se	vraa-tyit se	to return
vrchol	vr-khol	peak

vši	vshi	lice
všichni	vshi-knyi	all
vstoupit	vstoh-pit	to enter
vstup	vstup	admission
vstupné	vstup-neh	admission
vstupenka	vstu-pen-ka	ticket
vteřina	vte-rzhi-na	second (n)
vtip	vtyip	joke
vtipkovat	vtyip-ko-vat	to joke
vůdce	vood-tse	leader • guide (person)
vůz	vooz	car
vy	vi	you (pol)

výborný	vee-bor-nee	excellent
vybrat si	vee-braat si	to choose
východ	vee-khod	east • exit
východ slunce	vee-khod slun-tse	sunrise
vychutnávat	vi-khut-naa-vat	to enjoy (oneself)
výdej batožin	vee-dey ba-to-zhin	baggage claim
vydělat	vi-dye-lat	to earn
výhoda	vee-ho-da	advantage
vyhrát	vi-hraat	to win
vycházející	vi-khaa-ze-yee-tsee	outgoing

výkop	vee-kop	kick off
výlet	vee-let	trip
vylézt	vi-lehst	to climb
vyloučit	vi-loh-chit	excluded
výměna	vee-mye-na	exchange
vyměnit	vi-mye-nyit	to exchange
vyprávět	vi-praa-vyet	to tell
výprodej	vee-pro-dey	(on) sale
vyrážky	vi-raazh-ki	a rash
vyrábět	vi-raa-byet	to produce
výrobce	vee-rob-tse	producer
vyrobeno z	vi-ro-be-no z	made (of)
výron	vee-ron	a sprain
vyrovnat	vi-rov-nat	match
výška	veesh-ka	altitude
vysoký	vi-so-kee	high • tall
výstava	vee-sta-va	exhibition
vystavovat	vi-sta-vo-vat	to exhibit
vystoupit	vi-stoh-pit	to scale • climb
výstroj	vee-stroy	equipment
vysvědčení	vis-vyed-che-nyee	certificate
vyšplhat se	vish-plhat se	to scale • to climb
vytáčecí tón	vi-taa-che-tsee tawn	dial tone
výtah	vee-tah	lift (elevator)
výtěr z krčku mateřnice	vee-tyer s krch-ku ma-terzh-nyits-e	pap smear
výzbroj	veez-broy	equipment
vyzdvihnout	viz-dvi-hnoht	to pick up
vzácný	vzaats-nee	rare
vzadu	vza-du	at the back (behind)

vzdálený	vzdaa-le-nee	remote
vzdělání	vzdye-laa-nyee	education
vzduch	vzdukh	air
vždy	vzhdi	always
vzhůru	vzhoo-ru	up
vzít	vzeet	to take (food/the train)
vzít sebou	vzeet se-boh	to take (away)
vztah	vsta-h	relationship

Z

za (pět) minut	za (pyet) mi-nut	in (five) minutes
zábava	zaa-ba-va	fun
zábavní	zaa-bav-nyee	entertaining
zabít	za-beet	to kill

Zaboč vlevo.
za-boch vle-vo
Turn left.

Zaboč vpravo.
za-boch fpra-vo
Turn right.

zabránit	za-braa-nyit	prevent
začít	za-cheet	begin
zácpa	zaats-pa	constipation
záda	zaa-da	back (body)
zahájení	za-haa-ye-nyee	kick off
zahradničení	za-hrad-nyich-e-nyee	gardening
zahrady	za-hra-di	gardens
zahraniční	za-hrany-ich-nyee	foreign
záchody	zaa-kho-di	toilets
zachránit	za-khraa-nyit	to save
zajímavý	za-yee-ma-vee	interesting

zákazník	zaa-kaz-neek	client
zákon	zaa-kon	law
zákony	zaa-ko-ni	rules
zámek	zaa-mek	lock • padlock
zaměstnanec	za-myest-na-nets	employee
zaměstnání	za-myest-naa-nyee	job
zaměstnávatel	za-mest-naa-va-tel	employer
zamknout	zamk-noht	to lock
zamračeno	za-mra-che-no	cloudy
zamrznout	za-mrz-noht	to freeze
zaneprázdněný	za-ne-praaz-dnye-nee	busy
zánět močového měchýře	zaa-nyet mo-cho-veh-ho mye-khee-rzhe	cystitis
západ	zaa-pad	west
západ slunce	zaa-pad slun-tse	sunset
zapalovač	za-pa-lo-vach	lighter
zápas	zaa-pas	fight
zápasit	zaa-pa-sit	to fight
zápisník	zaa-pis-nyeek	notebook
zapomenout	za-po-me-noht	to forget
zapřít	za-przheet	to deny
zapsat se	za-psat se	check-in (desk)
zaregistrovat se	za-reg-is-tro-vat se	check-in (desk)
zařízení	za-rzhee-ze-nyee	equipment
zase	za-se	again
zasnoubení	za-snoh-be-nyee	engagement
zástava	zaa-sta-va	flag
zastavit	za-sta-vit	to stop
zastávka	za-staav-ka	station • stop
zásuvka	zaa-suv-ka	plug (electrical)

CZECH–ENGLISH DICTIONARY

zataženo	za-ta-zhe-no	cloudy
zátka	zaat-ka	plug (bath)
zavazadlo	za-va-za-dlo	baggage
závazek	zaa-va-zek	engagement
zavírat	za-vee-rat	to close
závislý na heroinu	zaa-vis-lee na he-ro-in-u	heroin addict
závod	zaa-vod	race (sport)
závodní kolo	zaa-vod-nee ko-lo	racing bike
zavolat	za-vo-lat	to shout
závrať	zaa-vraty	dizzy
zavřeno	zav-rzhe-no	closed
zavřít	zav-rzheet	to shut
zběr ovoce	zbyer o-vo-tse	fruit picking
zbylý	z-bi-lee	to be left (behind/over)
zbytek	z-bi-tek	rest (what's left)
zdarma	zdar-ma	free (of charge)
zdraví	zdra-vee	health
zdravotní sestra	zdra-vot-nyee ses-tra	nurse
ze zlata	ze zla-ta	of gold
zebra	ze-bra	zebra
zeď	zedy	wall (outside)
zelenina	ze-le-nyi-na	vegetable
zelený	ze-le-nee	green
zelovoc	ze-lo-vots	greengrocer
země	zem-ye	country • land
Země	ze-mye	Earth
zemědělství	zem-ye-dyel-stvee	agriculture
zemětřesení	ze-mye-trzhe-se-nyee	earthquake
zemřít	zem-rzheet	to die
zhulenej	z-hu-le-ney	stoned (drugged)
zima	zi-ma	winter
ziskovost	zis-ko-vost	profitability
zítra	zee-tra	tomorrow

> **zítra ráno**
> zee-tra raa-no
> tomorrow morning

> **zítra v poledne/večer**
> zee-tra fpo-led-ne/ve-cher
> tomorrow afternoon/evening

zkažený	ska-zhe-nee	gone off (food)
zkorumpovaný	sko-rum-po-va-nee	corrupt
zkusit	sku-sit	to try
zloděj	zlo-dyey	thief
zlomit	zlo-mit	to break
změnit	zmye-nyit	to change

> **Zmiz!**
> zmiz!
> Get lost!

zmrzlina	zmrz-li-na	icecream
znak	znak	a sign
znamení	zna-mye-nyee	a sign
známky	znaam-ki	stamps
znásilnění	znaa-sil-nye-nyee	rape
znát	znaat	to know (someone)
znečištění	zne-chish-tye-nyee	pollution
zničit	znyi-chit	to destroy
znovu	zno-vu	again
znuděný	znu-dye-nee	bored
zoologická zahrada	zo-o-lo-gits-kaa za-hra-da	zoo

zpáteční	zpaa-tech-nyee	return (ticket)
jízdenka	yeez-den-ka	(ticket)
zpěvák	spye-vaak	singer
zpěvák-písničkař	sye-vaak – pees-nyich-karzh	singer-song-writer
zpívat	spee-vat	to sing
zpověď	spo-vye-dy	confession (religious)
zpráva	spraa-va	message
zprávy	spraa-vi	news
zranění	zra-nye-nyee	injury
zrcadlo	zrts-ad-lo	mirror
zrcadlení	zr-tsad-le-nyee	reflection (mirror)
zrušit	zru-shit	to cancel
zub	zub	tooth
(přední)	(przhed-nyee)	(front)
zub	zub	tooth
(zadní/ stolička)	(zad-nyee/ sto-lich-ka)	(back)
zubař	zu-barzh	dentist
zubní kartáček	zub-nyee kar-taa-chek	tooth-brush
zubní pasta	zub-nyee pa-sta	tooth-paste
zuby	zu-bi	teeth
zůstat	zoo-stat	to stay (remain) • to stay (some where)
zvěrokruh	zvye-ro-kru-h	zodiac

zvířata	zvee-rzha-ta	animals
zvláštní	zvlaasht-nyee	unusual
zvonění	zvo-nye-nyee	ring (sound)
zvonit	zvo-nyit	ring (of phone)
zvuk	zvuk	sound

Ž

žádný	zhaa-dnee	neither • none
žárlivý	zhaar-li-vee	jealous
žárovka	zhaa-rov-ka	light bulb
žaludek	zha-lu-dek	stomach
žebrák	zheb-raak	beggar
železnice	zhe-lez-nyi-tse	railroad
žena	zhe-na	woman
židle	zhid-le	chair
žíla	zhee-la	vein
žiletky	zhi-let-ki	razor blades
žít	zheet	to live (life)
život	zhi-vot	life
životní úroveň	zhi-vot-nyee oo-ro-veny	standard of living
životopis	zhi-vo-to-pis	biography • resumé
žíznivý	zhee-znyi-vee	thirsty
žlutý	zhlu-tee	yellow
žokej	zho-key	jockey
ztráta	straa-ta	loss
ztratit	stra-tyit	to lose
žvýkačka	zhvee-kach-ka	chewing gum

INDEX

F
I
N
D
E
R

don't just stand there, say something!

To see the full range of our language products, go to:

www.lonelyplanet.com

What kind of traveller are you?

A. You're eating chicken for dinner *again* because it's the only word you know.

B. When no one understands what you say, you step closer and shout louder.

C. When the barman doesn't understand your order, you point frantically at the beer.

D. You're surrounded by locals, swapping jokes, email addresses and experiences – other travellers want to borrow your phrasebook.

If you answered A, B, or C, you NEED Lonely Planet's phrasebooks.

- **Talk to everyone everywhere**
  Over 120 languages, more than any other publisher

- **The right words at the right time**
  Quick-reference colour sections, two-way dictionary, easy pronunciation, every possible subject

- **Lonely Planet Fast Talk** – essential language for short trips and weekends away

- **Lonely Planet Phrasebooks** – for every phrase you need in every language you want

'Best for curious and independent travellers' – *Wall Street Journal*

Lonely Planet Offices

Australia
90 Maribyrnong St, Footscray,
Victoria 3011
☎ 03 8379 8000
fax 03 8379 8111
email: talk2us@lonelyplanet.com.au

USA
150 Linden St, Oakland,
CA 94607
☎ 510 893 8555
fax 510 893 8572
email: info@lonelyplanet.com

UK
72-82 Rosebery Ave,
London EC1R 4RW
☎ 020 7841 9000
fax 020 7841 9001
email: go@lonelyplanet.co.uk

France
1 rue du Dahomey, 75011 Paris
☎ 01 55 25 33 00
fax 01 55 25 33 01
email: bip@lonelyplanet.fr
website: www.lonelyplanet.fr

www.lonelyplanet.com